Praise for
Where's My Money?

"Bob Carlson is the world's #1 retirement expert. His new book is a gold mine of information that will save you tons of money and maximize your benefits from Social Security and Medicare. It includes tips and details you will never get from the government. Your spouse and family will forever be grateful!"
—Mark Skousen, editor of *Forecasts & Strategies*

"Having helped Americans plan their estates for over forty-eight years, I know first hand how confusing Social Security can be. And now, with all the new laws, it is a massive, mysterious maze. Bob's new book, *Where's My Money?*, clears up the confusion in an easy-to-understand format. It is, by far, the best work I have ever read on the subject. Considering that longevity risk (people outliving their retirement assets) is a serious problem, there has never been a more crucial time for us to prepare for the long haul. You must have Bob's book on hand to use as your guide, as it was written to help you get the most out of what is rightfully yours. Great job!"
—David T. Phillips, president of Phillips Financial Services

"Bob Carlson is my go-to resource for all things retirement, and especially for confusing topics like Social Security. He has detailed knowledge and presents information in a clear way that helps real folks make important decisions."
—Eric Tyson, bestselling author of *Personal Finance for Dummies* and *Investing for Dummies*

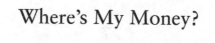

Where's My Money?

2021 EDITION

WHERE'S MY MONEY ?

Secrets to Getting the Most out of Your Social Security

BOB CARLSON

REGNERY
CAPITAL
Washington, D.C.

Regnery Capital™ is a trademark of Salem Communications Holding Corporation
Regnery® is a registered trademark of Salem Communications Holding Corporation

ISBN: 978-1-68451-050-4
eISBN: 978-1-68451-118-1
Library of Congress Catalog Number: 2020945138

Published in the United States by
Regnery Capital,
An Imprint of Regnery Publishing,
A Division of Salem Media Group,
Washington, D.C.
www.regnery.com

Manufactured in the United States of America

10 9 8 7 6 5 4 3 2 1

Books are available in quantity for promotional or premium use. For information on discounts and terms, please visit our website: www.Regnery.com.

To all the readers of *Retirement Watch* who over the years helped me identify the issues they face and develop practical solutions

CONTENTS

Key Social Security Lingo to Know   xi

Key Social Security Data and Changes for 2021   xiii

CHAPTER 1
You're Richer Than You Think—and Can Become Even Richer   1

CHAPTER 2
The Key to Making the Right Social Security Decisions for *You* 19

CHAPTER 3
You Can't Depend on the Social Security Administration
for the Right Answer   39

CHAPTER 4
What You Need to Know about Your Social Security Benefits   51

CHAPTER 5
What If I Keep Working?   77

CHAPTER 6
The Solo Years: Social Security When You're Widowed   91

CHAPTER 7
Benefits for the Divorced   113

CHAPTER 8
When Your Social Security Benefits Will Be Taxed   129

CHAPTER 9
How Social Security Is Different for Some Government
Employees and Other Non-Covered Workers   147

CHAPTER 10
Should You Take a Lump Sum?   157

CHAPTER 11
Can You Change Your Mind?   165

CHAPTER 12
How the Right Social Security Decision Will Make Your
Nest Egg Last Years Longer   177

CHAPTER 13
How to Fund a Social Security Delay and When Not to Delay 185

CHAPTER 14
The Future of Social Security and What It Means to You   195

CHAPTER 15
Social Security and Medicare: How Medicare Premiums
Could Wipe Out Your Social Security Income   207

CHAPTER 16
Thirty-Four Social Security Quirks, Surprises,
Misunderstandings, and Key Rules to Know   215

CHAPTER 17
Claiming Your Social Security Benefits: The Nuts and Bolts 235

CHAPTER 18
How to Avoid Social Security Scams   249

CHAPTER 19
How the Disabled Can Boost Their Benefits   259

APPENDIX
The Language of Social Security   269

NOTES   279
INDEX   285

Key Social Security Lingo to Know

As with other government programs, Social Security has its own vocabulary and lingo. Naturally, the words and terms that are unique to Social Security are turned into acronyms. In the book, I try to use the full term in each chapter before resorting to the acronym. But sometimes readers miss the first mention or get lost in frequent use of an acronym.

There's a more complete list of key Social Security terms and their definitions in the Appendix. But here in the front of the book I list the key acronyms that are used throughout the book so that you can dive in without first reviewing the Appendix and can quickly turn back to this page for a reminder of key acronyms.

SSA

Social Security Administration. This is the government agency that administers the Social Security program. It issues Social Security numbers and administers all the different benefits under Social Security: retirement, disability, survivor's and Supplemental Security Income. It is considered an independent agency, meaning it is not part of any cabinet department of the U.S. government. Its website is www.socialsecurity.gov. The main toll-free telephone number is 800-772-1213.

FRA

Full Retirement Age. This is the age at which you are eligible for full retirement benefits (FRB). FRA is the age at which you are eligible for the standard retirement benefit, without any reductions or additions.

FRA used to be 65 for everyone. But a rewrite of the Social Security law in the 1980s changed the rules. FRA now is between 66 and 67.

Your FRA depends on your year of birth. The schedule of FRAs is in chapter 4 in Table 4.1.

FRB

Full Retirement Benefit. This is the retirement benefit you receive if you begin claiming benefits at your FRA. The amount depends on your earnings history.

PIA

Primary Insurance Amount. This is another term the SSA uses for FRB. The calculation of the PIA, or FRB, is described in chapter 4.

AIME

Average Indexed Monthly Earnings. This is a number calculated from your earnings history and used to determine your monthly Social Security benefits. Your annual earnings are adjusted for general wage inflation during your career. Your highest thirty-five years of earnings, after the adjustment, are used to compute the AIME. A formula is applied to the AIME to determine your PIA/FRB. Details of the computations are in chapter 4.

COLA

Cost of Living Adjustment. Social Security benefits are adjusted, or indexed, for inflation each year. The Consumer Price Index is used to make the adjustment. Late each year the SSA announces what the COLA will be for the next year. Benefit payments for January are adjusted for the COLA.

DRC

Delayed Retirement Credits. When you delay the beginning of Social Security retirement benefits until after your FRA, the benefits are increased for each month of delay. A full year of DRCs increases your FRB by 8 percent. Further details are in chapter 4.

Key Social Security Data and Changes for 2021

Key parts of Social Security are adjusted for inflation late each year. These adjustments affect the taxes that workers and employers pay and the amounts beneficiaries receive. To ensure you have the latest data, I include the latest updates on this page. Compare any amounts listed in the book to the latest data here.

Cost of Living Adjustment (COLA)

1.3 percent

FICA Tax Rate

Employee	7.65 percent
Self-employed	15.30 percent

The 7.65 percent tax rate includes both Social Security and Medicare taxes. The Social Security portion, also known as OASDI or FICA, is 6.20 percent on earnings up to the maximum taxable earnings, or wage base, (listed below). Employers pay a rate matching the employee tax rate. The Medicare portion, also known as HI, is 1.45 percent on all earnings. Individuals with earned income of more than $200,000 ($250,000 for married couples filing jointly) pay an additional 0.9 percent in Medicare taxes.

Maximum Taxable Earnings for Social Security

$142,800

Earnings for a Credit toward Coverage

$1,470

Retirement Earnings Test Limits

Under full retirement age, annual limit	$18,960
Under full retirement age, monthly limit	$1,580
Year of full retirement age, annual limit	$50,520
Year of full retirement age, monthly limit	$4,210

Maximum Initial Social Security Benefit at Full Retirement Age

$3,148 per month

Estimated Average Monthly Social Security Benefits Payable in January 2021

All retired workers	$1,543
Aged couple, both receiving benefits	$2,596
Widowed mother with two children	$3,001
Aged widow(er) living alone	$1,453
Disabled worker, spouse, one or more children	$2,224
All disabled workers	$1,277

Bend Points

1st bend	$996
2nd bend	$6,002

The bend points are used in the SSA's formula for computing PIA, or FRB. The bend points ensure that the computation of Social Security benefits is progressive, meaning that workers with lower lifetime incomes receive a higher percentage of their average incomes in benefits than do workers with higher lifetime incomes.

CHAPTER 1

You're Richer Than You Think— and Can Become Even Richer

Shortly after I started working on this book, I mentioned it at a dinner party. A woman in her seventies quickly asked, "You're going to tell them to wait, aren't you?"

She explained that as they approached retirement, she and her husband had claimed their Social Security and other retirement benefits at the earliest possible dates. "We wanted that money as soon as we could get it. We thought it was great," she explained.

She no longer feels that way. A few years back, her husband passed away. At that point she discovered the long-term consequences of claiming Social Security benefits early. Her retirement benefit stopped and she now receives a surviving spouse's benefit based on her husband's earnings record and the age at which he claimed retirement benefits, because that amount is higher than her retirement benefit. If he had waited to claim Social Security benefits, her survivor's benefit would be much higher now. She now has to maintain the household on less money, though her costs have increased.

"Everybody wants the money as soon as they can get it, and it seemed great," she told me. "But you tell them they should be patient. I wish we had waited."

I had already determined that one of the themes of this book would be that many people make the wrong decisions about Social Security, and the most frequent mistake is to claim benefits too soon. Another frequent mistake is that married couples don't coordinate their benefits or put the emphasis that they should on maximizing the benefits of whichever spouse is the survivor.

It's understandable that people don't make optimum decisions about Social Security. The program is complicated, and your decisions have long-term consequences. Social Security is such a valuable asset that it's important to take the time to make better decisions.

Here are a few more anecdotes about Social Security decisions—in which I use fictional names—showing how these decisions can have significant and lasting effects on lifetime income and financial security.

Max Profits was retiring soon at age 62. His wife Rosie was 58. Max initially planned to do as most people do: begin his Social Security retirement benefits at the closest possible date to age 62. If Max began his benefits at 62, he would have received $1,500 monthly.

After doing some research, however, Max decided to delay claiming his benefits for as long as he could, hopefully to age 70, at which point he would receive a monthly benefit of $2,640. He would encourage Rosie, on the other hand, to begin her retirement benefits at age 62, when she would qualify to receive $1,200 monthly.

Max decided to delay his benefits because he realized that after either he or Rosie passed away, the surviving spouse would receive only one Social Security check. And if the surviving spouse had the smaller income, the amount she receives depends on the benefits of the spouse who has passed away. The rules can be complicated (I discuss them in detail in chapter 6), but in general the survivor's benefit is reduced if the spouse who has passed away began his retirement benefits before reaching full retirement age (FRA). It also can be further reduced if the surviving spouse has claimed her retirement benefits before full retirement age.

If Max began benefits at 62 and passed away at age 80, Rosie would stop receiving her own retirement benefit and instead receive about $1,650 monthly as a survivor's benefit. But by delaying his benefits to age 70, Max would increase his benefits to $2,640 a month, and if Max passed away first, Rosie would receive that amount (indexed for inflation) for the rest of her life.

That's about $990 more in benefits per month ($11,880 per year) that Rosie would receive compared to what she'd receive if Max had begun benefits at age 62. If Rosie lives to age 90, she'll receive more than $166,000 in additional lifetime benefits, before considering inflation indexing. By delaying his benefits to age 70, Max ensures his surviving spouse's income is substantially higher than if he began retirement benefits at age 62. If Rosie passes away first, Max would continue to receive his retirement benefit and Rosie's benefit would stop coming to the household.

After reviewing the alternatives, Max realized that delaying his retirement benefits would be the best way to increase the financial security of whichever spouse outlived the other.

Jess Makinit was still employed when he reached his full retirement age for Social Security benefits, and he planned to continue working for several more years. He didn't need his Social Security retirement benefits to support his lifestyle, so he delayed claiming the benefits. He decided to delay the benefits until age 70 so he could earn the maximum benefit amount.

Three months before turning 70 he met with a Social Security Administration (SSA) representative. The rep said that in addition to receiving his monthly benefits at age 70, Jess also would receive a one-time check that was a lump sum payment of six months of retro-active benefits. Jess was happy, until he started to receive his monthly retirement benefits. They were about 6 percent lower than the esti-mates he had received of his benefits at age 70.

After some investigation, Jess learned that when he accepted the lump sum of retroactive benefits his monthly benefits were reduced. As I explain in more detail in chapter 11, in exchange for receiving nine months of benefits as a lump sum, Jess reduced his monthly ben-efits for the rest of his life to the amount he would have received had he claimed them earlier than he intended. Also, when Jess accepted the lump sum, the SSA assumed he was requesting that his retirement benefits begin as of the date he applied, not when he turned 70.

The result was that Jess's monthly retirement benefit amount was adjusted to the level it would have been had he begun receiving benefits nine months before age 70 (the three months before his seventieth birth-day plus six months of retroactive benefits). His monthly benefits will be 6 percent less each month for the rest of his life. As a high-income earner receiving the maximum monthly benefit, Jess receives $2,160 less each year for the rest of his life.

Jess was never informed about the tradeoff. He didn't realize that accepting the lump sum of retroactive benefits meant lower monthly benefits. When anyone applies for benefits after full retirement age, under SSA policy he is automatically paid the lump sum benefit, and the monthly benefit amount is reduced accordingly, unless the appli-cant specifically declines the retroactive lump sum benefit.

Kim Kandu was newly widowed and a few months shy of her sixtieth birthday. Her late husband's passing had not been unexpected, and in the preceding months the couple had reviewed Kim's options and met with a financial planner to develop a plan. Unlike many wid-ows, when Kim went to her local SSA office to discuss her benefits as a surviving spouse, she was prepared with more than her late husband's death certificate.

Kim had worked for many years and had her own earnings record and earned Social Security retirement benefits. After reviewing Kim and her late husband's earnings records, the SSA rep insisted Kim shouldn't apply for survivor's benefits at age 60. Instead, she should return at age 62 and apply for her own earned retirement benefits. After Kim raised questions about the advice, the rep asked another rep to help explain why Kim should wait until age 62. In the course of that discussion, the first rep said that on second thought it would be even better for Kim to wait to claim her earned benefits at full retirement age, 66.

But because Kim had done her homework, she knew that if she claimed her survivor's benefit at age 60 and lived to age 80, she would receive at least $72,000 more in lifetime benefits than if she followed the Social Security rep's advice. The survivor's benefits she was entitled to receive upon turning age 60, based on her late husband's earnings history, would be $1,600 per month (as I explain in detail in chapter 6). If Kim waited until age 62 and claimed her own earned benefits, she would go two years without any benefits and then receive only $1,425 monthly.

Most People Misunderstand Social Security

Social Security benefits are one of the most valuable retirement resources many Americans have. They're a major source of income for most retirees. Even many well-off retirees receive a significant portion of their retirement income from Social Security. The longer a person's retirement lasts, the larger a share of their retirement income Social Security tends to become. That's partly because retirees will spend their other assets during retirement and partly because Social Security benefits are indexed for inflation, so they will increase most years.

About 86 percent of current retirees fund their retirement primarily with Social Security or a pension, according to a 2019 survey by Wells Fargo and the Harris Poll. Social Security and pensions will be the main retirement funding source for 60 percent of Baby Boomers, according to the survey.

Decisions about Social Security, especially when to claim retirement benefits, are some of the most important decisions about retirement finance that you will make. And most of those decisions, though not all of them, are irreversible.

Yet most people aren't well-prepared to make these important decisions, and there are few reliable resources available to advise them. Quite often these decisions are made quickly without careful analysis or assistance. People rely on conventional wisdom, rules of thumb, what friends did, and other shortcuts in making these critical decisions. They assume that Social Security is simple and their decisions about it are straightforward. In fact, most people have several options for their Social Security retirement benefits and the differences in lifetime income can be substantial.

Americans age 50 and older have significant knowledge gaps regarding their Social Security benefits, according to an annual survey sponsored by Nationwide Retirement Institute, a division of Nationwide Investment Services Corporation. Most Americans don't know key information. More important, most people believe they are well-informed about how to maximize their Social Security benefits, yet they give incorrect answers to basic questions about Social Security. In other words, they don't know what they don't know. That can lead to costly decisions that don't optimize Social Security benefits.

The 2019 survey found that about 70 percent believe they will be eligible for full retirement benefits years before they actually will be.

Fewer than 25 percent of older adults can identify their full retirement age for Social Security benefits. On average, future retirees believe they can begin full retirement benefits at age 63. In fact, those born in 1954 can't receive full benefits until age 66, and those born after 1954 won't receive full Social Security retirement benefits until later, as I explain in chapter 4. Retirement benefits can be claimed as early as age 62, but those benefits will be significantly lower than full retirement benefits.

How Much Will Social Security Pay You?

More than half of the survey respondents said they were confident they knew how to maximize their Social Security retirement benefits. When they were asked to name the factors that determine the maximum benefit, however, only 8 percent had the correct response.

Matching the overconfidence in their knowledge of Social Security, most future retirees are overly optimistic about the level of their retirement benefits.

For example, 56 percent of future retirees said they expect Social Security will pay more than half of their retirement expenses. And 26 percent believe Social Security alone will enable them to live comfortably in retirement.[1] But according to a 2019 study conducted by United Income, a financial services firm, Social Security is only about one-third of total income for retirees.[2] The SSA estimates that the average Social Security benefit replaces only about 40 percent of pre-retirement income. The higher a person's pre-retirement income was, the lower the percentage of it will be replaced with Social Security benefits.

Future retirees on average estimate their monthly benefits will be more than $1,800 per month. That's about 28 percent higher than the average monthly benefit reported by those who are retired already.

There are other basic features of Social Security that too many Americans don't understand well. A whopping 60 percent didn't know their Social Security retirement benefits are indexed for inflation. Under indexing, the dollar amount you're paid will be increased each year in line with the increase in the Consumer Price Index (CPI), but it won't decline if the CPI for the year is negative. It's a valuable benefit, because indexing preserves at least some of the purchasing power of monthly income.

Almost half of future retirees didn't know that Social Security retirement benefits are guaranteed for life. Social Security will be the only inflation-indexed guaranteed lifetime source of income for most retired Americans, yet a high percentage of future retirees don't know about these important features. Because it is the only income source guaranteed for life that many people will have, it is critical that the right decisions be made about claiming Social Security retirement benefits.

Another 40 percent of future retirees weren't aware of the benefits available to surviving spouses and divorced spouses. These benefits are often critical sources of income to unmarried retirees. Too often, however, these benefits aren't claimed or aren't maximized.

The survey covered only a few of the basic features of Social Security.[3] There's much more to the program, and a great deal more that most people misunderstand or are unaware of.

Don't Leave Thousands of Dollars on the Table

While the program was intended to benefit all Americans, Social Security's rules were written by armies of lawyers and Ph.D.s, then amended and adjusted many times over the decades since the program began. It's no wonder the average pre-retiree doesn't understand them all.

But the unfortunate result is that most people leave tens of thousands of dollars of lifetime income on the table. In fact, almost all American retirees claim Social Security benefits at the wrong time, shortchanging themselves by a collective $3.4 trillion in lifetime benefits, according to a 2019 report by United Income.

The United Income report used data from the University of Michigan Health and Retirement Study, a biannual survey of approximately twenty thousand Americans ages 50 and older. United Income took a sample of about two thousand of those households, which included both non-retired and retired individuals, and considered factors including income, wealth, taxes, health status, and longevity estimates. Using these factors, the report simulated the lifetime income that would have been paid to the individuals under different Social Security benefit-claiming scenarios. After running many simulations, the report determined what the optimal Social Security–claiming strategy would have been for each individual in the sample.

The study's key conclusion was stunning: 96 percent of retirees began Social Security benefits at the wrong time for them. If the households had claimed their benefits at the optimal time, the average lifetime income per household would have been higher by $111,000, or 9 percent. That's just the average shortfall; many households gave up even more lifetime benefits.

Remarkably, educated and affluent retirees are more likely to make the wrong decisions about their benefits than less wealthy and less educated retirees.

I won't hold you in suspense. The optimum decision for most individuals and households is to wait to claim retirement benefits. And yet most people do the opposite. A high percentage of people claim their retirement benefits as soon as possible, at age 62. According to the United Income survey, over 70 percent claim benefits before turning 64.[4] Full retirement age for people born from 1943 to 1954 is 66. At full retirement age you will be paid the normal or full retirement benefit. If you claim your benefits before full retirement age, they are reduced 5/8 of 1 percent per month for the first 36 months and 5/12 of one percent for each additional month. The result is that if you claim retirement benefits at age 62, you receive monthly benefits of about 25 percent less than your monthly full retirement age benefit. Other types of benefits also are reduced if you take them early. Spousal benefits claimed at age 62 pay 30 percent less per month than at full retirement age, and taking a survivor's benefit at 60 (the earliest possible age for most surviving spouses) instead of at full retirement age reduces the monthly benefit by 28.5 percent.

You can further delay claiming benefits past full retirement age. For each year you delay benefits, up to age 70, your benefits increase 8 percent per year through what are known as delayed retirement credits. That means if you delay claiming benefits until you turn 70, you'll receive about 32 percent more than your benefit at full retirement age.

Your full retirement age depends on your birth date, so the exact increase or decrease for you is determined by your year of birth. Those with FRAs after age 66 will lose more by claiming benefits at age 62 and gain a little less by waiting until age 70 to claim benefits.

There's a tradeoff to delaying Social Security benefits: you won't receive any benefits during the delay period. That will cost you money in the short term. But the increased benefits from delaying are generous. You'll lose some wealth in your sixties and seventies, but you'll make up for it later. The longer you live, the greater the gain from delaying benefits. Many people will more than make up for the benefits they do not receive while waiting to make their claim.

There are additional reasons to delay benefits. We saw one of those reasons in the example of Max and Rosie Profits: if you're married, you and your spouse should coordinate your decisions about when to claim Social Security in order to maximize your joint lifetime income and ensure that whichever spouse survives the other has the highest possible survivor's benefit.

Why Most People Make the Wrong Social Security Decisions

There are many reasons people don't capture the full amount of Social Security retirement income that they're allowed. As I said before, Social Security is a complicated program, written primarily by lawyers and Ph.D.s. The law, rules, and regulations governing the program take up about twenty thousand pages. We aren't taught even the basics of Social Security in our schooling. And if we were, most people would forget the details by the time they approached retirement.

Most financial professionals don't make Social Security planning part of their services. They focus more on investment management, estate planning, and other financial issues. The two foundations of Americans' retirement security—Social Security and Medicare—receive far less attention from most financial professionals than they should. (Luckily, that is beginning to change.)

You're Probably a Social Security Millionaire

I think a significant reason people don't take the time to make the right decisions about Social Security is that they don't realize either how much their Social Security benefits are worth or how much optimal decisions about them could increase that value. (Some studies have concluded that the benefit estimates from the Social Security Administration understate the amount of benefits you'll be paid, and some analysts argue the understatement is deliberate. That's why I discuss how to interpret Social Security benefit estimates in chapter 3.)

Social Security retirement benefits are paid monthly, and benefit estimates are expressed as a monthly payment. Most people focus on that monthly amount. This benefit can seem like a helpful amount of money, but not a large sum. The average Social Security benefit in

2020 was $1,503 per month, and the maximum amount for a beginning beneficiary was $3,011. But multiply the monthly benefit by twelve months in a year, and it starts to seem like a substantial amount of money. Then multiply that amount by twenty or thirty years of retirement, and you start to see the real value.

Also, remember that Social Security benefits—unlike most annuities, pensions, and bond interest—are indexed for inflation each year. When the CPI rises, your benefits increase.

Another overlooked factor is that the monthly benefits are guaranteed for life, no matter how long you live and no matter how the markets perform. Those are significant advantages that most people aren't aware of. The value of a guaranteed lifetime income usually isn't appreciated until some years into retirement.

Consider how large an investment portfolio would be needed to generate the level of income paid by Social Security. A married couple with average Social Security benefits receives over thirty-six thousand dollars each year. To generate an annual income of this amount, they would need an investment portfolio of more than one million dollars, earning at least 3.6 percent annually plus an additional return to ensure future income keeps up with inflation. And neither the investment return nor the safety of the principal would be guaranteed. Or they could purchase an annuity from an insurance company. A joint life annuity that pays thirty-six thousand dollars annually would cost about seven hundred thousand dollars, but it's not indexed for inflation. Inflation-indexed annuities aren't widely available in the U.S.

And those comparisons are to average Social Security benefits. If the couple were to increase their lifetime benefits above the average by using some of the strategies you'll learn in this book, they would need a nest egg of $1.5 million or more to produce the same cash flow.

Because few people do this analysis, most people don't realize the value of their Social Security benefits or see the value in taking the time to learn how to maximize their benefits.

I'm from the Government and I'm Here to Help You

Another reason people shortchange themselves when it comes to Social Security is that the SSA itself doesn't provide good information to many retirees. Many financial advisors have heard from people who were told by Social Security representatives that they couldn't use strategies that clearly are allowed under the law. I've been told by readers of my *Retirement Watch* newsletter that they asked different SSA reps the same question and received different answers from each of them.

The Inspector General of Social Security has found instances when the program routinely underpaid benefits that people were entitled to. Social Security's representatives are overworked, and often not as well trained and informed as we would like. (I discuss the issue of the SSA's mistakes in more detail in chapter 3.)

Another reason people don't maximize their Social Security benefits is that they underestimate how long they are likely to live. As I pointed out earlier, the optimum claiming strategy results in a loss of wealth during your sixties and seventies but more than makes up for that loss in your later years. Many people wrongly assume that they won't live long enough to reap the rewards of claiming benefits later. This misunderstanding of longevity and how it relates to claiming Social Security benefits is so widespread that I discuss it in detail in chapter 2.

The longer you live, the more important guaranteed, inflation-indexed lifetime income becomes. And it's generally more important to women than to men, because women on average live longer than men.

I want you to be among the 4 percent of Americans who optimize their Social Security benefits. I want to help increase the percentage of Americans who select the right benefit-claiming strategy for them, or at least choose a better strategy than they would have. I want the percentage of retirees who make the right Social Security decisions to be far higher than the paltry 4 percent revealed in the United Income report.[5]

An estimated ten thousand Baby Boomers become eligible for Social Security retirement benefits every day. The peak of the baby boom generation now is reaching Social Security–claiming age. Yet, few of them will seek informed advice about when to take benefits. They'll make the wrong decisions—meaning they won't optimize their benefits. They'll receive much lower lifetime benefits than they could have. They'll have a lower standard of living than they could have had, especially in their later years, and might even struggle financially. With married couples, the burden of this poor decision making will fall more on the surviving spouse. Most of the Baby Boomers don't know how much their benefits will vary based on key decisions they make.

The greatest fear that future retirees have is running out of money in retirement. This book was written for those who want to reduce that risk and maximize their retirement security and independence.

Optimizing Social Security benefits isn't a rich person's problem. Quite the opposite. It's an important goal for everyone, but it is especially critical for middle-class and upper-middle-class Americans.

In this book you'll learn that in many cases the best strategy is to delay beginning Social Security benefits past the age when you're first eligible to begin them. For a married couple, it's especially important for the spouses to coordinate benefits. Usually at least one spouse (the one with the highest lifetime earnings) should delay benefits as long as possible. But delaying benefits isn't always the best solution. I'll explain how to make the optimum decision for you (and your spouse if you're married). You'll also learn when taking benefits sooner rather than later can be the optimum solution.

Yes, you'll lose some money in the short run by not starting those benefits as early as possible. But if you're among the half of your age cohort who lives to life expectancy and beyond, you'll more than make up that money. In fact, the payoff for those who optimize their benefits and live beyond life expectancy is significant, and it increases for each additional year you or your spouse lives.

How to Beat the Three Greatest Retirement Risks

Optimizing Social Security retirement benefits significantly reduces the three greatest risks of retirement:

- Maximizing Social Security benefits reduces what economists call "longevity risk." No matter how long you live, you won't run out of money. Your Social Security benefits will continue for life, and because you maximized benefits, those payments will be higher than if you had joined the crowd and claimed benefits early.
- Your risk of losing purchasing power to inflation will be reduced. Social Security benefits are indexed for inflation each year. Social Security is the only inflation-indexed income most people have. While it's not a perfect inflation hedge, optimizing Social Security benefits causes you to lose less purchasing power over time.
- You'll depend less on investment markets for retirement security. Many retirees depend on healthy investment markets to finance their retirement lifestyles. But investments can go through extended periods of below-average returns, or even negative returns. U.S. stocks suffered

two significant bear markets from 2000 through 2019. Stock market returns from the beginning of that period through the end were little better than the return from short-term treasury bills, and returns were negative for extended times. Social Security benefits are paid without regard to what's happening in the investment markets. In fact, maximizing guaranteed Social Security benefits can allow you to take more risk with the rest of your nest egg and possibly earn higher returns than you otherwise would have.

Social Security seems boring to many people. I suspect some of them were turned off to the program from the time they received their first paycheck and saw that mysterious "FICA" deduction taken right out of their gross income. Schools never did much to alert us to the importance of Social Security benefits. The government certainly hasn't alerted people to the importance of making their benefit choices wisely. Even many retirement-planning professionals and programs downplay or ignore the subject.

As you have learned, Social Security benefits are a significant asset, and for many of us they are the largest retirement resource. They're the only source of inflation-indexed guaranteed lifetime income many people have. In a period of volatile, uncertain investment markets and a weak global economy, guaranteed lifetime income is an important source of security.

Why to Continue Reading
In the rest of this book, you'll learn how to enhance this source of lifetime income. The right decision (or at least a better decision) will

reduce the risk of running out of income in retirement and increase your independence and security.

I cut through the confusing rules and hard-to-understand terms so you can choose the best Social Security benefits decision for you. You'll learn that the right decision for you might not be the right decision for others. I explain the factors that make the difference.

You'll also learn about special situations, such as those for surviving spouses, the divorced, and other family members. I explain what happens to your benefits if you continue working while receiving Social Security. You'll discover how Social Security benefits might be taxed and how to avoid or minimize those taxes.

I also address the financial solvency of Social Security. Many people say they won't put much thought into Social Security strategies because the program is insolvent. I look behind the scary headlines and give you the straight facts. You'll learn what to be afraid of, what not to worry about, and how to adjust your plans.

I cover all that and more in the rest of this book, which is written so that you can maximize your Social Security benefits without reading the chapters in order. You can read the chapters that interest or affect you the most and still be able to understand the material and make wise choices.

It's time to learn how to bolster the financial foundation of your retirement and maximize the return on decades of paying all those FICA or self-employment taxes on your earnings by choosing the right Social Security strategy for you.

CHAPTER 2

The Key to Making the Right Social Security Decisions for *You*

I believe there's one overriding reason people make mistakes about claiming their Social Security benefits.

In chapter 1 we learned that 96 percent of Americans don't make the optimal decisions about claiming Social Security benefits, according to a report from the financial services firm, United Income. The report's authors obtained data on about two thousand Americans, including their income, wealth, taxes, health status, and life expectancy estimates, and then simulated the results of different Social Security–claiming decisions. The report's conclusion was that only 4 percent claimed Social Security benefits at the optimal time.

The authors found that not making the most advantageous Social Security decision has significant lifetime consequences. The average retiree gives up more than $100,000 of guaranteed lifetime income. And many give up significantly more. Depending on longevity and lifetime income, the difference between a poor claiming decision and the optimum decision can be $200,000 or more.[1]

There are two mistakes made most commonly. Surveys of long-lived retirees show that claiming benefits early is one that retirees regret more as the years pass.[2] Studies by economists and financial advisers also demonstrate that claiming benefits early is a choice that results in much lower lifetime benefits for most people.[3] The other frequent mistake is that spouses fail to coordinate their benefit-claiming decisions. The harm from this mistake usually isn't apparent until one spouse passes away.

Of course, other claiming mistakes are made, and I'll discuss them—and also other opportunities—in this book. But those two are the most frequently made errors.

You can avoid these mistakes and the others.

Yes, Social Security is a complicated program with over twenty thousand pages of rules and regulations. It's also true that schools, employers, and even the Social Security Administration don't do enough to help people maximize their Social Security benefits. Those are obstacles to making good decisions about claiming Social Security benefits, but the obstacles can be overcome.

The Key Question

Early in the retirement planning process, you need to ask: How long will my retirement last? To put it another way, how long are you likely to live?

Someone anticipating a short retirement isn't likely to worry about the long term. He is likely to be comfortable spending more than others in the first years of retirement and to put less value on guaranteed, inflation-adjusted lifetime income. On the other hand, someone anticipating a longer-than-average life expectancy knows his income and assets have to last decades. More importance will be given to controlling spending, avoiding investment losses, and setting up one or more streams of income guaranteed to last for life, no matter how long that might be.

Unfortunately, most people enter retirement with misconceptions about their probable life expectancy. Some people don't seriously attempt to answer the question of how long their retirement might last. Others develop answers, but their answers are off base.

Americans most often significantly underestimate their life expectancy—something that can have serious adverse consequences. When they're asked about their greatest retirement fear, most people answer either that they're afraid of running out of money or that they're afraid medical expenses will absorb their savings. Either way, people are afraid their savings will be exhausted in retirement.

An important step in avoiding running out of money in retirement is to develop a reasonable estimate of your life expectancy. If you underestimate your life expectancy, you're more likely to run out of money. You'll spend too much money in the early years of retirement, invest too conservatively, or take other actions that limit your income or deplete your nest egg too rapidly. You're also likely to make a Social Security–claiming decision that is beneficial in the short term but harmful in the long run.

An important step in having a financially successful retirement and making the right decisions about Social Security is to develop a reasonable estimate of life expectancy.

How Most People Get It Wrong

People generally use two methods to estimate the length of their retirement.

The first method is to look at the ages to which their parents and grandparents lived. Then they'll estimate their own life expectancy with reference to those ages.

That's a bad system. Insurance companies have to make highly accurate estimates of how long people are likely to live. If they make the wrong estimates, insurers misprice life insurance and annuities. They'll soon run out of money if they routinely make bad estimates of how long people are likely to live. And insurance companies don't put much emphasis on how long someone's ancestors lived. The insurers know that medical care and personal health habits were different for previous generations. Genetics and heredity influence longevity, but more significant influences are environment, lifestyle, and improvements in medical care. Insurers know that many diseases and conditions that led to early death in past generations now are curable or treatable. The life spans of ancestors are at most only a small factor in developing a reasonably accurate estimate of an individual's life expectancy.

The second frequently used method is to apply the life expectancy estimated for the individual's age group when they were youngsters. Many of today's Baby Boomers, who are in or entering the traditional retirement years, remember that in their youth their generation's life expectancy was projected to be their late seventies.

That's a bad estimate to use in your retirement planning. The average life expectancy estimated at birth for an age group assumes that many members of the cohort will pass away before reaching retirement age. Because of illness and accidents, a number will pass away during childhood. Many others will face their demise before reaching their sixties.

The average life expectancy for the surviving members of the age group increases each year that they live. Baby Boomers who have made it this far are likely, on average, to live into their eighties. That significantly exceeds the life expectancy that was projected when they were born.

How You Can Get It Right

Another frequent misunderstanding is about the meaning of life-expectancy estimates for people of a particular age. The frequently cited estimated life expectancies are properly stated as "average life expectancy." An average life expectancy for an age group means that is the average life expectancy of all the members of the group. Roughly speaking, about half the members of the age group will live longer than the average, and half will have shorter lives. Of the half who will live longer than the average, a meaningful percentage of them will live much longer than the average.

How much longer will the fortunate 50 percent live?

A man who is 65 years old today has a 22-year life expectancy. That means he has a 50 percent probability of living to age 87 or longer, according to the LIMRA Secure Retirement Institute. Yet, one in four men age 65 today are expected to live to age 93. Among women aged 65 today, one in four will live to age 96 or longer.[4] (Despite a narrowing of the gap in recent years, women still are likely to live several years longer than men.)

Those who are in good health at age 65 need to add additional years to the estimates. The 65-year-olds in good health today are likely on average to live two to four years longer than the entire group. Also, data show that people with more education or higher lifetime incomes or both tend to live longer than the age group average life expectancy. So if you are in good health, have a college education (or beyond), and have an above-average lifetime income, you should assume that you'll live years longer than your age-group average, unless there are reasons to believe that you won't benefit from those advantages.

Married couples need to consider their joint life expectancy, something that can be significantly different from a single life expectancy. There's a significant probability that at least one spouse will live beyond the average for the age group. In a married couple age 65 today, there's a 75 percent probability at least one spouse will live to age 88 or longer. At least one spouse has a 50 percent probability of living to age 93, and there's a 25 percent probability at least one spouse lives to 98.

I have emphasized that a major mistake in Social Security claiming is for spouses to make their claiming decisions independently instead of coordinating their decisions. That's because when one spouse passes away, one Social Security benefit will end. The surviving spouse will have only one Social Security benefit to maintain a household that was previously supported by two benefits.

The surviving spouse may have to live with only one Social Security check for a considerable time. In almost 75 percent of married couples, one spouse will outlive the other by at least five years. In about 50 percent of couples, the surviving spouse will outlive the other by at least ten years. That's a long time to make ends meet on a substantially reduced household income. It's important to consider the long term when making decisions about Social Security and other retirement finance issues.

What's Your Longevity Risk?

One thing that should be clear at this point is that when planning for retirement, you can't treat life expectancy as a fixed period. The best we can do is establish probabilities. You have a 50 percent probability of living beyond the life expectancy for your age group, unless you have an underlying health concern. You also have a lower, but still meaningful, probability of living well beyond life expectancy, well into your eighties, nineties, even beyond one hundred.

You need to decide which probability to include in your planning. If there's a 25 percent probability you or your spouse will live into your nineties, do you want to accommodate that possibility in your plan? Or do you want to assume that's too low a probability to affect your retirement decisions? That's a key question to answer before deciding when to claim Social Security benefits.

Science and medicine have done a lot to extend life expectancy, which has increased dramatically over the last fifty years. In addition, people are likely to be healthier and more active during these extended years than in the past. Increased longevity is a major benefit of living in these times.

Yet longer life expectancy can be a financial risk. Economists and financial advisors refer to "longevity risk." The longer you are going to live, the more assets and income you will have to accumulate during your working years in order to pay your expenses during those additional years.

A longer lifespan also means more inflation risk. The prices of most things you buy are likely to rise during retirement. The purchasing power of your dollars is going to decline, so you'll need more dollars in the later years of retirement to buy the same goods and services you purchased in the early years of retirement. The longer you live, the more purchasing power you are likely to lose to inflation.

In addition, though an older person today is likely to be healthier and more active than someone of the same age was decades ago, he or she will still need help over the years. As you age, there will be things that you're no longer able to do or shouldn't try to do. You'll need to have other people do those things, and often you'll have to hire someone.

Beating the Curse of the Average

Longevity risk is one of the greatest retirement risks. Living longer than the average life expectancy greatly increases the risk of exhausting your financial resources. You can plan your retirement based on the average. You can assume average life expectancy, average investment returns, and so forth. I call this The Curse of the Average. It makes planning easy, but it's risky.

The average is derived from a large number of individual instances. Most of those individual events differ greatly from the average. That's true of life expectancy, investment returns, and other factors used in retirement planning. Collectively and over the long term, the average is the right number. But each individual's experience is likely to differ from the average, and it will often differ greatly.

Very few people live to the average life expectancy for their age group. Most live for shorter or longer periods, so most likely your life expectancy will differ from the average. That's not a problem when your experience differs from the average by a modest amount. But there's going to be a wide variation. A significant percentage of people will have life spans much longer than the average. If you plan only for the average life span, you greatly increase the probability that you'll run out of money in retirement.

Social Security is insurance against a long life. It's one source of money you can't outlive, because it is guaranteed to be paid monthly for life, no matter how long you live. If you're in the half of your age group that lives to life expectancy or less, you'll come out ahead by claiming Social Security benefits at an early age. But those who live beyond average life expectancy will realize, as the years go by, that their monthly income would be higher if they had waited. As they live longer and spend down their assets and see other sources of income lose purchasing power to inflation, the importance of Social Security benefits increases. Your monthly benefit is higher the longer you wait to begin taking your Social Security benefits, and the advantage of that higher monthly benefit will increase the longer you live.

Tools You Can Use

Before making a decision about when to claim your Social Security benefits, develop a realistic estimate of your life expectancy. The average life expectancy for your age group is only a starting point. There are ways to arrive at a better estimate of your life expectancy.

The Society of Actuaries and the American Academy of Actuaries jointly developed an online tool, the Actuaries Longevity Illustrator (ALI). It's available free online at https://www.longevityillustrator.org. The actuaries sorted through the data and concluded that a reasonable estimate of an individual's life expectancy can be determined from four factors: age, gender, smoking habits, and whether his current health is poor, average, or excellent. You enter these factors in the ALI, and it gives you an answer.

The ALI gives you more than a simple estimate of life expectancy. It shows you your probability of living to different ages. In addition, a couple can enter the data for each individual. The ALI will not only give probable life expectancies for each spouse. It also will answer the questions "How long can we expect to live as a couple?" and "By how many years might one spouse outlive the other?"

Another way to obtain a personalized estimate is to use one or more of the many individual life expectancy calculators available for free on the internet. They ask a series of questions about your health and lifestyle. Some ask only a few basic questions while others ask a greater number of questions about lifestyle, health, and recent medical tests.

One popular calculator is at www.livingto100.com. Social Security has a life expectancy calculator on its website, and many life insurance companies do as well. The calculator at the Wharton School at the University of Pennsylvania has received good reviews. You can access several well-regarded calculators in one place at www.lifeexpectancycalculators.com. You also can search for "life expectancy calculators" or something similar on your favorite search engine.

The Tools Have Limits

While they are better than life expectancy tables and averages, the calculators also have shortcomings.

Some of the calculators aren't updated often enough to reflect the latest research and findings. In a quest to be user-friendly, many limit the number of questions they ask. Many calculators, for example, don't ask if the person ever had cancer.

Some of the calculators make arbitrary decisions. For example, research shows that calcium-rich diets improve bone density and reduce hip fractures late in life. Avoiding a hip fracture can increase life expectancy. But the research doesn't show how much a calcium-rich diet and avoiding hip fractures increase life expectancy. Yet at least one calculator asks about calcium in the diet and arbitrarily adjusts life expectancy based on the answer.

The calculators also rely on self-reported information, which can be incomplete or inaccurate.

Perhaps most important, the online calculators generally treat each factor in isolation and adjust life expectancy higher or lower based on each answer. In the real world, factors often interact. Two or more factors together can increase or decrease life expectancy more than each factor alone.

Online calculators are valuable tools. They're a better way to estimate life expectancy than the methods most people use. But I recommend that if you go this route you use more than one calculator. You'll see different results, sometimes differences of a decade or more. Then you can decide if you want to be conservative and use the longest projection, average the results, or use another method.

You also can consider one of the scientific services known generally as DNA testing services. You submit some genetic material, usually saliva or blood. You may need to go to a medical lab to submit the sample, though many of these services now use the mail or commercial shipping services. The scientific service will examine your DNA or run blood panels and compare your results to those in its database.

These services purport to offer a more scientific and personalized estimate of longevity. Some also say they can point to health or medical issues before you display symptoms or they are detected by standard tests associated with routine medical exams. Your life expectancy could be extended by having these issues addressed now instead of later when symptoms arise.

These are new services, so they are a long way from having a record of accurately estimating the longevity of individuals. Their accuracy depends on the size of their databases as well as the methods they use to sort the data and develop links between different factors and life expectancy.

Some General Rules to Use Carefully

Once you have a reasonable estimate of your life expectancy, you are closer to making the optimum decision about claiming your Social Security benefits.

The general rule is that for single people with no reason to expect a below-average life expectancy, it's better to wait to claim retirement benefits. Each year you wait after full retirement increases your benefits by 8 percent. That's an 8 percent return on your money, and it's both guaranteed and tax-free. Not many people have another way to earn a guaranteed 8 percent after-tax return. And if your full retirement age (FRA) is 67 and you wait the full three years to 70 to maximize your benefits, you'll increase your monthly benefits by *29 percent.*

Married couples should coordinate their benefits taking into account their life expectancies. Usually one spouse earns significantly more during the working years and will have a higher Social Security retirement benefit. Usually, the best strategy for these couples is for the higher-earning spouse to delay benefits as long as possible. The other spouse can claim benefits earlier: it may even make sense for the spouse with lower benefits to begin benefits as soon as allowed at age 62.

How Break-Even Analysis Can Break Your Retirement

Many people make their decisions about Social Security benefits using what is called break-even analysis, which is widely used by financial advisors. In the past it was the primary tool the Social Security Administration (SSA) used to help people decide when to begin their benefits.

Break-even analysis is simple to work with and explain, which is why it is widely used. But the method has significant shortcomings and can lead people to make the decision that isn't best for them in the long run.

Here's how break-even analysis works.

Suppose your full retirement benefit at 66 would be $1,400 per month. Waiting until age 70 would entitle you to $1,820 monthly. So waiting until 70 gets you an extra $420 a month, while taking benefits at 66 means you receive payments 48 months earlier.

To find the break-even point, multiply the normal retirement benefit by the number of extra months that you'll receive Social Security payments before age 70. In this example, the calculation is $1,400 times 48 months for a total early payment of $67,200. Divide that total by the $420 increase in the monthly benefit you would receive by waiting until age 70 to claim benefits. The result is 160. That is the number of months you have to live after age 70 for the total lifetime payments from waiting until age 70 to catch up with the lifetime payments you would receive from starting benefits at 66. Adding 160 months, or 13 years and 4 months, to 70 years takes you to age 83 and 4 months. That's the age you have to live to for waiting to claim benefits to pay off. If you die before age 83 and 4 months, you will receive lower lifetime benefits than you would have by claiming benefits earlier. Every month you live past 83 and 4 months increases the lifetime benefit of claiming benefits at age 70.

The formula is set up so that the benefit for waiting to receive benefits closely follows the actuarial tables used to develop the Social Security benefit formula. The Social Security system should come out whole on average. Those who outlive the life expectancy will come out ahead by waiting to receive benefits, and those who do not will lose money by waiting.

Here's another example. Suppose you turn 62 and your FRA is 66. If you started taking benefits at age 62, your benefits payable would be 77.5 percent of full retirement age, meaning that if your FRA benefit were $1,400 per month you would receive $1,085, or $315 less monthly. But by taking benefits at 62, you will receive the benefits for an extra 48 months before FRA. The total benefits you would receive before your FRA would be $52,080. Divide that amount by the $315 additional benefit you would receive by waiting until FRA. You'll find that it will take 165 ⅓ months (or almost 14 years) to make up for waiting until FRA to claim benefits. You will have to live to almost 80 to break even for waiting until FRA to begin benefits.

Live till 80, and waiting until full retirement age to take your benefits will have paid off: you will receive higher total lifetime benefits than you would have if you had claimed them at 62.

As in the other example, the break-even point is designed to be around average life expectancy for the age group. The system breaks even on average, so the half of the age group who live beyond life expectancy receive higher lifetime benefits than they would have by claiming earlier.

Break-Even Analysis Gone Bad

So what's wrong with break-even analysis?

For one thing, research demonstrates that how the Social Security decision is framed or presented to people makes a difference. People tend to begin their Social Security benefits earlier when the break-even analysis is used to help them decide. But when people are told that the amount Social Security will pay out over the average life expectancy is the same regardless of the choice they make, they tend to delay taking their benefits.

Also, break-even analysis makes the decision about when to begin Social Security seem like something between an investment and a bet. Some people conclude that if they delay benefits, they're making a bet that they will live until at least the break-even age. As we have seen, many people don't have a strong grasp of the life expectancy data and believe they are unlikely to live to average life expectancy. They are unwilling to make what they view as a bet that they will live to average life expectancy or beyond, though half of them will.

The break-even analysis also plays into two human traits that, behavioral finance shows, cause people to make bad financial decisions.

One of those traits is "loss regret." Most people regret an investment or financial loss more than they appreciate a gain. It's not clear why that's the case, but a number of studies have found that people in general have stronger regrets about losses than they have appreciation of gains. Some ways of couching the Social Security decision make it appear that the individual is losing or giving up something by delaying Social Security benefits. Break-even analysis begins with the understanding that that you could have a stream of payments beginning at age 62, and that you lose that revenue stream by delaying Social Security benefits to full retirement age or later. Presented with the example above—of the individual who can choose between retiring early with a benefit of $1,085 per month or waiting until full retirement age for a $1,400 monthly benefit—most people will focus on the fact that waiting till full retirement age means losing more than $52,000 the individual could have received between ages 62 and 66. That "loss"—which will be locked in only if the person dies at age 66, much earlier than the average life expectancy—resonates more than the gain in lifetime benefits (from higher monthly payments) that he will enjoy if he lives beyond the average life expectancy.

Another trait that interferes with clear-eyed analysis of Social Security options: most people have difficulty delaying gratification. The relatively low savings rate and the small amount of money that most people have put aside for retirement are but two examples. And there is no denying that taking Social Security benefits at FRA or later means you are delaying for years the receipt of money you could have had.

Thus, many people will find it difficult to delay receiving over $52,000, even if that delay means receiving more money later.

While break-even analysis can be a helpful tool, it frames the decision in a way that biases many people toward claiming benefits early. So break-even analysis shouldn't be the only or even the primary tool used to make decisions about Social Security.

Longevity Insurance for Longevity Risk

You should remember that Social Security retirement benefits are an insurance program. For most people during their working years, each paycheck has a box or line labeled "FICA" that states the amount of money withheld for Social Security taxes. FICA stands for Federal Insurance Contributions Act. Insurance is right there in the name.

In its early days, Social Security was called "old-age insurance." Many economists and financial advisors still call it longevity insurance. Over the years, however, the general public has come to view Social Security as a savings account that they want access to as soon as possible.

But your Social Security retirement benefits insure against the possibility that you'll live to the average life expectancy of your age group or beyond. Most important, the program insures the percentage—still a minority, but increasing—of people who live well beyond life expectancy. The program ensures they will receive a minimum amount of income no matter how long they live, even if they spend all their other assets.

As we have seen, the greatest fear of those planning for retirement is running out of money. Social Security provides guaranteed lifetime benefits that are indexed for inflation, so your Social Security benefits won't run out and will preserve at least a portion of their purchasing power. Even better, if you delay receiving the benefits as long as you can, the benefits you will receive in those extended years will be much higher than if you took the benefits at an earlier age.

Consider what your life and finances will be like should you live to your late eighties or early nineties. At age 62 or so, it is tempting to begin your retirement benefits and start receiving that extra monthly payment. But at age 85 or 90, you'd probably much rather have a monthly check that's considerably higher.

Once you have lived to the average life expectancy for your age group, as projected in Social Security law, the additional lifetime benefit from delaying benefits increases rapidly. Each monthly check adds to the amount. You'll be much more financially secure in those later years if, when you were younger, you delayed claiming benefits in return for those higher monthly payments.

Longevity Insurance

You probably have other types of insurance, such as for your autos and home. Most people hope that they never receive payments from a claim because they don't want to experience a casualty. But they still pay the insurance premiums and generally don't look at them as money wasted or thrown away. They know they are buying protection from a significant financial loss, even if it has a low probability of occurring.

Social Security provides a similar insurance benefit, and you increase the benefit by delaying the receipt of the retirement benefits. For many people, the probability of receiving an enhanced benefit by delaying Social Security benefits is higher than the probability they'll receive a substantial claim payment against their auto or homeowner's insurance.

Social Security provides a second type of insurance for married couples. As we have seen, when a spouse passes away, one Social Security benefit stops coming in to the household. The surviving spouse must maintain the household with less income from Social Security.

No matter which spouse survives, you both probably want to ensure that spouse has the highest income possible. The way to do that is for the spouse with the highest lifetime earnings to delay Social Security benefits as long as possible so that his or her monthly benefit will be as large as possible and thus the survivor's benefit will be as high as possible.

Keep in mind that there's a high probability at least one spouse will live beyond the average life expectancy and a significant probability one spouse will live well beyond it. Whichever one of you is the survivor will likely be much more secure with the higher income during the solo years than they would be from beginning a lower benefit a few years earlier.

For married couples, delaying the higher of the two Social Security benefits is a very inexpensive form of life insurance. As I showed in chapter 1, Social Security benefits have substantial value over a lifetime. You would need a large sum of money—for most people, one million dollars or more—to buy a commercial annuity with the same monthly income that's guaranteed for life and indexed for inflation. Or a substantial investment portfolio would be needed to generate the same lifetime monthly income, and the investment return won't be guaranteed as Social Security is.

When people run low on money in retirement, it often is after one spouse has passed away. There are several reasons the money might run out. But near the top of the list is that income has declined drastically after one spouse passed away. The surviving spouse is more likely to run out of money if both spouses took their Social Security benefits early because that decision results in a much lower survivor benefit.

Profit from Government Sloth

There's another reason to consider delaying Social Security benefits.

The Social Security Administration and many other sources will tell you that it doesn't matter to the system when you begin retirement benefits. The benefit levels for different ages were set using life-expectancy data, so Social Security will pay the same total amount to the age group over its lifetime, regardless of when the individual members begin their benefits.

The Social Security benefit levels, however, were last updated in 1983. The SSA's actuarial data and benefit levels at different ages haven't changed since then. Yet life expectancy has increased since then, and private insurers have updated their actuarial tables to reflect that fact.

What this means is that more than half of any age group is likely to live past the average life expectancy that was used to determine the benefit levels. Now those who delay benefits have on average—setting aside their individual health and other factors—a greater than 50 percent probability of receiving higher lifetime benefits as a result of the delay.

Government moves slowly. And this is one instance when its sluggishness can work in your favor. The average life expectancy for your age cohort is likely to be longer now than it was when your Social Security benefit levels were set. Thus the increase you receive by delaying the receipt of your benefits is probably larger than it would be if updated life expectancy data were used. In other words, you will receive a larger bonus from delaying benefits than Congress intended.

Maximize Your Longevity Insurance

One of your greatest risks in retirement is that you will outlive your income and assets. Few people realize that optimal Social Security benefits can reduce that risk. Thus, a high percentage of people claim Social Security benefits well before FRA, and only a small minority wait to maximize benefits at age 70.

Life expectancy has increased, and that has many benefits. But it increases the risk of outliving your money.

Making a reasonable estimate of your life expectancy and of the probability that you will live a long time is key to making the right decision about when you should claim Social Security benefits. Optimal Social Security–claiming decisions, both for individuals and for married couples, depend on developing that reasonable estimate, as you have learned to do in this chapter.

CHAPTER 3

You Can't Depend on the Social Security Administration for the Right Answer

You wouldn't ask the Internal Revenue Service for advice and recommendations on how to minimize your income taxes. So why would you go to the Social Security Administration to learn how to maximize your retirement income?

Unfortunately, you can't expect the SSA even to give you accurate information about your benefit options in response to your inquiries. You rely on the SSA at your own risk.

There's substantial documented and anecdotal evidence that SSA staff regularly give people information and advice that can cause them to make bad decisions about their benefits.

As the editor of *Retirement Watch*, a popular monthly newsletter and website devoted to retirement finances, I regularly write on Social Security and hear from readers about their experiences with the SSA. And it's not unusual for me to hear from a reader who has contacted the SSA two or three different times about the same issue and received two or three different answers, or who has been given incorrect advice.

One reader, for example, was delaying his Social Security benefits until age 70 and was interested in the option of taking six months of benefits in a lump sum. He understood from my writing that by taking the lump sum he would be treated as though he had applied for benefits six months earlier. (See chapter 11 for details.) In August 2019 he wrote the following to me:

> I turn 70 in January 2020 and have waited to take my social security until then.
>
> Last Spring I had an appointment at my local SS office to gather information. It was there that I was told about the 6 month cash lump sum payment, going back to age 69 ½ for monthly payments beginning with January 2020.
>
> I have one debt left and the cash would wipe it out.
>
> Yesterday I called SS to make an appointment to file in October for January. I made an appointment for a face to face meeting on October 8th, and mentioned my plan to apply for the lump sum. The phone counselor said that if I do that, my SS monthly payments reverts to the amount due to me at age 66. He assured me that he is correct.
>
> How can I apply for SS and be assured of accuracy?

Unfortunately, he can't. In fact, as we have seen, his benefits should revert to the amount he would have received if he had claimed them at age 69 ½, not at age 66. Even more unfortunate is that this experience isn't unusual. I regularly hear similar stories from other readers and from audience members when I make public presentations. I regularly see anecdotes from financial advisors reporting errors or conflicts in the advice that they or their clients have received from the SSA.

Social Security's Mistakes Documented

But you don't have to rely on anecdotes to know that advice and information from the SSA should be treated skeptically. The Office of Inspector General (OIG) of the SSA has issued reports documenting and detailing some of the mistakes.

On February 14, 2018, the OIG issued a report blandly titled, "Higher Benefits for Dually Entitled Widow(er)s Had They Delayed Applying for Retirement Benefits" (A-09-18-50559). The report concluded that the SSA, in violation of its own policy and procedures, didn't inform widowed beneficiaries of an option that would increase their lifetime guaranteed income.

As we will see in more detail in chapter 6, a widowed person is entitled to either his or her own retirement benefit or the survivor benefit—whichever is higher. Plus, unlike other Social Security benefits, a surviving spouse can first claim one type of benefit and later claim the other benefit if it is higher.

For example, a widow might first claim the survivor's benefit—which is available to her at age 60, two years before the earliest she can claim retirement benefits—to ensure receiving some monthly income. This also allows the widow to delay claiming her own retirement benefit until that benefit reaches the full retirement benefit or delay it even longer until it is maximized at age 70. At that point the widow can switch from the survivor's benefit to the higher retirement benefit. The reverse also is possible, if the survivor benefit is higher than the retirement benefit.

SSA policy is that employees must explain the different filing options available to a claimant and the advantages and disadvantages of each option. If the claimant chooses a filing option that doesn't maximize benefits, the SSA employee is supposed to document the facts and decision in the SSA's automated system.

But when the OIG selected a sample of widowed beneficiaries who were eligible for both retirement benefits and survivor's benefits before age 70 and examined their records, it found that the SSA had failed to inform 82 percent of the claimants of the strategy that would maximize their lifetime benefits. Specifically, these claimants should have filed initially for survivor's benefits and later filed for their retirement benefits at age 70. But only 18 percent of the sample made the optimum claiming decision for them.

The OIG applied these findings to the entire Social Security population and estimated that the failure to follow SSA policy and give claimants correct information and advice had resulted in 11,123 beneficiaries receiving lower lifetime benefits than they were entitled to. About 9,224 beneficiaries age 70 and older were underpaid about $131.9 million in aggregate. Another 1,889 who were under age 70 at the time of the study would be underpaid about $9.8 million annually beginning the year they turn 70.[1]

And this is not the first or the last time the OIG pointed out this error to the SSA. A similar report was filed in 2015, and the SSA has done little or nothing to improve its operations since then. The OIG revisited the issue again and published another report on June 9, 2020. This latest report found that almost half of the surviving spouses weren't informed that they were eligible for higher benefits after their spouses passed away. The OIG estimated that, as a result, more than 12,000 beneficiaries would be underpaid cumulatively more than $530 million in lifetime benefits.[2]

To date, the SSA has done nothing to compensate the beneficiaries who are being underpaid for life because of SSA's failure to follow its policies and give accurate information to the claimants. In early 2020 a law firm was trying to put together a class action lawsuit against SSA to compensate those underpaid as a result of these mistakes.

As you may have surmised, this is not the only mistake the SSA has made. It's not unusual for the SSA to miscalculate someone's benefits and begin sending monthly benefits greater than the program mandates. After a while, the SSA catches the error and sends the beneficiary a letter explaining the mistake and demanding repayment of the excess payments. The SSA also sends people letters stating they might be entitled to a higher benefit if they file a claim, but these letters frequently contain mistakes. The benefit estimates that the SSA mails out can also contain errors.

It may be hard to believe in this day of smartphones that are more powerful than the supercomputers of a few decades ago, but SSA's computer system is so antiquated that SSA staff often calculate benefits manually. Sometimes they make mistakes in those calculations.

In addition, as we have seen, the Social Security program is detailed and complicated, with source documents covering more than twenty thousand pages. At the same time, the SSA is understaffed, and its workers are poorly trained and underpaid for the work they do. One thing the SSA staff seem to be trained in is to assert absolute certainty, even when their accuracy is questionable or they are saying something different from what they told others.

You should take three steps to protect yourself from the SSA's shortcomings. Step One is to research your options, learn what benefits you are entitled to, and determine which benefit you want to claim and how to file for it. Step Two is to file the appropriate application, preferably online rather than over the telephone or in person at an SSA office. Though many SSA employees are well-intentioned and hardworking, the information I have says that it's not a good idea to ask questions at the office or over the telephone, or to rely on the SSA for guidance.

Then, Step Three: you have to follow up and monitor your case. Remember that SSA's technology isn't up to date. Your case is likely to be reviewed manually by SSA employees. Sometimes the SSA employees reviewing the case will decide you didn't choose the best claiming strategy, or that you aren't allowed to claim the benefits as you did, and will change your application. Sometimes an SSA employee will contact you to discuss the changes. But other times SSA staff will simply process the revised application. You won't know it has been changed until the benefits start arriving for a different benefit than the one you claimed.

How to Read Those Benefit Estimates

At some point you have probably received a printed estimate of your future Social Security benefits in the mail. There was a time, beginning in 1999, when the SSA mailed a statement every year to everyone who might be eligible to receive retirement benefits in the future. But the cost of preparing and mailing those statements didn't fit into the SSA's budget for long, and the SSA curtailed the practice. No statements were mailed in 2011, and then the mailings were off and on for a few years. The current policy is for written statements to be mailed annually to everyone 60 or older who meets the minimum qualifications for benefits and has not claimed them.

There are other ways to obtain estimates of your benefits, regardless of your age. You can call Social Security or visit a local SSA office and ask for a benefit estimate. You also can register on the Social Security website for a *"my* Social Security" account. Once registered, you won't be mailed benefit estimates. Instead, you can go online and obtain the latest estimates at any time.

The benefit-estimate statements provide useful information. As you probably have been told, you should take a look at the estimates at least every few years, regardless of your age. Once you're age 52 (and thus within ten years of the point at which you're first allowed to claim retirement benefits), an annual review of the estimates is a good idea.

The most important part of the statement for most people is the earnings history. Social Security benefits are based on the highest thirty-five years of earnings. Mistakes in the earnings history, especially years when earnings are missing and recorded as zero, can reduce benefits every month for the rest of your life. So be sure to review the earnings history and contact the SSA to correct any errors. SSA will require documentation of the error, such as an income tax return or W-2 statement. The longer you wait, the less likely it is that an error can be corrected.

Sometimes there's a lag of a year or so before the SSA posts earnings. That's especially true of self-employment income. The SSA doesn't receive that information from the IRS until after a tax return has been filed and processed.

The part of the SSA statement that's key for your retirement planning is the estimate of future benefits. You'll see an estimate of the monthly benefit that you'll receive at full retirement age, which varies by your year of birth. There is also an estimate of the monthly benefit that will be paid if you claim benefits as early as possible, at age 62. And the statement will also give you an estimate of the monthly benefit that will be paid if you wait until age 70 to claim the benefits. That's the maximum amount possible, because you get no additional delayed retirement credits for waiting beyond age 70 to begin receiving benefits.

You also will find estimates of disability benefits, child benefits, and benefits payable to your surviving spouse.

But some key types of benefits aren't estimated on the statements. Those estimates are available only after someone files to receive the benefits. In other words, you don't have a good idea of what the benefit will be until you, or someone who can receive benefits based on your earnings history, applies to receive the benefits. In this category are spousal benefits, benefits you might receive as a surviving spouse, and divorced-spouse benefits.

About Those Assumptions

When someone says a number is an estimate, that should trigger an immediate question. An estimate is based on assumptions, often about the future. The question to ask is: What are the assumptions?

The assumptions that the SSA uses in the benefit estimates are conservative—far too conservative in the views of some analysts, who judge that most workers are likely to receive higher monthly benefits than in the estimates. The assumptions used for economic growth and inflation, in particular, are low, causing benefits to be understated. These are calculated from your earnings history indexed for wage growth during your lifetime. There are also estimates about your future earnings history, which I'll discuss shortly, that are unrealistic or misleading for many people and likely to cause benefits to be understated.

Some analysts even argue that the SSA is deliberately underestimating future benefits to encourage people to save more for retirement or to dampen people's expectations about how much they will receive in Social Security benefits. Other analysts say conservative estimates are a good idea: the SSA shouldn't risk overstating what people are likely to receive. They will base their retirement plans on those estimates, and they could be in trouble if their Social Security benefits are less than the estimates they're depending on.

In any case, the benefit amounts in the statements are estimates that could be very different from the benefits you receive. And the further you are away from retirement, the less accurate the estimates will be. The closer you are to retirement, the less room there is for the estimates to vary from the final results.

But there is an exception to that rule. When the SSA estimates your benefits it uses only your earnings history through age 62. Let's say you're 65, still working, and considering whether to claim benefits now or wait until later, perhaps as late as age 70. The SSA's benefit estimate won't include your earnings after 62. The difference between the estimate and your actual retirement benefit could be substantial, especially if these are higher-earnings years that are knocking low-earnings years out of your highest thirty-five years. You won't know the real benefit until after applying to receive it.

Because a very high percentage of people claim their benefits at age 62 or shortly thereafter, ending the benefit estimates with the data available as of age 62 will be accurate for most people. But it's possible that some people claim their benefits early because the estimates underestimate the gains from waiting. People might wait longer to claim benefits if they knew how much more the payment would be as a result of additional income earned after age 62.

This assumption also distorts the planning of younger workers. They don't realize that the earnings assumption stops at age 62 and that their benefits could be substantially higher if they worked for years after that and replaced lower-earnings years with higher-earning years after age 62.

Another assumption, which can cause the SSA estimates to be either too high or too low, is that you'll continue to earn essentially the same amount for the rest of your career through age 62 as you earned in the latest year. That amount is indexed for inflation, but it doesn't take into account future promotions or job changes that will increase earnings more than simple inflation—or, on the other hand, the possibility of leaving the workforce early, whether temporarily or permanently, voluntarily or involuntarily.

As we have seen, Social Security benefits increase in line with the Consumer Price Index (CPI) each year but aren't reduced for any decrease in the CPI. But these cost of living adjustments (COLAs) aren't taken into account in the SSA's benefit estimates. This is an understatement of future benefits, which could be significant if the rate of inflation is high.

The bottom line is that the annual benefit estimates you receive are ballpark numbers, not numbers you can take to the bank. The younger you are, the more the estimates can vary from the final benefit. Of course, low, conservative estimates can be good. You're less likely to plan on receiving an artificially high benefit and have to scale back your retirement spending plan once the final estimate is received.

The disadvantage of these conservative estimates is that in many cases they understate the advantages of delaying benefits until full retirement age or later. That's especially true for people who can continue to earn an annual income after age 62 that would exceed the earnings of earlier years in their careers. Many people planning their retirements never know how much their Social Security benefits could be increased by the combination of delayed retirement credits from waiting to claim benefits and knocking lower-earning years out of their thirty-five highest-earning years with higher-earning years after age 62.

How to Get Better Estimates

You don't have to settle for using the official annual benefit estimates from SSA. As I said, these can be useful ballpark estimates. But you should use better estimates when you're at the point of making detailed retirement plans. It's especially important to look at more accurate estimates before deciding when to claim Social Security retirement benefits and when to stop working.

Despite the imperfection of SSA's annual benefit estimates, you can obtain better estimates through SSA—by registering on SSA's website for a *"my* Social Security" account. Once you open the account, you'll have access to your lifetime earnings record, and it's worth your while to register and obtain estimates from the calculator there. Log into that account, and you have access to a retirement-benefits estimate calculator tied directly to your current earnings. Because of the updated earnings history, the SSA calculator at *"my* Social Security" will give you more accurate estimates than the benefits estimates that the SSA mails out. The calculator will also estimate benefits under different scenarios you create. It also lets you incorporate your spouse's earnings record so that you can see the results of each of you claiming benefits at different times. But it will still make potentially inaccurate assumptions about future earnings and inflation.

While the SSA calculator is good, I recommend using more than one calculator to make your decision. The calculations can be complex, and they depend on a number of assumptions that vary from calculator to calculator. Some calculators allow you to change all the assumptions, while others don't. That's why I recommend using at least one calculator in addition to the SSA's and comparing the results.

Private firms also offer software that will generate benefit estimates under different scenarios. They also let you include the earnings history of your spouse so you can determine the best claiming strategies for both of you. These programs are better described as Social Security–optimization programs than as benefit-estimation programs, because they try to determine the best Social Security–claiming strategy under likely scenarios. The goal of these programs is to maximize lifetime benefits. The programs also give you more freedom to change the assumptions than the SSA does.

There are several commercially available Social Security calculators well worth your consideration. (I have no financial relationship with either company or the experts who have worked on them.)

"Maximize My Social Security" is a comprehensive calculator developed with economist Laurence Kotlikoff, a Social Security expert. It's available at https://maximizemysocialsecurity.com and costs $40 per year.

Another comprehensive calculator that would be a good choice is "Social Security Solutions," developed with economist and Social Security expert William Reichenstein. Several different packages of this tool, starting at $19.95, are available at www.socialsecuritysolutions.com.

I usually recommend using more than one of these programs, if you can afford it, along with the "my Social Security" calculator. Though the programs are very similar, there are differences in the details. It's good to see whether they generate significantly different results for the same scenarios. These programs also give you a way to check the benefits SSA pays you after filing your claim.

You also can work with a financial planner who has expertise in Social Security and uses professional versions of the Social Security calculators. If you can't find a planner through recommendations and references, the websites for the two Social Security calculators just mentioned offer to connect you to advisors who use the professional versions of their calculators.

Making the optimum decision about claiming Social Security benefits can change your lifetime benefits by a substantial amount. For most people it's worth using all three of these calculators and comparing the results, or even working with a financial planning professional.

CHAPTER 4

What You Need to Know about Your Social Security Benefits

To really understand Social Security and be sure of maximizing your lifetime benefits, you need to dig into the details. In this chapter I explain the basics of how Social Security benefits are calculated and how to use this knowledge to your advantage. Let's dive into the details and learn more about the program that is the foundation of retirement income for many Americans.

A Few Basics

Social Security was intended to provide a basic minimum income for older Americans. But over the years the program has expanded to include a range of other benefits. You may receive only one type of benefit during your lifetime, or you may receive several over time, as you qualify for different benefits. The SSA will pay a beneficiary only one benefit at a time. If you qualify for several benefits at the same time, you'll generally be paid the highest of the benefits.

You qualify for benefits based on your earnings history. You also may qualify for benefits based on the earning history of another person, such as a spouse or parent. The main kinds of benefits available under the program are:

- retirement benefits
- spousal benefits
- child benefits
- disability benefits
- survivor's benefits
- ex-spouse's benefits (technically, part of spousal benefits)

The minimum qualification to be eligible for retirement benefits based on your own work history is to have forty credits of covered employment. Covered employment is any work for which you are subject to Social Security taxes—also known as FICA (for Federal Insurance Contribution Act) or OASI (for Old Age & Survivors Insurance). Self-employment for which you are required to pay self-employment taxes also qualifies.

Most but not all jobs in the United States are covered work for Social Security purposes. As you'll see in chapter 10, some jobs aren't subject to Social Security taxes—primarily jobs with state and local governments or tax-exempt organizations. Jobs outside the U.S. usually aren't covered employment, and neither are many jobs at U.S. subsidiaries of foreign companies.

A "credit" used to be referred to as a "quarter." Originally, to earn one you had to be paid at least $50 for covered employment during a calendar quarter. To qualify for Social Security retirement benefits, you had to earn forty quarters—a total of ten years of covered work, but the quarters didn't have to be consecutive.

In 1978, the forty quarters was changed to forty credits. A credit is an amount of earnings, which changes each year with inflation. In

2020, $1,410 in covered earnings amounted to a credit. You earned four credits of coverage with your first $5,640 of covered work during the year.

You can't earn more than four credits of coverage during a calendar year. The first $5,640 of covered employment or self-employment income for the year earned four credits of coverage in 2020, even if you earned that much in the first month of the year. No matter how much money you earn the rest of the year, you don't receive more than four credits for that year. Most people earn the forty credits required to qualify for Social Security retirement benefits with ten years of four credits in each year. There are different minimum credit levels for disability and survivor's benefits, which are discussed in the appropriate chapters.

Your AIME

Now you know how you qualify for Social Security retirement benefits. You should also know how the benefits are calculated—so you can judge whether the estimates you're receiving from the Social Security Administration (SSA) are accurate, and so you'll have a good idea about how to increase your benefits by making savvy decisions.

Social Security benefits aren't anything like the benefits of a 401(k) plan or other savings plans with which most people are familiar. Your Social Security retirement benefits are calculated on the basis of your lifetime earnings. But the taxes you and your employer pay on those earnings aren't going into a separate account to be accumulated and invested until you're ready to retire. You can't cash the benefits in as a lump sum at retirement. You receive them in monthly payments for life.

And in contrast to how an investment account works, there's an inverse relationship between the amount of taxes you pay into Social

Security and the "return" you receive in benefits. Social Security is a progressive system, so those who have the highest lifetime earnings and pay the most into the system receive a lower benefit for each dollar paid in. Those who didn't earn as much during their careers, and therefore paid fewer taxes into the system, receive a larger benefit for each dollar paid in. They don't receive a larger absolute benefit, but they do get a larger benefit for each tax dollar they paid into the system.

The calculation of your benefits begins with your lifetime earnings from covered employment and self-employment. Specifically, the SSA takes your highest thirty-five years of earnings—after indexing them for wage inflation, as I will explain below. If you have fewer than thirty-five years of covered earnings, zero-earnings years are also included in the calculations. But if you have more than thirty-five years of covered earnings, only the thirty-five years with the highest earnings are used in the calculation.

Before the highest thirty-five years of earnings are selected, each year of earnings through age 60 is adjusted for inflation. A dollar of earnings in 1975 was worth more than a dollar of earnings in 2020 is worth because of inflation. So to equalize the annual earnings, the SSA adjusts your earnings for wage inflation—using not the Consumer Price Index (CPI) but instead the National Average Wage Index, which is generally higher than the CPI. If you want, you can search the SSA website to find the adjustment factor used for each year. Earnings after age 60 aren't indexed; the SSA calculation uses the amount you actually earned each year beginning at 61.[1]

Once the indexing is done, your highest thirty-five years of earnings are identified and added. The total is divided by 420, which is the number of months in thirty-five years. The result is your Average Indexed Monthly Earnings, or AIME—a critical number. Your AIME is the basis for calculating all Social Security benefits that depend on your earnings record. You have probably heard advice that you should review the earnings record the SSA has for you from time to time and try to correct any errors in it. And now you should see the importance of a correct earnings record. If SSA credits you with lower earnings for a year than you actually had (and paid FICA taxes on), your Social Security retirement benefits and all benefits paid to others based on your earnings record will be lower than they should be.

How AIME Becomes PIA (a.k.a. FRB)

The AIME is used to compute your retirement benefits, but the calculation isn't straightforward. Remember, Social Security retirement benefits are progressive. Higher earners receive lower benefits for each dollar of earnings and taxes paid than lower earners do. To establish that progressivism, SSA does a little work with the AIME. Instead of applying a simple factor to AIME to arrive at your benefit level, SSA uses a multistep equation to arrive at your primary insurance amount, or PIA, which is also known as your full retirement benefit (FRB) because it's the amount you will receive at your full retirement age (FRA).

The AIME is divided into what the SSA calls "bend points" or "break points." The bend points in the PIA calculation change with inflation each year. Your actual PIA isn't calculated until you turn 62. Before that, any estimate of future benefits from SSA is made using a series of estimates of what your future AIME and PIA will be. Estimates at age 62 and later use the real computation of PIA.

There are three bend points. For someone who turned 62 in 2020, the first $960 of AIME is multiplied by 0.90. The amount between $960 and $5,784 (the next $4,825) is multiplied by 0.32. Any AIME amount over $5,784 is multiplied by 0.15. The results are added together, and the sum is the PIA, or the FRB, the monthly retirement benefit the person will receive if benefits are claimed exactly at your FRA.

Let's look at two examples to show how the calculations work and how they make the system progressive.

Lo Profits and Hi Profits are twin brothers who turned 62 in 2020. Lo has been working since 1980, when he turned 22, and he has consistently earned exactly half the maximum Social Security wage base each year. (The Social Security wage base is the maximum pay on which Social Security taxes are imposed. FICA taxes are taken from each dollar of that amount, but once someone's total earnings for any year reach the maximum wage base, additional earnings that year aren't subject to Social Security taxes.) After his highest thirty-five years of earnings are identified and adjusted, Lo has an AIME of $5,195. SSA will compute his PIA or FRB to be $2,219. That's the amount he will receive each month in retirement benefits if he waits until full retirement age to claim his benefits. Full retirement age for Lo is 66 years and 8 months. (I explain below how full retirement age is determined.)

Hi Profits is naturally the same age as his twin brother Lo, but Hi earned exactly the Social Security maximum wage base during his career—twice as much as Lo. So Hi's covered earnings were twice those of Lo. SSA will compute Lo's AIME to be $10,683. But Hi's PIA is only $3,143. Though Hi earned twice what Lo did during their careers, Hi's PIA is only about 42 percent higher than Lo's.

Note that these calculations were made when the twins reached age 62. That's the first age at which SSA will make an official calculation of AIME and PIA. But if you keep working past age 62 and have covered earnings, those additional earnings will eventually be factored in to determine your benefit.

There's an additional limit on your retirement benefit. Regardless of the PIA that is calculated for you, your actual benefit cannot exceed a maximum monthly Social Security initial retirement benefit, which changes with inflation each year. In 2020, the maximum initial full retirement benefit was $3,011 per month. (This was first time the maximum initial benefit exceeded $3,000.) Some beneficiaries receive more than this amount because they've been receiving benefits for years and their benefits have increased annually with cost of living adjustments (COLA). The maximum monthly limit only applies to first-time beneficiaries.

Another way to conceive of the progressive nature of Social Security is through what's called the replacement ratio. That's the percentage of your income from your last year of covered work that is paid out to you in your first year of Social Security retirement benefits.

The SSA says the average Social Security beneficiary receives about 40 percent of his final covered earnings in retirement benefits. But the replacement ratio gets higher as covered income falls below average. The lowest income workers receive about 90 percent of their final covered earnings in retirement benefits. Those who earned the maximum Social Security wage base, on the other hand, receive only about 15 percent of their final covered earnings in retirement benefits. The highest-earning retirees have an even lower replacement ratio when all their income is considered, because their earnings exceeded the maximum wage base. They didn't pay Social Security taxes on those excess earnings, and they also don't receive any Social Security retirement benefits based on them.

Know Your FRA and Understand Why It Matters

Another concept you need to understand is full retirement age (FRA). When you claim retirement benefits at your FRA, you receive the full retirement benefit (FRB). When you claim benefits before FRA, they are reduced. The reduction is a percentage amount for each month you claim benefits before FRA. When you delay claiming benefits until after FRA, the monthly amount you'll receive is increased for each month of that delay. But the increases, known as delayed retirement credits (DRC), stop at age 70. So there's no reason to delay claiming retirement benefits past age 70 since benefits won't increase any more after that point. In a moment we'll go into the details of how much benefits increase or decrease when you claim them late or early.

FRA used to be the same for everyone: age 65. But when Social Security was reformed in 1983 in order to make it more financially stable, one of the reforms was to increase the FRA, which now increases on a sliding scale based on the year of birth. People born in 1937 or earlier retained the traditional FRA of 65. FRA increased gradually for those born in 1938 or later years. Those born from 1943 to 1954 have an FRA of 66. Those born from 1955 to 1959 have FRAs of 66 years and 2, 4, 6, 8, and 10 months, respectively. For those born in 1960 or later years, FRA is 67.

Table 4.1 shows the FRA schedule.

Table 4.1: What's Your Full Retirement Age?

Year of Birth	Full Retirement Age (FRA)
1943–1954	66
1955	66 and 2 months
1956	66 and 4 months
1957	66 and 6 months
1958	66 and 8 months
1959	66 and 10 months
1960 and later	67

Note: If you were born on January 1 of any year, use the previous year as your year of birth.

FRA has nothing to do with your work status. Your FRA is a particular age, whether you are working or not. You could stop working years before FRA or continue working years past FRA, and your FRA won't be affected. The FRA is determined by your year of birth and isn't affected by whether or not you actually are retired on that date.

How Benefits Change Based on Your Claiming Age

When you claim Social Security retirement benefits at FRA you receive the FRB. But, as we have seen, you don't have to wait until FRA to claim your retirement benefits. You can claim the benefits as early as age 62. You can also delay claiming the benefits after the FRA.

The benefits are reduced below the FRB for each month you claim them before FRA. The early retirement reduction, or penalty, for claiming benefits before FRA is 5/9 of a percent for each month claimed before FRA, up to 36 months. When the benefit is claimed more than 36 months before FRA, the benefit is further reduced by 5/12 of a percent for each of the additional months.

For someone born in 1960 who claims benefits as early as possible, at age 62, the benefit paid will be 30 percent less than the FRB. In other words, the person will receive only 70 percent of the FRB. The reduction is calculated as 36 months times 5/9 of a percent *plus* 24 months times 5/12 of 1 percent.

When you delay benefits until after FRA, the amount of your benefits is increased above the FRB, or PIA. For people born in 1943 or later, each year that benefits are delayed increases them by 8 percent, or each month of delay increases benefits by 2/3 of 1 percent. These monthly increases for delaying benefits are known as delayed retirement credits (DRCs).

The maximum increase for delaying the benefits claim also depends on your year of birth. Because the FRA is later for people born after 1954, there's less time between FRA and age 70. That means there are fewer months to delay benefits, and that reduces the amount of delayed retirement credits you can receive.

Table 4.2: Social Security Retirement Benefits Beginning at Each Age, Expressed as a Percentage of the Full Retirement Benefit (FRB)

Year of Birth	Full Retirement Age (FRA)	Annual Credit for Delayed Retirement	Benefit as a Percentage of Full Retirement Benefit (FRB), Beginning at Each Age						
			62	63	64	65	66	67	70
1943–1954	66	8	75	80	86⅔	93⅓	100	108	132
1955	66, 2 mo.	8	74⅙	79⅛	85⁵⁄₉	92²⁄₉	98⁸⁄₉	106⅔	130⅔
1956	66, 4 mo.	8	73⅓	78⅓	84⁴⁄₉	91⅑	97⁷⁄₉	105⅓	129⅓
1957	66, 6 mo.	8	72½	77½	83⅓	90	96⅔	104	128
1958	66, 8 mo.	8	71⅔	76⅔	82²⁄₉	88⁸⁄₉	95⁵⁄₉	102⅔	126⅔
1959	66, 10 mo.	8	70⅚	75⅚	81⅑	87⁷⁄₉	94⁴⁄₉	101⅓	125⅓
1960 and later	67	8	70	75	80	86⅔	93⅓	100	124

Source: Social Security Administration website

Someone born in 1958 has an FRA of 66 years and 8 months. Delaying the claim of retirement benefits to age 70 increases them to 126.66 percent of the FRB. Delaying them to 67 increases them to 102.66 percent of FRB.

Table 4.2 shows the effects of claiming benefits at different ages. You also can go to the SSA website and use a calculator that shows how much benefits will change if you claim them at different ages: https://www.ssa.gov/OACT/quickcalc/early_late.html.

There's no additional increase for delaying benefits past age 70, so there's no reason not to claim benefits by then. Technically, the benefits are maximized while you're still age 69, because the increases stop on your 70th birthday, so you receive the maximum retirement credits at the end of your 69th year.

Special Rules for Spouses

There are a few special rules for married couples, which Congress changed in 2015. So, if you're married you need to be especially careful not to base your decisions about Social Security on an older source.

A married person has choices when claiming Social Security benefits. If the person worked in covered employment and acquired at least forty credits, he or she can claim retirement benefits based on that work history. Or a married person can claim spousal benefits instead. A spousal benefit is normally 50 percent of the other spouse's FRB. In other words, the spousal benefit is half of the benefit the other spouse would be entitled to at FRA.

The SSA deems that a person has filed for all the benefits he or she qualifies for, and pays whichever is the highest benefit. So most people don't decide whether to claim their own retirement benefits or the spousal benefits; the SSA determines which benefits the applicant qualifies for and pays the higher one.

But there are a few caveats. You don't qualify for spousal benefits until your spouse has claimed his or her retirement benefits. So, if you want to claim Social Security benefits and your spouse hasn't filed to claim his or her retirement benefits, you can claim only your own retirement benefits. But later, when your spouse does claim retirement benefits, you can switch to spousal benefits if they're higher than your retirement benefits.

Another caveat is that the early retirement reduction for claiming benefits before FRA applies to spousal benefits as well. So, if you qualify for spousal benefits but are younger than your FRA (not your spouse's FRA), you can receive the spousal benefits but they'll be reduced because you claimed them early. In that scenario you'll receive less than 50 percent of your spouse's FRB.

Let's look at Jim and Sherry Snow. They're both 62. Jim is still working and has decided not to claim his retirement benefits until later, perhaps as late as age 70. Sherry no longer is working and wants to receive benefits from SSA.

When Sherry applies for benefits, she won't qualify for spousal benefits because Jim hasn't filed to claim his retirement benefits. Sherry will be paid her retirement benefits, but they'll be reduced below her FRB because she claimed them early.

When Jim claims his retirement benefits at age 70, he'll receive the maximum benefit available to him. And at that point Sherry will become eligible to switch to the spousal benefit if it is greater than her retirement benefit. Her spousal benefit would normally be 50 percent of Jim's FRB (not 50 percent of his higher benefit for claiming at age 70). But because Sherry first claimed her own retirement benefit early, at 62, her spousal benefit will be reduced. She'll receive less than 50 percent of Jim's FRB.

Another rule spouses should know is that only one spouse at a time can claim spousal benefits. One spouse has to claim his or her retirement benefits to allow the other spouse to claim the spousal benefit.

As we have seen, when a person applies to claim benefits, he or she is deemed to have applied for all benefits available. That is a feature of the 2015 Social Security reforms. Before those changes, when Sherry applied for her benefits at 62, Jim could have applied only for spousal benefits. He could have received the spousal benefits for years and then later, at FRA or even age 70, he could have applied for his own retirement benefits and received them without any reduction for claiming the spousal benefits at 62. That strategy no longer works because now a person is deemed to have applied for all benefits available. He or she can no longer file a restricted claim for only one type of benefit. (There is an exception for surviving spouses, which you'll read about in chapter 6.)

Now you are deemed to have applied for every Social Security benefit you qualify for, but, as I have explained, you will be paid only one of those benefits at a time, even if you're eligible for more. For example, a married person might qualify for both his or her retirement benefit and a spousal benefit, but only the higher of the two benefits will be paid.

Here's how that works. Suppose a lower-earning spouse chooses to apply for his or her retirement benefits before the other spouse claims benefits. At that point, the lower-earning spouse is eligible only for the retirement benefit. But once the higher-earning spouse claims his or her retirement benefit, the lower-earning spouse becomes eligible for the spousal benefit. Let's say the spousal benefit is greater than the lower-earning spouse's retirement benefit, so the lower-earning spouse will switch to the spousal benefit. This switch is allowed only once.

That's how it works in practice. But the issue is confused by the way SSA chooses to label benefits. Because of SSA's choice of phrasing, you might be told at times that you are receiving an "excess spousal benefit." The SSA says that the lower-earning spouse continues to receive his or her retirement benefit but also will receive an "excess spousal benefit" that will boost the monthly benefit to an amount equal to the full spousal benefit. SSA uses similar phrasing about survivor's benefits and some other benefits. But that's just a matter of semantics; it doesn't change the amount of the benefit. But it does confuse many people. They may wonder why a program with solvency problems is knowingly paying them "excess benefits," and their friends may want to know how *they* can receive excess benefits, too.

How You Should Decide

That's a lot of information to digest. Yet the basic points to take away are fairly simple:

- The amount of your Social Security FRB is based on your earnings history. The more you earn, the higher your benefits will be—with some limits.
- You can enjoy retirement benefits before FRA by claiming them any time between ages 62 and your FRA, but you'll receive a lesser amount. In other words, you can opt to receive a smaller monthly amount for a longer period of time.
- On the other hand, you can delay retirement benefits until after your FRA and receive a higher monthly amount. You will receive more money each month but for a shorter period of time.

Before you make a decision, you need to ponder some important factors.

The first factor to consider is longevity. Specifically, how long will you live? We don't know the answer, of course. But as I said in chapter 2, we can look at probabilities.

Your decision about when you claim benefits will make a big difference. If you wait until FRA or later to claim benefits and pass away before average life expectancy, then you'll receive lower lifetime benefits than were estimated when the law was written. This is the scenario that most people seem to be worried about: they believe they won't live to average life expectancy and thus won't receive as high of a lifetime benefit. That worry would explain why the majority of beneficiaries claim benefits before FRA, and most of them well before FRA—the vast majority between ages 62 and 64. Only 6 percent of women and 4 percent of men waited to claim the maximum benefit at age 70 in 2018.[2]

I believe that most people aren't making the optimum long-term decision. As I explained in chapter 2, all other things being equal—unless you have particular health issues, for example—there's a *more* than 50 percent probability you'll live to at least average life expectancy, because SSA uses outdated life average expectancy numbers to set the break-even point. If you wait to claim your benefits and live at least that long, you will receive a greater lifetime benefit than if you had claimed earlier. Live beyond that (outdated) average life expectancy, and the delay in claiming benefits puts you ahead of the game.

There's a greater than 50 percent probability of living to average life expectancy, because the life expectancies used in Social Security benefit formulas are from 1983 and earlier. Life expectancies have increased since then, and the benefit formulas haven't been adjusted. The difference isn't great, but more than half of Social Security beneficiaries today are likely to live beyond the average life expectancy used to compute the benefit formulas.

The key point to keep in mind, though, is that the Social Security retirement benefit is longevity insurance. It's not an investment, and you shouldn't attempt to recoup the lifetime taxes you paid as soon as possible. Social Security is to protect you from the risks of living a long life. Sure, if you claim benefits at age 62 and pass away at 72, you'll benefit from claiming those benefits early. But you need to consider the other scenarios.

Suppose you claim benefits at 62 and live to age 80 or beyond. Suppose also that after retiring you spend down some of your assets and your other sources of income are eroded by years of inflation. At that point, you'll likely regret claiming the retirement benefits early. As other sources of cash dwindle, you'll wish that your Social Security retirement benefits were substantially higher. Instead of the benefit you're receiving because you claimed at age 62, you could have waited until age 70 and be receiving a benefit that's about 176 percent higher. That's the difference between an age 62 benefit and an age 70 benefit for someone born in 1958. And the benefit is increased for inflation each year. Even if you had delayed claiming the benefit from age 62 only until your FRA of 66 years and 8 months, the increase in your monthly benefit would have been substantial.

Also keep in mind that in those later years, when other sources of cash could be dwindling, your medical expenses are likely to be increasing and you could be facing long-term care expenses at some point. Maximizing Social Security benefits can reduce the pain from being pinched by the combination of rising expenses and shrinking resources.

Delaying Benefits Yields High Returns

Delaying benefits gets you a return on your money like an investment. You receive an 8 percent increase in lifetime income for each year you delay benefits from FRA to 70. That 8 percent increase is guaranteed, and it is tax free—unlike most investment income.

Many people don't think delaying retirement benefits will make a big difference. One reason, I believe, is that they focus on the monthly amounts in the Social Security estimates. The difference in the monthly benefits between retiring at ages 62 and 70 or between 62 and FRA may not look like much. But you have to remember that these amounts are paid each month for the rest of your life, and they are indexed for inflation each year. Those small amounts mount up over time.

Let's turn back to Lo Profits. Throughout his career he earned exactly half the maximum Social Security wage base. If he claimed his benefits at age 62, he'd initially receive $1,600 monthly. If he lived to age 90 and had annual COLAs averaging 2.6 percent, he'd receive $812,680 in lifetime benefits. Yet if Lo had delayed claiming benefits to age 70, his monthly benefit would have started at $3,451. His lifetime benefits to age 90 would total to $1,134,453.

That's a substantial difference. It would pay for a lot of food, medicine, and other expenses. It would allow Lo to spend less of his nest egg after age 70, perhaps saving it to pay for long-term care or to leave as an inheritance for his children. Most importantly, the higher monthly benefits later in life make it more likely that Lo can maintain his financial independence.

The factor you should be looking at is total lifetime benefits received through different ages, and you should assume that you'll live at least to life expectancy. As I showed in chapter 2, the probability of living beyond average life expectancy is significant. After all, half your age cohort will live at least that long. And the probability of living to a ripe old age is rising. Unless you have reasons to believe you personally won't live to average life expectancy, your plans should assume you'll live to average life expectancy or longer.

As you learned in chapter 2, in a married couple, there's a very significant probability at least one spouse will live beyond life expectancy. That brings us to my next point.

Consider the Others in Your Life

Maybe you still aren't persuaded to delay claiming Social Security retirement benefits. Consider another factor. Consider the other people in your life who might claim benefits based on your earnings history and when you claim benefits.

A spouse is the most important person to consider. The biggest mistakes made in claiming Social Security benefits are the failure to coordinate claiming decisions with a spouse and to consider how one spouse's decision to claim benefits affects the other spouse over the long term.

The important consideration is not how much money comes into the household when both spouses are living. The key period to consider is after one spouse passes away. As I explain in detail in chapter 6, a surviving spouse receives only one Social Security benefit. In most cases, the surviving spouse receives the higher of his or her own retirement benefit and what the other spouse was receiving at the time of death. There are some exceptions, as you'll see in chapter 6, but that's the basic rule that affects most surviving spouses.

While both spouses were alive, two Social Security checks were coming into the household. After one spouse passes away, one Social Security benefit ends. The surviving spouse must maintain the household on only the remaining benefit. If the higher-earning spouse claims benefits early, that one check is going to be much less than it could have been.

It doesn't matter whether the surviving spouse is you or your partner. The survivor is likely going to regret the decision to grab those Social Security benefits as soon as they were available and wish the survivor's benefit check were a lot higher. Remember from chapter 2 that the surviving spouse often lives alone for five years or longer, and often much longer. That's a long time to try to maintain a household on the survivor's benefits of someone who claimed benefits early.

Some Key Lessons and Guidelines

I'll say at the outset that it frequently is a mistake to use general rules to make a financial decision such as when to claim Social Security benefits. The details of everyone's situation are different. While details of everyone in a group can be compiled to determine an average, almost none of these individuals actually resemble the average. It's wiser to dive into the details of your own situation, compare the numbers, and make a careful decision.

Even so, many people want to know some rules of thumb and general principles. In this section I boil down the key points of my research and this book to a few important lessons. I hope you'll read the rest of the book to learn the details and ensure your situation isn't an exception to the general rules. But this guidance will serve most people well.

Principles for Single Individuals

I recommend that single individuals make Social Security-claiming decisions with two goals in mind. The first goal is to maximize lifetime cumulative benefits. The second is to reduce "longevity risk"—that is, the risk of running out of money and having to reduce your standard of living if you live well beyond life expectancy.

For most single persons, each of these goals is achieved by waiting to claim Social Security retirement benefits.

The crossover or break-even point for single individuals claiming benefits is between ages 78 and 80, depending on their year of birth and FRA. If you live longer than that crossover point, waiting to claim benefits maximizes your total lifetime benefit. The longer you delay claiming Social Security, the greater the lifetime benefits you'll be paid once you live beyond the crossover point. The added lifetime benefits from delaying benefits compound, so that the longer you live after the crossover point the greater the cumulative benefit compared to claiming early. If someone with an FRB of $2,000 claims benefits at 70 instead of 62 and then lives into his 90s, that person's lifetime benefits will be $150,000 more than if he had claimed benefits at age 62.

Claiming benefits later also reduces longevity risk. That is, you make it less likely that you will outlive your money. The greater your monthly Social Security benefit, the less money you need to spend from your retirement nest egg and any other resources you have. Chapter 13 gives more detail and cites several studies on this issue. Delaying benefits also means your monthly income is much higher in the later years. If your nest egg has been reduced and other sources of income lost purchasing power due to inflation, the additional monthly income from a higher Social Security benefit will be very welcome.

High income in your oldest years is the way to reduce longevity risk. But claiming Social Security benefits early reduces your monthly income in those additional years, whereas delaying your claim of Social Security benefits increases that income and provides more security in later years.

Principles for Married Couples

There are special considerations for married couples. The best strategy for spouses can be different from the best strategy for singles. It's important, as I have pointed out, for married couples to coordinate their Social Security–claiming decisions. And yet often each spouse makes a claiming decision based on his or her goals, assumptions, and outlook, independent of the other spouse.

The basic goals for a married couple are the same as those of an individual. You want to maximize lifetime cumulative benefits received and minimize longevity risk. But the actions that spouses need to take in order to accomplish those goals may be slightly different from the right decisions for single people.

For most married couples, one spouse has higher lifetime earnings and a higher FRB than the other. Sometimes the gap between the two is substantial, and other times the gap isn't as large. The difference can change the optimum claiming decisions for the spouses.

As I mentioned earlier, the important consideration for married couples is what I call the solo years—the time after one spouse has passed away and the other is still living. When one spouse passes, one Social Security benefit ends. The surviving spouse receives only the higher of the two benefits that were coming into the household, as a general rule.

To maximize the monthly benefit to the surviving spouse, regardless of which spouse it is, the spouse with the higher lifetime earnings and higher FRB needs to delay claiming benefits as long as possible, ideally to age 70.

The best decision for the lower-earning spouse isn't as clear-cut. The ideal decision can depend on the age difference and the difference between the spouses' earnings. Often, the right decision for the couple is for the lower-earning spouse to claim Social Security benefits early, even as early as age 62, while the higher-earning spouse delays benefits.

Because the higher-earning spouse is claiming benefits late and ensuring the highest monthly benefit for the surviving spouse, the goal of reducing longevity risk is achieved. The couple also is a long way toward maximizing lifetime benefits. Thus, it can make sense for the lower-earning spouse to claim benefits early so that benefits begin flowing into the household.

When the lower-earning spouse claims benefits early, the couple can spend less from their nest egg without reducing their standard of living. This makes the nest egg last longer and reduces longevity risk.

There's another trick for married couples. Once the higher-earning spouse claims retirement benefits, the other spouse may receive a bump in monthly benefits. That's because a spouse receives the higher of his or her own retirement benefit or the spousal benefit. But the spousal benefit can't be received until the other spouse claims his or her benefits. So if the lower-earning spouse claims retirement benefits early while the higher-earning spouse waits, the lower-earning spouse can't receive the spousal benefits at first.

Once the higher-earning spouse claims retirement benefits, the lower-earning spouse can begin receiving the spousal benefit—one half of the spouse's retirement benefit—if it is higher than his or her retirement benefit. When there's a meaningful gap between the lifetime earnings of the two spouses, one-half of the higher-earning spouse's FRB will be higher than the lower-earning spouse's benefit. The couple receives a boost in monthly income when the lower-earning spouse switches from his or her retirement benefit to the spousal benefit of one-half the other spouse's FRB. One caveat: that spousal benefit will be reduced to less than half the other spouse's FRB when the lower-earning spouse first claimed retirement benefits in advance of his or her FRA before later switching to spousal benefits. How much the spousal benefit will be reduced will depend on how long before FRA the spouse first claimed his or her retirement benefits.

The bottom line for married couples is that the higher-earning spouse should delay retirement benefits as long as possible. The ideal time for the lower-earning spouse to take benefits depends on the difference between the ages and earnings of the two spouses. The best way to make the decision is to use the Social Security calculators I discuss below.

How to Decide

Those are the basic scenarios—and the general principles for maximizing benefits and achieving other important retirement benefits. As I said, everyone's situation is different. The general rules might not be the best solutions for you. I'm sure you've also realized that there are a lot of elements to the Social Security–claiming decision, and it shouldn't be a snap decision.

That's why I recommend that you not make a decision based on intuition or by simply reviewing the rules. The best approach is to crunch the numbers and look at what the lifetime benefits would be under the different scenarios.

Fortunately, you don't have to do the calculations by hand—a process that would take quite a lot of time if you want to see the results under a range of different assumptions about life spans and claiming dates. As we have seen, there are very good and low-cost tools available to you. The time and money you spend on them will be worth it. As we have seen, the optimum claiming decision will increase lifetime benefits by an average of more than $100,000. And for some people the difference can be twice that, or more. As we saw at the end of chapter 3, the first step is to go to the SSA website at www.socialsecurity.gov, open a *"my* Social Security" account, and use the calculator there. And then you should also use at least one commercially available benefits calculator such as Maximize My Social Security (www.maximizemysocialsecurity.com) or Social Security Solutions (www.socialsecuritysolutions.com). I have worked with both programs, and found them to be useful, but I have no financial relationship with either of them or the experts who created them. You may also want to work with a retirement planning professional.

What About Claiming Early and Investing?

Periodically I hear people say that they plan to claim Social Security benefits as early as possible and invest them. Often they don't plan to retire from working until some years later, perhaps as late as 70. They believe their investment returns in the interim will exceed the additional benefits from claiming Social Security later. You can find books and articles advocating this strategy.

There is no doubt that you can develop a spreadsheet showing that claiming benefits early and investing them generates superior results than simply claiming the benefits later. But there are key points to keep in mind before pursuing this strategy.

- The increased income from delaying a claim for Social Security benefits is guaranteed. Investment returns aren't.

Someone who began the claim-early-and-invest strategy in March 2009 or almost any time in the next ten years probably did well. Someone who began the strategy in the mid-to-late 1990s likely also had good results.

But the results almost certainly weren't as positive for anyone who initiated the strategy in 1999 or early 2000. And they were likely even more dismal for someone who began the strategy in 2007 or so. For the strategy to work, both your investment strategy and your timing have to be good.

- You have to take some risks to earn an investment return that beats the gains from delaying Social Security benefits. You can't achieve superior results by claiming early and investing conservatively. So you're comparing a guaranteed return from delaying Social Security benefits with the uncertain return of investing in risky assets.
- Don't forget about taxes. The investment returns will be taxed. You might earn long-term capital gains and qualified dividends, so the tax rate is lower than the ordinary income tax rate. Yet you're still taxed, and you can spend only the after-tax amount. Your after-tax return, not the pre-tax return, from the investments has

to exceed the increase in Social Security benefits for the investment strategy to pay off.

In addition, if you're still working you're probably earning enough that some portion of your Social Security benefits will be taxed. If so, you're really not investing the full amount of the Social Security benefits even if you pay the taxes with money from other sources.

A few years ago, economist James Poterba surveyed the data and concluded that the average American passes away with few assets. At the end of life most Americans had their Social Security benefits, perhaps some home equity, and about $10,000 in cash and other assets. Most people enter retirement with what appear to be adequate savings and income. But surprises and changes during retirement deplete most of their resources. A major reason people's assets are depleted in retirement is that they live longer, and accrue more ensuing costs during those longer lives, than they expect.[3]

A good way to reduce the chances of this happening is to maximize lifetime Social Security benefits and the monthly income you'll receive late in life. You learned how to do that in this chapter and will learn more in later chapters.

You know the fundamentals of Social Security now. In the following chapters you will learn more details, including the benefit rules for special situations, and more strategies for how to maximize your Social Security benefits.

CHAPTER 5

What If I Keep Working?

What happens if you claim your Social Security benefits and stay in the workforce? How will working after age 62 affect your retirement benefits? What if you keep working after full retirement age, or even after 70?

These are important questions, and they are among the most misunderstood aspects of Social Security. The consequences of working while receiving Social Security benefits or during the traditional retirement years aren't well known, and they can be complicated.

Your Social Security benefits will be affected if you keep working and you should use that knowledge as you decide when to begin receiving benefits and when to stop working.

Many people today want to continue working past the traditional retirement age, at least according to surveys. Department of Labor data also indicate that the number of workers older than 65 is increasing, both absolutely and as a percentage of the work force.

Yet the vast majority of people continue to claim their Social Security retirement benefits well before full retirement age. Some of them claim benefits while still working.

If you want to maximize your Social Security benefits and don't want to leave money on the table, it's crucial to know how continuing to work after age 62 affects Social Security retirement benefits. You need to consider some important questions.

Do you lose Social Security benefits if you work while receiving benefits? Social Security has an earnings limitation that in some cases reduces or eliminates the Social Security retirement benefits of someone who is working. The earnings limit and its effects are widely misunderstood. How exactly does continuing to work after age 62 affect the amount of benefits you receive? Consider two different scenarios:

- You continue to work and delay claiming Social Security benefits.
- You receive Social Security retirement benefits while continuing to work.

By the end of this chapter you should have a good understanding of how working will affect your benefits and be able to make wiser decisions about when to begin your benefits and when to stop working.

(There is another issue related to working while receiving Social Security benefits: Will your benefits be taxed? The simple answer is that whether or not you will have to pay income tax on your benefits depends on the amount of your non-Social Security income, regardless of whether that income is from working, investments, or from other sources. Income tax issues are discussed in detail in chapter 8.)

Let's first be clear what I'm *not* talking about in this chapter. You already know that each month you delay claiming Social Security benefits after age 62 up to age 70 increases the monthly amount you'll be paid. This chapter does not address how *delaying the claiming decision* affects the amount of benefits you will be paid. In this chapter we discuss how *continuing to work* affects the amount of benefits paid. I will address how continuing to work affects the benefits whether you claim benefits early or delay claiming them. You'll also learn how continuing to work can affect both the current amount of benefits you receive and your future benefits.

Continuing to Work Affects the Amount of Future Benefits

As you know by now, the amount of Social Security benefits you receive is based on your lifetime earnings. In particular, your thirty-five highest-earning years are used to determine the retirement benefits you'll be paid. As we have seen, the nominal dollars earned each year are the starting point, but the earnings are indexed for wage growth (also known as wage inflation), over the years. But the indexing stops after age 60. Your earnings after 60 aren't indexed when the lifetime calculation is made, and earnings before that date aren't indexed any further.

If you have zero-wage or lower-wage years in your earnings record, or if your pay continues to increase past the age of 60, then the years you work after that time will replace earlier, lower-wage years in the computation of your retirement benefits, which will be higher as a result. So depending on your work history, working a few years longer may increase your lifetime retirement benefits, or an additional year or two (or more) of earnings may not boost your benefits by much.

Social Security looks at your annual earnings from the year when you first paid Social Security taxes on earnings to the day you claim retirement benefits. As we have seen, if you don't have thirty-five years of earnings at that point, Social Security will use a zero for each year your record is short of thirty-five. By continuing to work, you can replace those zeros with whatever your earnings are in the additional working years.

Even if you don't have zeros for any of the thirty-five years, there might be a benefit to continuing to work. Most people have low-earnings years early in their careers. There might be years of part-time jobs and summer jobs during school years. Also, earnings in the first years after leaving school are likely to be much lower than earnings later in your career. If you continue to work for several more years, years with low earnings might be replaced by years with higher, perhaps much higher, earnings.

Replacing those lower-earnings years with new higher-earnings years will increase your lifetime Social Security benefits. The amount of the monthly increase in benefits will depend on the number of low-earnings years that are replaced and the dollar differences between the new higher-earnings year and the lower-earnings years.

Another factor is your income level. Middle- and lower-income workers receive benefits that replace a higher percentage of their working years' income than upper-income earners. Someone who has had a lot of earnings years at or above the maximum Social Security wage base probably already qualifies for the maximum monthly benefit or is very close to it. Working a few more years might increase his or her monthly benefit by only a few dollars. But for middle- and low-income workers, replacing a few low-earning years with higher-earning years can generate a meaningful increase in lifetime benefits.

The Continuous Benefit Recalculation

After you turn 62, Social Security recalculates your benefits every year that you don't claim benefits. It takes your pay for the latest year, adds it to your record of lifetime earnings, selects the thirty-five years with the highest inflation-adjusted earnings, and recalculates your projected retirement benefits.

This recalculation is especially helpful to people who had poor earnings years during what could have been some of their prime working years. There are parents who stopped working or took lower-paying jobs to help raise their children. Other people stepped out of the workforce to care for aged parents or others. Many people lost jobs in recessions, industry disruptions, or the bankruptcies of their employers. It's not uncommon in those situations for it to take a year or longer to find employment with remuneration comparable to the pay of the lost position.

Here's an extreme but unusual example. Consider two women who are the same age and had similar career paths. After college each worked for a few years and then left the workforce to be full-time mothers. Both women returned to the workforce the same year, after their children had grown.

Now both are 62 and contemplating retirement. Because they had comparable earnings histories, Social Security tells each woman she would receive a monthly benefit of $1,049 if she claimed benefits at full retirement age (age 66, not age 62). At age 70, she would receive $1,700. Claiming at age 70 would pay lifetime benefits of about $568,000, assuming 2.5 percent annual inflation increases, through age 90.

But suppose instead of retiring at 62 or 66, one of the women continues to work at the job at which she has been earning about 75 percent of the Social Security wage base. She doesn't stop working or claim her Social Security benefits until age 70. Because her additional years of work replaced years when she had no income in her earnings record, her monthly benefit increases substantially. She'll receive about $3,200 monthly beginning at 70—more than twice what she would have received if she had stopped working at 62 and retired at age 66.

By age 90, she will have received lifetime benefits of about $1,070,000, assuming 2.5 percent inflation each year. That's substantially more than she would have received if she had stopped working at age 62, even if she had delayed claiming her benefits until age 70.

As I said, that's an extreme example because this worker is replacing years of no earned income with years of an above-average salary. That's a scenario in which working longer can boost retirement security significantly; in that case working after age 62, past your full retirement age, or even up to age 70 can be the best way to close the gap in an underfunded retirement. According to the report "The Power of Working Longer," written by Gila Bronshtein et al. and published by the National Bureau of Economic Research, in some situations working longer is so powerful that delaying retirement by only three to six months has the same impact on a retirement standard of living as saving an additional percentage point of earnings for thirty years.[1]

The impact that working longer will have on the level of your Social Security benefits also depends on your income level. The lower your earnings, the higher the impact additional earnings have on your retirement benefits. Higher-income earners receive a smaller increase in retirement benefits from additional earnings.

Additional Benefits from Working Longer

Even when the increase in monthly benefits from working longer is small, that's not the end of the story. You'll receive those higher benefits every month for the rest of your life, no matter how long you live. And don't forget that Social Security retirement benefits are indexed for inflation. A small increase in benefits can compound to a meaningful lifetime sum when you're retired for a couple of decades or longer and the benefits increase with inflation.

You should also consider the potential effects additional working years will have on the rest of your retirement nest egg. While the topic of this book is maximizing Social Security, it's likely that part of the earnings from working additional years will be saved, added to existing retirement savings, and invested to earn additional returns. In addition, if you continue to work and pay current expenses with income, you should be able to delay drawing down your existing retirement savings. Either way, your nest egg will rise in value before you begin drawing from it in retirement.

You don't have to guess how much additional years of work might add to your Social Security benefits. The calculators I discussed near the end of chapter 4 can be used to make the estimates under different scenarios. You can open a *"my* Social Security" account on the Social Security Administration (SSA) website at www.ssa.gov. Or you can use the commercial Social Security calculators, such as Maximize My Social Security and Social Security Solutions.

Delaying Benefits, but Not Retirement

Though they're called Social Security retirement benefits, you don't have to stop working and be retired to claim them. You can claim Social Security retirement benefits as early as age 62, whether or not you continue to work for a salary.

As long as you keep working, your Social Security benefits won't be a fixed amount that's indexed for inflation each year. Instead, your retirement benefits will be adjusted each year as you extend your earnings record—assuming the earnings from your latest year are higher than the inflation-adjusted earnings of at least one of the previous thirty-five highest-earnings years in your record.

Like delaying your Social Security retirement claim, working after you have begun to receive the retirement benefits will boost those benefits in the long run. Remember that your Social Security benefits are calculated using the thirty-five highest-earnings years from your earnings record. Each additional year you work has the potential of knocking out a year of low earnings or zero earnings and replacing it with a year of higher earnings.

The calculation of your Social Security retirement benefits is a rolling, annual process as long as you keep working. Each year, Social Security reviews the records for all Social Security recipients who work. If your latest year of earnings turns out to be one of your thirty-five highest years, Social Security will refigure your benefit and pay you any increase due. This is an automatic process. The additional benefits will be paid in December of the following year. For example, if you received Social Security retirement benefits in 2020 and also worked and earned enough income in that year that it replaced one of the thirty-five previously highest years in your earnings record, you should receive an additional payment in December of 2021 reflecting an increase in your 2020 benefits. The increase would be retroactive to January of the year in which the higher wages were earned.

As we have seen, the additional benefits can be substantial if the additional year of work replaces a zero- or very low-earnings year. If, on the other hand, you already have thirty-five years of earnings at or near the maximum Social Security wage base each year, an additional year of earnings near or above the wage base will increase your benefits only a little.

In either case, don't forget that the accumulated increase over potentially many years of retirement and the fact that it will be indexed for inflation can make the final result from working additional years meaningful. Remember that with Social Security you should focus on maximum lifetime benefits received. Because benefits and benefit estimates are usually expressed in monthly amounts, they can seem less significant than the cumulative lifetime cash flow they'll amount to.

The Earned Income Limit: The Penalty for Working

But do you also lose Social Security benefits if you work while receiving them?

Once you reach age 62, you can claim Social Security retirement benefits. As we've seen, you don't have to retire to receive retirement benefits. You can continue to work and still receive the benefits.

But working while receiving benefits is something that Social Security law historically discouraged—by a provision known as the earned income limit, or earnings test. At certain ages, if you earn "too much" money while claiming retirement benefits, your retirement benefits will be reduced. As we'll see, though, any decrease is only temporary. You'll get it back later.

The earnings limit used to be more onerous than it is now. Originally, it applied no matter how old you were. That put Social Security recipients who needed both their retirement benefits and earned income to make ends meet in a difficult position. The more they earned from working, the more their Social Security benefits were reduced. The earned income limit also discouraged work by people who didn't really need the additional income but wanted to hold jobs to stay active or have a purpose in life. Under the old earnings limit, they would essentially be working without compensation, because their earnings reduced their Social Security benefits. So they were unlikely to work.

The earnings test is a relic of the Great Depression era when Social Security was created and one purpose of the program was to encourage older workers to leave the work force so that jobs would open up for the many younger people who were unemployed at the time.

Congress scaled the earned income limit back significantly in the 1990s, believing it was largely obsolete and not liking the disincentives it created. Now the earnings limit applies only until the year you reach full retirement age. If you are considering both claiming your benefits before full retirement age and continuing to work, you need to know the consequences of the earnings limit for your situation.

If you're already older than your full retirement age, or you don't plan to claim Social Security benefits before your FRA, then you don't have to worry about the earned income limit. (See chapter 4 for your FRA, which is based on your birth year.)

There is a limit to how much you can earn and still receive the full Social Security benefit due for your age when you're younger than your FRA. If you're younger than FRA during the entire calendar year, Social Security will deduct $1 from your benefits for each $2 you earn above the earnings limit. The limit, which is indexed for inflation each year, was $18,240 in 2020.

Suppose someone was 64 years old in 2020 and receiving Social Security retirement benefits. He was also working and earned $19,240. His earnings were $1,000 above the earnings limit. He lost $1 of benefits for each $2 of earnings above the limit. That means he lost $500 of his benefits for the year.

The limit is different for the year you reach your FRA. The reduction in your benefits is only for the months of the year before you reach your FRA. You lose only $1 of benefits for each $3 you earn above the limit up to that point. And the earnings limit for that year is much higher than for the earlier year—$48,600 in 2020. Plus, only the earnings from the beginning of year to the day you reach your FRA count towards the earnings limit. If you don't exceed the earned income limit by the day you reach full retirement age, you don't lose any benefits for the year, even if you keep receiving earned income for the rest of the year and the total exceeds the limit.

Suppose you reached your FRA in August 2020. You earned $63,000 in income during the year, but only $49,040 of it was earned from January through July. That put you only $440 over the earnings limit ($49,040 minus $48,600). Your benefits for the year were reduced by only $146.70.

Both earnings limits apply only during months when you're both working and receiving retirement benefits. If you don't claim retirement benefits until some time after January 1, then your earnings before you began receiving benefits don't count toward the limit. Instead, the annual limit will be prorated based on the number of months you receive retirement benefits. You'll forfeit benefits only if your earnings during the period when you are both working and also receiving benefits exceed the prorated limit.

Only wages and salaries from jobs you work and your net profits from self-employment count towards the earned income limit. Earned income includes bonuses, commissions, and vacation pay. Income that isn't counted towards the earnings limit includes pensions, annuities, investment income, interest, jury duty pay, and veterans' or other military or government retirement benefits.

The Mechanics of the Earned Income Limit

Once you claim benefits, the SSA will send you a letter late in each year asking for an estimate of the earned income you expect to receive the following year. If it exceeds the limit, your monthly benefits will be reduced on the basis of the formulas above. In addition, the SSA will check your annual earnings with the IRS each year and determine whether you retroactively forfeited benefits by earning above the limit during a previous year.

But remember, losing some or all of your benefits because of the earnings limit isn't a disaster. The loss of benefits is only temporary.

First, as we have seen, the additional earnings are added to your lifetime earnings record. Whenever the current year's earnings exceed the earnings of a year that was included in your highest thirty-five years of earnings, the SSA will recalculate your earnings record and increase your future Social Security benefits.

Second, after you reach your FRA, the benefits forfeited in earlier years will increase your future benefits. Exceeding the earned income limit is more like a deferral or withholding of benefits than a loss of benefits.

Here's an example provided by Social Security. Let's say you claimed retirement benefits upon turning 62 in 2020, and your benefit payment was $931 per month. But you continued to work. Because your earnings greatly exceeded the earnings limit, all twelve months of benefits were withheld.

Social Security would recalculate your benefit due at your FRA of 66 years and 8 months and pay you $998 per month instead of $931. That amount is in 2020 dollars; the SSA would adjust the amount for inflation, so you would receive a higher amount.

To take the example further, suppose you continue working between the ages of 62 and FRA while claiming benefits and earn so much that all benefits in those years are withheld. In that case, Social Security would pay you $1,300 a month starting at age 66 and 8 months.

Once again, you don't have to guess how your earnings might affect your retirement benefits. The Social Security website has a Retirement Earnings Test Calculator. Enter your birth date and a few other details into the calculator, and it will tell the amount, if any, by which your benefits would be reduced by the amount of earnings you expect. You don't have to open a "*my* Social Security" account to use this calculator.

You can see that there's a lot of interplay between the different rules, and it can be difficult to estimate the net effects of different choices about your benefits. The best approach is to use the Social Security benefit calculators available on the web—the one that's available on the Social Security website after you establish a *"my Social Security"* account—and also the commercially available tools available at sites such as www.maximizemysocialsecurity.com and www.socialsecuritysolutions.com (see chapter 4). Run different scenarios through the calculators to get an idea of the likely results of your different choices.

CHAPTER 6

The Solo Years: Social Security When You're Widowed

By understanding these unique advantages of survivor's benefits and applying the rules to your situation, you can develop a strategy that will maximize your lifetime benefits.

As I have emphasized, married couples need to coordinate their Social Security–claiming decisions. But as important as that is, it isn't the only thing that they need to do to maximize their lifetime Social Security benefits. Surviving spouses are in a unique position under Social Security, and they need to know the special rules and options regarding survivor's benefits.

To recap: few married couples coordinate their decisions because the importance of coordinating claiming decisions often doesn't become apparent until after one of the spouses passes away and one Social Security benefit ends. The cessation of one Social Security benefit and other changes that occur at the same time cause many surviving spouses to struggle financially.

Coordinated decisions among spouses make it possible for the survivor, whichever spouse it is, to receive the maximum possible benefits from Social Security for the rest of his or her life. When spouses don't coordinate benefits, the surviving spouse often finds that the one benefit check supporting the household is substantially less than it could have been if they had made different decisions years earlier.

But even when spouses coordinate their claiming decisions, the work that needs to be done to maximize survivor benefits still isn't over. When it comes to Social Security benefits, survivor's benefits are unique in their complexity—and in the opportunities they offer. A surviving spouse can often choose from among benefit options—and, as with spousal benefits, may be able to change the benefit choice over time. The decisions made after one spouse passes away can make a substantial difference in the lifetime income of the surviving spouse. The choices facing the surviving spouse can also be among the more difficult Social Security decisions.

Recall that I opened this book with a few stories of Social Security claiming. One of them involved the widow, Kim Kandu, who had difficulty convincing the SSA representative that the claiming strategy that she wanted to pursue was a wise one. We shouldn't blame the Social Security rep in that anecdote too harshly; the survivor's benefit rules are confusing and difficult even for those who work with them regularly. The options simply aren't straightforward or intuitive.

The advantage of these complex rules is that they give surviving spouses more options than other beneficiaries have. The surviving spouse has more ways to maximize the amount of that monthly benefit he or she will receive. When spouses coordinate benefits before claiming them, and then the surviving spouse makes wise choices, lifetime benefits can be significantly higher. Coordination is important, but it's also important for a surviving spouse to take some time to select the right benefit, or series of benefits. A surviving spouse needs to be prepared to research the choices and possibly even seek help from a financial professional.

Survivor's Benefit Basics

Survivor's benefits are available to both married and divorced widows and widowers. That's right—there are times when a divorced spouse can claim survivor's benefits based on the earnings of a deceased former spouse. To minimize confusion, however, this chapter will focus on survivor's benefits available to someone who was married at the time the other spouse passed away. (Divorced spouses' survivor benefits will be discussed in chapter 7.)

Survivor's benefits sometimes are called widow's benefits, for good reason. The odds are that the husband will be the first spouse to pass away. Though the gap is slowly closing, demographic data still indicate that, on average, women live longer than men. Social Security's data say that about 80 percent of surviving spouse benefits are paid to women. Since the surviving spouse is highly likely to be the wife, I'll often refer to the deceased spouse as "he," "him," and "his" and to the survivor as "she" and "her."

But don't let that make you believe that only women qualify for survivor's benefits. Any surviving spouse (or ex-spouse) can be eligible for Social Security survivor's benefits. Both widows and widowers will have the same choices.

First, I'll outline the basic rules. Then we'll look at some examples that demonstrate how you can use the rules to maximize survivor's benefits.

To qualify for survivor's benefits, a widow or widower must have been married to the deceased for at least the nine months just before he passed away. (The nine-month requirement is waived if the deceased spouse's death was accidental.) In addition, in order for the survivor to claim benefits, the deceased spouse must have been fully insured under Social Security. As we saw in chapter 4, a person is fully insured after paying enough taxes into the Social Security system to receive forty credits. This generally means earning a minimum amount of income in jobs covered by Social Security for at least ten years.

When you're a qualified surviving spouse of a fully insured worker, you can claim survivor's benefits as early as age 60 (or age 50 if you're disabled and the disability started either before or within seven years of the other spouse's death). But although you are allowed to begin receiving survivor's benefits as early as age 60, you'll receive lower benefits than you would be paid if you waited to receive them at a later age. The benefits are reduced by 0.396 percent for each month you claim them before your FRA. The reduction comes to 4.75 percent for each year. If your FRA is 66, the maximum reduction, which is incurred by claiming benefits at age 60, is 28.5 percent.

The Many Levels of Survivor Benefits

The amount of survivor's benefits that you are eligible for depends on your age, your deceased spouse's earnings record, and his age and benefit status at the time of his passing. These variables often create a range of benefit choices for the surviving spouse.

I'll break down the different benefit levels and options.

If One Spouse Passes Away before Age 62

If the deceased spouse was younger than 62, he didn't have the opportunity to claim retirement benefits. The survivor's benefits will be based on his earnings record.

The SSA will compute the primary insurance amount (PIA) of the deceased spouse. This also is known as the full retirement benefit (FRB), or the amount the worker would have been eligible to receive at full retirement age (FRA). As we have seen, the PIA is based on the lifetime earnings of the worker. For surviving spouses in this situation, the PIA (or FRB) will be computed two different ways, and the higher of the two will be the amount payable in survivor's benefits. (We don't need to get into the differences between the two methods because there's nothing you can do to affect the results. If you want to check SSA's arithmetic, I suggest using one of the available benefit calculators I've mentioned.) If no reductions for early claiming are made, the widow or widower's survivor benefit will be the full retirement benefit of the deceased spouse.

The surviving spouse has two immediate claiming options. She can claim the survivor's benefits based on the deceased spouse's PIA. As we have seen, these survivor's benefits can be claimed as early as age 60 (or 50, for the disabled). The other option is for the surviving spouse to claim her own earned retirement benefits, which she can do as early as age 62. But if you claim either benefit before your FRA, you won't receive the full benefit amount. The benefits, whether survivor's benefits or retirement benefits, will be reduced if they are claimed before the survivor's full retirement age.

This is not the end of the choices for the surviving spouse. A surviving spouse, unlike most people applying for Social Security benefits today, can choose which benefit to claim. She can even first claim one type of benefit and later switch to the other benefit. Thus she can choose one benefit first and delay the other benefit in order to maximize her benefits under her second claim. Later in this chapter I will discuss how a surviving spouse can maximize benefits using this powerful option.

If the Deceased Spouse Was at Least 62 and Had Claimed Benefits

If your spouse passes away after age 62, you can claim survivor's benefits based on his work history. But if he claimed retirement benefits before his FRA, your survivor benefits will be reduced below the FRA amount because of his early claim. That's one reason it's important for spouses to coordinate their Social Security benefits. By waiting to receive benefits until at least FRA, the higher-earning spouse ensures that a surviving spouse doesn't receive a reduced survivor's benefit.

Again, the surviving spouse has the choice of receiving the survivor's benefits as early as age 60. If the surviving spouse elects to claim benefits before her full retirement age, the amount of the benefits will be reduced for each month they are claimed before FRA. If she claims the benefits when they're first available, at age 60, then she will receive only 71.5 percent of the deceased spouse's PIA. In other words, there's a 28.5 percent reduction for taking the survivor's benefits as early as possible. The benefit amount is increased gradually for each month the claim is delayed.

This is where things can get complicated for a surviving spouse. As we have seen, her survivor benefit can be reduced not only by her own early survivor claim, but also by her husband's early retirement claim. Social Security has a special formula that limits the benefits paid to surviving spouses whose deceased spouses had claimed retirement benefits before their FRAs. The formula is called the Retirement Insurance Benefit Limit, or RIB-LIM. Some also call it the widow's limit. SSA says about one-third of surviving spouses currently receive reduced benefits because of RIB-LIM.

Under this widow's limit, the surviving spouse of a deceased person who claimed retirement benefits before his full retirement age can't receive the deceased spouse's full retirement benefits. The maximum survivor benefit that you can receive is the higher of the reduced amount that your spouse was receiving at the time of his demise and 82.5 percent of his PIA.

Because claiming survivor benefits early also reduces survivor's benefits, it's generally true that the closer you are to your full retirement age when you claim as a widow or widower, the more likely you are to receive the maximum amount. But in some cases your survivor benefit may hit a maximum point before your FRA. That happens if both of two conditions are met: 1) You are close enough to your FRA that the penalty for your own early claim will reduce your survivor benefit to no less than 82.5 percent of the deceased spouse's FRB, and 2) your spouse claimed retirement benefits so many months before his own FRA that his retirement benefit was less than 82.5 percent of his FRB. If those things are true, 82.5 percent of his full retirement benefit is the maximum you can receive, and there's no point in delaying your claim any longer than the point at which you reach that number.

Suppose a man claimed his retirement benefits at age 63. He passed away, leaving a widow who is age 59. If she claims survivor's benefits at age 60, they'll be reduced to about 71.5 percent of her husband's full retirement benefit because of her early claim. If, on the other hand, the widow delays claiming survivor's benefits for thirty-two months, those benefits will be 82.5 percent of her husband's FRB. Because that's the maximum she's allowed to receive under the RIB-LIM, there's no advantage to her delaying any later to claim her survivor's benefits. They're capped at that 82.5 percent.

You don't need to know all the details of how the RIB-LIM is calculated and applied. But you do need to know that if you're a surviving spouse and the deceased spouse claimed benefits before FRA, then the limit might apply to you.

And if it does, you need to determine how your benefits will be reduced and when you'll reach the crossover point after which survivor's benefits won't increase with any further delay in claiming them. You can start by working with SSA representatives, either on the phone or at the local office. You can open a "*my* Social Security" account on the Social Security Administration website and use the online calculator to estimate the benefits under different scenarios. You also can purchase one of the commercial software programs discussed in chapter 3, or work with a financial planner who has an expertise in Social Security benefits.

If the RIB-LIM applies, the surviving spouse needs to consider a two-step strategy. This strategy is most likely to be beneficial when the surviving spouse has retirement benefits based on her own work history and they aren't substantially lower than her late husband's benefits. In this situation, it can make sense to claim survivor's benefits initially. Then, after the surviving spouse's FRA and preferably not until age 70, the surviving spouse switches over to her retirement benefits—if by that point the retirement benefits have increased to the point that they are higher than her survivor's benefits. The reverse strategy also should be examined. The surviving spouse should consider claiming her retirement benefits first and later claiming her survivor's benefits after they reached the maximum level.

If the Deceased Spouse Was 62 or Older but
Had Not Claimed Benefits

The options are much simpler if the deceased spouse was at least 62 but had not claimed Social Security benefits. There are two possible scenarios.

If your spouse has turned 62, has not claimed benefits early, and passes away before his FRA, you'll receive his whole earned PIA.

If, on the other hand, your spouse passed away after reaching his FRA and still had not claimed his retirement benefits, you'll be paid the monthly benefits that he would have received, if he had applied as of the day of his death, including any extra for delayed retirement credits.

But remember that your survivor benefits are reduced if you claim them before your own FRA.

If the Deceased Spouse was Older than FRA and Receiving Benefits, but Hadn't Claimed before FRA

This is another fairly simple situation. In this case the deceased spouse died after his FRA. He was receiving benefits at the time of his death but hadn't claimed benefits until his FRA or later. In other words, he had no reduction below his full FRB and may even have been receiving an increased benefit because of delayed retirement credits.

In this case the surviving spouse generally receives the amount the deceased spouse was receiving at the time of his death. But don't forget that the survivor's benefit is reduced if the surviving spouse claims the benefits before her FRA.

Why Delaying Benefits Matters

Once again you can see how important it is for spouses to coordinate their benefit decisions, and for the higher-earning spouse to claim benefits based on what would be best for the surviving spouse, regardless of which spouse it is. That usually means delaying the claim for benefits as long as possible up to age 70. It's important for the higher-earning spouse to delay receiving retirement benefits to boost the monthly amount because the benefit the higher-earning spouse was receiving or would have been entitled to at FRA is likely to be the basis of the survivor's benefit.

Remember, after one spouse passes away, only one Social Security check comes into the household. In most cases, the amount paid to the survivor is the higher of the survivor's benefits as outlined above and the surviving spouse's earned retirement benefits. The surviving spouse's income is already going to be reduced because the passing of one spouse eliminates one monthly benefit that was coming to the household. If the higher-earning spouse claimed benefits before FRA, then the single SSA payment still coming as income to the survivor—whether that's the higher- or lower-earning spouse—is reduced below what it could have been if the higher-earning spouse had claimed at FRA or later, further reducing the survivor's income.

Also remember the key point I made in chapter 2. It's vital to make a reasonable estimate of life expectancy before making a claiming decision. The key point for married couples is that in many couples, at least one spouse has a significant probability of living beyond average life expectancy for his or her age group. The surviving spouse could live well into her eighties. Many widows will outlive their husbands ten years or longer. That's a long time to live on substantially reduced Social Security benefits.

So unless there are good reasons to believe both spouses will live to less than average life expectancy, my recommendation is that married couples should claim benefits with the assumption that at least one spouse will live well beyond life expectancy. The highest-earning spouse should choose a claiming decision that is likely to maximize lifetime benefits over an above-average life expectancy instead of maximizing short-term benefits.

Remember that Social Security retirement benefits are guaranteed for life, no matter how long that life lasts, and are indexed for inflation. These features become more valuable the longer one of you lives. In fact, those features are so valuable over the long term that it can make sense to work longer or to draw down your nest egg or both to pay your living expenses while waiting to claim Social Security benefits. I discuss these strategies in chapter 12.

You Can Also Switch

You can be paid only one Social Security benefit at a time, but as with spousal benefits, you can switch between survivor's benefits and retirement benefits one time. You can start with either benefit and switch to the other. It doesn't matter in which order you receive the benefits.

And also as with spousal benefits, the language SSA uses to describe survivor's benefits can be confusing.

Suppose you're a widow receiving retirement benefits based on your own earnings record. The survivor's benefits to which you're entitled are higher than the retirement benefits. At some point, you ask to switch to the survivor's benefit. You'll receive a check (or an electronic deposit to your bank account) equal to the survivor's benefit.

But SSA will say that you're receiving two benefits simultaneously. In SSA's accounting, a widow is receiving her own retirement benefit plus an "excess survivor's benefit" (like the "excess spousal benefit" I explained in chapter 4). The amount she receives is the exact amount of the survivor's benefit, but SSA chooses to describe it as two benefits. It's a technical point, but you might need to know it when reviewing some of the Social Security Administration's literature, either in print or on its website.

Which Benefits to Claim and When to Claim Them

The strategies I have explained apply primarily to surviving spouses between the ages of 60 and 70. Before age 60 (50 if you are disabled), you can't claim survivor's benefits. After age 70, there is no additional benefit from delaying either survivor's or retirement benefits.

But in the intervening decade, the choices can be quite complicated. Let's consider an example in detail to see how the different rules work together and can be used to develop a strategy that generates the highest guaranteed lifetime income.

Mary Anne Croker is nearing age 62 and recently widowed. She was the lower-earning spouse. Her husband, Bill, didn't claim Social Security benefits during his lifetime and passed away before his FRA.

Mary Anne now has choices. At age 62, her survivor's benefit will be $2,000 and her retirement benefit will be $1,800. Remember that either benefit will be reduced if she claims it before her FRA.

If Mary Anne claims the survivor's benefit, she'll receive $200 more per month than her retirement benefit. (Confusingly, if Mary Anne opts for the survivor's benefit, the SSA will tell her that she's receiving her own retirement benefit plus a $200 excess survivor benefit, but she's really receiving the survivor's benefit and nothing from her own work history.) But it doesn't make sense for Mary Anne to take the survivor's benefit now and switch to her own retirement benefit at FRA, because her full retirement benefit is less than her survivor's benefit.

A better strategy for Mary Anne is to start by claiming her own retirement benefit at age 62. This will be lower than it would be at her FRA, but at least she will be receiving $1,800 per month, indexed for inflation. Then, when she reaches FRA at age 66, Mary Anne can switch to the survivor's benefits. At that point she'll be at FRA, and because her survivor's benefits won't be reduced by a penalty for taking her own retirement benefits first at age 62, her survivor's benefits will now be $2,469—23 percent higher than they would have been if she had taken them at age 62.

There's no benefit to waiting until age 70 to begin the survivor's benefit, because unlike the retirement benefit, the survivor's benefit is maximized at FRA.

Under this strategy, Mary Anne receives $1,800 monthly (plus inflation indexing) for four years. Then she switches to the higher survivor's benefit. She'll receive that amount, indexed for inflation, each month for the rest of her life no matter how long she lives.

As attractive as that strategy is, there's a third option that might be even better for Mary Anne.

Mary Anne can start receiving the $2,000 survivor's benefit at age 62. She can receive that amount, indexed for inflation, for eight years until she reaches age 70. At that point, Mary Anne's earned retirement benefits will be at their maximum level, $3,168 per month, which is even higher than the maximum survivor's benefit of $2,469 that she could have received by switching from retirement to survivor's benefits at her FRA. Again, the benefit will be indexed for inflation after that and guaranteed for life, no matter how long Rosie lives.

The third option is probably the best for Mary Anne. She receives $2,000 per month beginning at age 62. Then at age 70 she locks in the maximum monthly amount available to her for the rest of her life.

The Lessons to Learn

As you can see from this example, a good general rule for a surviving spouse is to determine which benefit will top out at the highest level, and then delay taking that benefit until it is maximized. In this case, Mary Anne's retirement benefit at age 70 is the highest of the possible benefit amounts. Because Bill died before his FRA, Mary Anne's survivor's benefit will be based on Bill's PIA and won't increase once she reaches her FRA at age 66. And her retirement benefit, based on her own earnings record, will be higher at 70 than her survivor's benefit. So, it makes sense for Mary Anne to take the survivor's benefit at 62 and delay her own retirement benefit.

It is important to look at the numbers over the long term. Many people take the highest benefit available at the time they claim benefits (in this case at age 62) and don't revisit the decision. As you can see, they may be shortchanging themselves. The longer the survivor lives, the more money she leaves on the table by not making the optimum decision in the first place—and by not considering the option to change benefits in the future.

Survivor's benefits provide unique opportunities, but they also create unique perils. This is one of the few times you can begin receiving one type of benefit and later switch to another. In addition, the second benefit isn't reduced because you began taking the other benefit before your FRA. At a minimum, surviving spouses should estimate what each benefit would pay now, at age 62, at FRA, and finally at age 70. When in doubt, delay the benefit that will be maximized at the highest level and take the other first.

The strategy laid out here assumes that the surviving spouse isn't in dire need of cash and can afford to delay one benefit while receiving another benefit at a lower level for a period of years. In this case, the late husband's survivor's benefit provides a cash flow sufficient to enable the widow to delay her own retirement benefit until it is maximized at age 70. (If, on the other hand, her maximum survivor's benefits were higher than her own retirement benefits and the latter were enough for her to live on in the interim, it could make sense for her to take her retirement benefit for a period of years and later switch to the survivor's benefit.)

But sometimes a surviving spouse needs to maximize current cash flow because she has few or no other sources of income available. The strategies recommended here are for someone who has enough resources to forego the maximum current benefit in exchange for receiving a higher benefit later.

Of course, the best scenario of all would have been for Bill to live until at least age 70 and not take his retirement benefits until then, because he was the higher earner. That would have guaranteed Mary Anne an even higher survivor's benefit for the rest of her life.

Claiming Situations for Survivor's Benefits: The Basic Possibilities

The good news about Social Security survivor's benefits is that there are several options for claiming the benefits, so you can find a choice (or choices) that optimizes lifetime cash flow and financial security for you. The bad news is that all the options make the decision more complicated. And, as we have seen, the Social Security Administration doesn't make it easy to understand and compare your options.

So to help you weigh your options, I provided brief summaries below of the most likely situations in which a widow or widower can claim survivor's benefits. (Keep in mind that the key factors that determine the amount of your survivor's benefits are the age at which you claim them and the age at which your spouse began claiming retirement benefits.)

<u>Situation 1</u>: The husband died after he became eligible to begin retirement benefits, and he had begun receiving his benefits before his FRA. The widow is age 60, and because she needs the income, she will take her survivor's benefits sometime before her FRA. This way her survivor's benefit will be less than what her husband was receiving, which was already less than his full retirement benefit due to his early claim. How much less the benefit will be depends on how early the widow takes the survivor's benefits. If the widow begins benefits at age 60, she'll receive only 71.5 percent of her husband's FRA benefit, or PIA. When the widow begins benefits sometime after age 60 but still before her FRA, she'll receive the higher of 82.5 percent of the spouse's PIA and whatever he was receiving at the time of his death.

<u>Situation 2</u>: As in Situation 1, the husband died after becoming eligible to receive retirement benefits and he had begun receiving them before his FRA. But in this case, the widow can afford to wait to receive her survivor's benefit until it is maximized.

The trick in this case is that it is likely the widow won't have to wait until reaching her own FRA to receive the highest possible amount. She needs to delay only until she is eligible to receive the higher of either the amount her husband was receiving at his death, or

82.5 percent of the husband's PIA, because that's the maximum she will ever be eligible for, on account of his early retirement claim.

The amount of time the widow has to wait to receive the maximum amount depends on the age at which her husband began claiming benefits. The earlier the husband began claiming benefits, the less time the widow has to wait to receive the maximum survivor's benefit. She can use one of the Social Security benefit calculators I described in chapter 3 to determine the age at which she'll maximize the survivor's benefit.

Situation 3: The husband began his retirement benefit at his FRA, but the widow plans to begin the survivor's benefit before reaching her FRA. The base survivor's benefit will be the amount the husband was receiving at the time of his death, but it will be reduced for each month the widow begins the survivor's benefits before her FRA. If she begins survivor's benefits when first eligible at age 60, the survivor's benefit will be reduced the maximum 28.5 percent.

Situation 4: The husband began his benefits after his FRA, and the widow plans to begin survivor's benefits at or after her own FRA. The survivor's benefits will be the amount the husband was receiving at his death, which will include any increases for delayed retirement credits the husband received by claiming benefits after his FRA. There won't be any reduction, because the widow will be at her own FRA or older when claiming the benefits. Once the widow reaches her FRA, however, there's no benefit to delaying any further. Her survivor's benefits won't be increased above what the husband was receiving at the time of his death.

Situation 5: The husband was older than his FRA and no older than 70 but had not begun his retirement benefits. The widow plans to begin survivor's benefits at or after her own FRA. In this case, the survivor's benefits will be whatever amount the husband would have received had he applied to begin benefits on the day he died. The benefit will include delayed retirement credits for beginning the benefit after FRA. There won't be any reduction, because the widow is claiming at her FRA or later. And as in situation 4, there's no advantage for the widow from delaying her claim of benefits after her FRA.

Situation 6: The husband passed away after age 62 but had not claimed Social Security retirement benefits. If the husband died before his FRA, the widow will receive the full PIA that he would have received at his FRA. If the husband died after his FRA, the widow will receive what he would have received had he applied for retirement benefits on the day he died, including delayed retirement credits. If the widow hasn't reached her FRA before claiming the survivor's benefits, the benefits will be reduced based on the number of months she claims the benefits before her FRA.

In each of these situations, as we have seen, the widow has the choice of receiving either her own retirement benefits or the survivor's benefits first and then switching to the other benefit. In cases when the widow is younger than her FRA at the time her husband passed away, the strategy most likely to maximize her lifetime benefits is to receive the lower benefit first and switch to the other benefit at the age at which it is maximized and is greater than the first benefit.

Life Insurance on the Cheap

An important point to note about these scenarios is that if the husband (assuming he's the higher-earning spouse) claims his retirement benefits before his FRA, the widow will never receive more than 82.5 percent of his PIA, which is the full benefit he would have received at his FRA. Because so many people claim their retirement benefits before reaching FRA, Social Security data indicate about 60 percent of widows receive survivor's benefits that are less than what their late husband's benefit would have been at his FRA.[1]

That's one reason I emphasize that the higher-earning spouse should delay receiving retirement benefits as long as possible. Given the probability that, in most marriages, at least one of the spouses is likely to live well beyond average life expectancy, it makes sense to ensure the survivor's check is the highest amount you can make it— unless the couple has such substantial assets that Social Security benefits aren't significant to them. Remember, the surviving spouse will receive only one Social Security check.

The higher-earning spouse should think of delaying the retirement benefit as an affordable life insurance policy. The delay will increase the amount paid to the surviving spouse every month for life, no matter how long that life lasts. The longer the surviving spouse lives, the longer that higher benefit will be received. As I explained in chapter 1, most people don't realize the value of that benefit. You would have to purchase a significant life insurance policy to fund an annuity that would pay the higher benefit amount indexed for inflation and guaranteed for life. It's much more affordable to delay retirement benefits for a few years.

Social Security is an insurance program, and the primary risk it insures against is the risk inherent in living a long life: the possibility that you will outlive your assets. Unless there's a significant probability that neither spouse will live to at least average life expectancy, you can maximize the longevity insurance benefit by delaying the benefits of the higher-earning spouse.

Pitfalls to Avoid

It's important to know that survivor's benefits are treated the same as retirement benefits for most purposes. This causes a couple of other rules to come into play, which you need to know in order to make the best decision about when to begin taking different benefits.

One rule that applies to survivor's benefits is the earned income limit. As we have seen, if you claim benefits and also continue to be either employed or self-employed before FRA, your benefits will be reduced if you earn "too much" money. (But remember, as you learned in chapter 5, the earnings limit applies only to earnings from a job or self-employment, not to investment income. Also, the Social Security benefits are only delayed until a later year when you no longer exceed the earnings limit or have reached FRA. Then, they are paid back over time in the form of higher monthly benefits.)

The other rule is federal income taxation of Social Security benefits. When income exceeds certain levels, some of your Social Security benefits are included in your gross income and subject to federal income taxes. Income tax issues are discussed in chapter 8.

What Happens When a Widow Remarries?

There are some situations in which the Social Security rules seem more generous than you would expect—allowing different benefit options based on the earnings histories of different people. In this chapter you have seen how surviving spouses can claim retirement benefits on the basis of their own earnings or survivor benefits based on the earnings of a deceased spouse, and even switch from one to the other. In chapter 7 I'll explain how divorced people have similar options.

But what about when a widow or widower remarries? How does remarriage affect the choices available under Social Security law and regulations?

The answer is that if a surviving spouse remarries after age 60, there is no change to his or her benefits. The widow or widower still is entitled to survivor's benefits based on the deceased spouse's earnings and claiming record.

Because of this rule, some surviving spouses are entitled to claim benefits based on the earnings records of more than one spouse. You can receive only one benefit at a time, but you can look to several spouse's earnings histories to maximize your benefits.

For example, suppose you were widowed in your early sixties and began collecting survivor's benefits based on your late husband's earnings history. You remarry after your FRA. If your spousal benefit based on your new husband's earnings record is higher than your current survivor's benefit, you can apply for and receive it instead. That spousal benefit will not be reduced for early claiming, because at this point you have reached FRA. The penalty for claiming the survivor's benefit from the previous marriage early, before your FRA, won't carry over to reduce your new spousal benefit.

If the second spouse also passes away before you do, you can claim survivor's benefits based on either of the two deceased spouses' earnings record, and you will receive the higher of the two benefits.

But you don't have those options if you remarry before age 60. In that case, you're not entitled to survivor's benefits on the basis of your first husband's earnings unless your second marriage ends by death, divorce, or annulment. Then you might be eligible for survivor's benefits based on your first spouse's earnings record.

The Lump Sum Survivor's Benefit

A surviving spouse who lived in the same household with the deceased spouse can also receive a one-time lump sum payment of $255. If there's no surviving spouse, the lump sum can be paid to a dependent child (usually a child under age 18) who is eligible to receive benefits based on the deceased's record.

This lump sum used to be considered money to pay for a funeral, but funeral costs now far exceed $255.

What if you were married to the deceased spouse and weren't living with him at the time of death? You're still eligible for the $255 lump sum if you were receiving benefits based on the deceased's earnings record or became eligible for the benefits upon his death.

Widows Beware

Unfortunately, as I explained in chapter 3, you can't depend on the Social Security Administration for the right answers. It has been demonstrated—by the SSA's own Office of Inspector General (OIG)—that SSA representatives often give the wrong answers when asked about benefits. The 2018 OIG report showed that surviving spouses in particular had been recipients of bad advice and service from the SSA. The SSA had systematically failed to inform surviving spouses of their benefit choices. As a result, 82 percent of surviving spouses were underpaid, receiving lower benefits than they were eligible for. Specifically, SSA didn't inform surviving spouses that they could delay their own retirement benefits until age 70 while claiming survivor's benefits in the interim. And, as we have seen, a 2020 follow-up report found that the SSA still hadn't remedied the situation.

The lessons to take away are that Social Security is complicated and you can't rely on the SSA to give you accurate and complete advice. Educate yourself about the options and seek help from knowledgeable sources to ensure that your lifetime guaranteed benefits are maximized.

CHAPTER 7

Benefits for the Divorced

In this chapter I will explain how and when a divorced spouse can receive benefits based on an ex-spouse's earnings history. There's no such thing as "divorce benefits" in Social Security. But spousal benefits are often available to ex-spouses, and they're available on fairly liberal terms. Divorced spouses, in fact, sometimes have more options and flexibility than current spouses. At other times, a small difference in timing can leave a divorced spouse without benefits, or with lower benefits than would be available with different timing.

The topic of Social Security benefits for ex-spouses is becoming more important with the increase in late-in-life divorces. An internet search for "gray divorce" reveals that, though divorce still is less common after 50 than at younger ages, the divorce rate for those over 50 is rising. It has doubled since 1990, and in 2010 one in four divorces in the United States involved couples older than 50. Divorce is more likely for those who have been divorced previously. The Baby Boomers are now older than 50, and a higher percentage of them divorced earlier in life than in previous generations. So, Social Security's rules for divorced spouses are more important to the boomers than to previous generations.

You may expect Social Security policy to be neutral toward marriage and divorce. But as you'll see in this chapter, this often is not the case. People who review Social Security's rules before changing their marital status will find that the rules encourage marriage in some cases and discourage couples from marrying in other cases. And if the rules don't encourage divorce, at least there's no penalty for divorcing.

Collecting on a Former Spouse

A person can collect Social Security spousal benefits based on the earnings record of a former spouse under certain circumstances. The basic requirements are:

- The marriage must have lasted at least ten years
- The couple must have been divorced for at least two years, in most cases
- The ex-spouse claiming benefits must still be unmarried—again, in most cases
- The ex-spouse on whose earnings history the benefits are based must be at least age 62

An ex-spouse also might be able to claim survivor's benefits after the other ex-spouse passes away, which is another possibility I explore in this chapter.

Some of the claiming rules for married spouses don't apply to former spouses. You may recall from chapter 4 that when a couple is married, a spouse can't claim spousal benefits unless the other spouse has claimed his or her retirement benefits. If the spouse drawing a retirement benefit suspends that benefit or withdraws the claim, the spousal benefits to the other spouse also will end. When a divorced spouse claims spousal benefits, however, it doesn't matter whether the worker whose earnings history is the basis of the claim has filed to claim benefits or when that worker plans to claim benefits. The ex-spouse can claim benefits based on that earnings history anyway.

In other words, a divorced person is independently entitled to claim benefits on the earnings history of his or her former spouse. The worker whose earnings history is the basis for the claim doesn't have to be consulted and isn't even informed by Social Security that the former spouse is taking the benefits. The spousal benefits drawn by an ex-spouse also don't affect the amount of the benefits paid to the worker or any current spouse of the worker.

It also doesn't matter whether the ex-spouse whose earnings record is the basis of the other former spouse's claim has remarried. Thus, three or more people can claim benefits based on the same earnings record: the worker with the earnings record can claim his or her own benefits. That worker's current spouse can file for spousal benefits based on that record. In addition, the former spouse—or former spouses—of the worker can claim benefits on that record if the eligibility rules are met.

In case you're worried, the primary worker's benefits aren't reduced when other people claim benefits based on his or her earnings history. A worker's retirement benefits are calculated based on his or her earnings history. The amount of those benefits doesn't change based on the number of spouses and ex-spouses who also claim benefits on that earnings history. (That, incidentally, is evidence that you don't have a separate Social Security account with a sum of money in it.)

Suppose that Will and Marilyn were married for more than ten years and then divorced. Each of them also meets the other requirements for an ex-spouse to claim spousal benefits on the other ex-spouse's earnings record. Let's say Will had the higher lifetime earnings, so that Marilyn's spousal benefit based on Will's earnings record would be higher than the retirement benefit based on Marilyn's earnings history.

Marilyn can collect spousal benefits on Will's earnings record. Marilyn's spousal benefit at her full retirement age will be one-half of Will's full retirement benefit, no matter when he claims. As we have seen, an early retirement claim on his part won't reduce her spousal benefits. But by the same token, if Will delays collecting benefits beyond his FRA and receives delayed retirement credits that increase his monthly benefit, Marilyn won't gain an increase from that delay. Marilyn receives half of Will's FRA benefit, regardless of when Will actually claims benefits and how much Will receives.

Marilyn's spousal benefits will be reduced, however, if she claims benefits before her own FRA. Just as retirement benefits are reduced when you claim them before FRA, spousal benefits are reduced before FRA—whether you claim them as a current spouse or former spouse.

The rate of reduction for spousal benefits, whether we're talking about spouses or ex-spouses, is greater than for claiming your own retirement benefits before FRA. The spousal benefit is reduced by 8.33 percent annually for the first three years benefits are claimed early (that's 25/36 of 1 percent for each of the first 36 months) and 5 percent for each additional year (that's 5/12 of 1 percent for each additional month). A divorced spouse who claims the spousal benefit as early as possible, at age 62, will have the benefit reduced by 30 percent, whereas a retiree who claims early will receive a benefit reduced by only about 25 percent.

Because the reduction for taking benefits early is greater for spousal benefits, it usually makes sense for a former spouse to delay claiming the benefits until FRA if he or she can live without the income. The longer the former spouse lives, the greater the payoff from waiting to begin those benefits.

The Two-Year Rule

What if the couple was married for at least ten years, but they've been divorced less than two years? I said earlier that for a former spouse to claim spousal benefits, the couple must have been divorced for at least two years "in most cases." Being divorced for at least two years provides the most flexibility in claiming benefits, but claiming benefits on the record of a former spouse may not be foreclosed by the fact that the divorce was finalized fewer than two years ago.

When the two-year requirement hasn't been met, a former spouse still can collect spousal benefits on the earnings history of the other ex-spouse when the latter has filed to claim his or her retirement benefits.

Suppose Dale and Debbie recently had their divorce finalized. Dale is 63 and Debbie is about to turn 65. Debbie would like to claim Social Security benefits based on Dale's earnings history, because the spousal benefit of one-half Dale's benefit would be significantly more than the benefits based on Debbie's earnings history, whether she claims the benefits now at age 65 or at her FRA.

But Dale hasn't applied for his Social Security retirement benefits and doesn't plan to claim before full retirement age. He might even wait until age 70 to maximize his monthly benefit.

So Debbie's only option at this point is to file a claim for her own retirement benefits. If she claims them now, Debbie will receive less than the full retirement benefit, because she's filing before her FRA, which is age 66 and four months.

After the divorce has been finalized for at least two years, however, Debbie can claim benefits on Dale's earnings history and receive half of his benefit payable at his FRA. At that point, she'll be approved for the benefits even if Dale hasn't claimed benefits or reached his FRA, because they've been divorced at least two years. She will reach her FRA by then, so there won't be a reduction to her spousal benefits for claiming them early.

The Remarriage Rule

To claim benefits on the earnings history of an ex-spouse, you can't be remarried at the time the claim is filed. It doesn't matter what age you are, how long you were married, or how long you've been divorced. If you remarried, and still are married, you can't claim benefits on the earnings history of an ex-spouse. You can claim benefits only on your own earnings record or that of your current spouse.

One source of confusion is that the rule for divorced people is different from the rule for widowed people. A widowed person who remarried after the age of 60 can claim benefits on the earnings history of the late spouse. In fact, as explained in chapter 6, a widow or widower who has remarried can file benefits based on the earnings history of several people: the late spouse, the current spouse, and himself or herself.

In some situations, the remarriage rule can discourage a divorced person from remarrying. Suppose Ron and Rhonda are in their sixties. They're both divorced from their first spouses and considering marrying each other. Rhonda's earnings history would entitle her to only a low retirement benefit.

And after looking closely at Ron's finances, Rhonda realizes that Ron's earnings history entitles him to a much lower Social Security retirement benefit than her ex-husband's. If Rhonda remains unmarried, she can claim spousal benefits as a former spouse equal to one-half her ex-husband's full retirement benefits. But if she marries Ron, she loses the ability to claim on her ex-husband's earnings and can claim only spousal benefits equal to one-half of Ron's full retirement benefit. She'll have a higher monthly benefit if she claims on her ex-husband's earnings history instead of Ron's.

Looking to the longer term, Rhonda realizes that if she outlives her ex-husband, she'll be able to claim survivor's benefits on his earnings history. They're likely to be higher than the survivor's benefits she could claim from Ron's earnings history. The difference in survivor's benefits will be even greater if Ron claims his benefits at FRA or earlier and Rhonda's ex-husband waited until 70 to claim his retirement benefits.

A substantial difference between the benefits of the two men could discourage Rhonda from marrying Ron. It might even cause Ron to discourage Rhonda from marrying him. They could live together as an unmarried couple and have higher joint Social Security income from Rhonda's spousal benefits on her ex-husband's earning history than on Ron's.

The remarriage rule even gives some people a financial incentive to divorce. Let's say Rhonda didn't research Social Security's benefit rules beforehand and married Ron. After the marriage, Rhonda takes a look at the claiming rules and realizes she'd be eligible for a higher benefit as her first husband's ex-spouse than as Ron's current spouse.

Under the rules, she is ineligible to claim benefits under her ex-spouse's earnings history if she is remarried at the time the claim for benefits is filed. But if she divorces Ron, even if she keeps living with him, she'll be eligible for spousal benefits based on the earnings record of either ex-spouse and will receive whichever benefit is higher—in this case, the spousal benefit based on the earnings of her first ex-spouse.

Thus it could make financial sense for Rhonda to divorce Ron. Then she'll be eligible to claim benefits on the basis of her first ex-husband's higher earnings record.

A Divorced Person's Claiming Strategies

A divorced person can maximize lifetime benefits through careful decisions over the years about which benefits to claim.

Let's go back to Dale and Debbie and add some dollar amounts to the situation. Debbie is estimated to receive $1,100 monthly if she waits until her FRA to claim her earned benefits. If she claims the benefits now, she'll receive about $900 monthly. Dale will receive an estimated $2,700 monthly at full retirement age and $3,537 if he waits until age 70.

To maximize her lifetime benefits, Debbie should wait until full retirement age and claim her $1,100 monthly benefits. After the divorce is finalized for two years, Debbie can apply for her spousal benefits. She'll receive one-half of Dale's full retirement benefit, even if Dale hasn't filed for benefits yet. Since Dale won't have reached FRA yet, he won't have filed for benefits unless his plans have changed. Debbie will receive $1,350 monthly at this point.

Suppose Dale doesn't claim his benefits until age 70. Debbie would not benefit from waiting until then to claim her spousal benefits. As we have seen, the spousal benefits for an ex-spouse are fixed at one-half of Dale's full retirement benefit. They don't increase if the other spouse claims the benefits at a later age and receives a higher benefit.

Note that this is one instance in which a divorced spouse has an advantage over a married spouse. If Dale and Debbie were still married, Debbie couldn't claim spousal benefits until Dale claimed his benefits. Debbie would only be able to claim her own retirement benefits. But once they have been divorced for at least two years, Debbie can claim the spousal benefits regardless of what Dale does.

Ex-spouses born on or before January 1, 1954, have even more options. Unlike people born after that date, they have the option of applying for one type of benefit at a time, making a restricted claim for the first benefit and then switching to claim the other benefit later, when it is maximized. They can either apply for spousal benefits on the basis of their ex-spouse's earnings first and later apply for retirement benefits based on their own earnings, or else make those two separate claims in the opposite order, whichever is more beneficial.

But people born after January 1, 1954, however, don't have that option. They are deemed to apply for all available benefits and will be paid the higher of the two. Social Security doesn't allow them to make a restricted claim. They can't switch from one benefit to another. (As we saw in chapter 6, the exception to that rule is in the case of survivor's benefits.)

George and Martha, for example, were married for ten years and have been divorced for two. But they, unlike the ex-spouses in the example above, were born on or before January 1, 1954. Thus, Martha is able to maximize her benefits by switching between claiming retirement benefits on her own earnings record and claiming spouse's benefits on the earnings of her ex-husband George. For example, let's suppose Martha's work history entitles her to a benefit of $2,500 at full retirement age, which she reached when she turned 66. But if she delays her retirement claim until she turns 70, her benefit will increase to about $3,300. And further, suppose that Martha's spousal benefits, based on the earnings record of her ex-spouse George, are $1,350, one-half of her ex-husband's FRB of $2,700.

Here's where this scenario gets really interesting. Because both George and Martha were born on or before January 1, 1954, they can make restricted claims for either their spousal or their retirement benefits, instead of only being able to claim and receive the one highest possible benefit for them at the time of the claim. If they had been born after January 1, 1954, any Social Security claim by either of them would result in their being paid their own retirement benefit, which is higher than their spousal benefit. But because they were born on or before that date, they each have the option to receive the lower spousal benefits now in order to maximize their retirement benefit by waiting to claim it until age 70. The retirement benefits will be increased, because George and Martha have waited to receive them. In the meantime, though, each will have received some monthly benefit from the spousal benefits claims.

Thus, Martha's optimum strategy is probably first to file a restricted claim for her spousal benefits based on George's earnings history. She'll receive $1,350. Then, at age 70, Martha can file a retirement claim for benefits based on her own earnings history and receive about $3,300 monthly.

Both ex-spouses can use the restricted claim strategy, because they were both born no later than January 1, 1954. And as ex-spouses they are both eligible to file for spousal benefits—one-half of the ex-spouse's full retirement benefit—at the same time. (This option would not be available to them if they were still married to each other because only one married spouse in a couple can claim spousal benefits at a time.) Each of them also has the option of filing for retirement benefits based on his or her own earnings record. They have both reached their full retirement age but not yet reached age 70, at which point their retirement benefits will be maximized.

Remember, the restricted claim strategy is available only to those born on or before January 1, 1954. If you were born after that date, you can't file a restricted claim for only one type of benefit. You are deemed to file for all the types of benefits for which you are eligible and you'll be paid the highest of them. The only exception is for a surviving spouse, who can file a claim for only one type of benefit (either retirement or survivor's) and later switch to the other benefit, as discussed in chapter 6.

The Widowed Ex-Spouse

Martha will have another option if George predeceases her. As an ex-spouse, Martha likely will qualify for survivor's benefits. She can't have remarried before age 60, which wouldn't be a problem in her case. (See chapter 6 for full details about eligibility for surviving spouse benefits.)

As a surviving ex-spouse, Martha generally would be entitled to either George's full retirement benefit or whatever he was collecting at death—whichever amount is higher. That's the same survivor's benefit that she would qualify for if she had still been married to George when he died. Before his death, she was receiving only one-half of his full retirement benefit as a spousal benefit. But now that George has passed away and Martha qualifies for survivor's benefits equal to what he was receiving at the time of his demise, instead of her spousal benefits, her monthly income is boosted substantially—especially if her ex-spouse had delayed his claim past his FRA and was receiving more than his FRB of $2,700.

There's another trick in the Social Security rules that can help surviving ex-spouses who are in the right circumstances. And it applies even to people born after January 1, 1954, who generally can't restrict their benefits application to one type of benefits at a time. They are deemed to file for all the benefits available to them and will be paid only the one that is the highest. But that "deemed filing" rule doesn't apply to survivor benefits, as we have seen. The exception from the deemed filing rule can come in handy.

And a surviving ex-spouse who was born on or before January 1, 1954, has even more options. So after George dies, Martha can now switch from the spousal benefit of $1,350 per month that she has been receiving to either her retirement benefit based on her own earnings record *or* to survivor's benefits set at the higher of her ex-husband's FRB or what he was actually receiving at the time he passed away. The right choice for Martha will depend on which is higher, the survivor's benefits or her own earned retirement benefits.

She can even switch twice—from spousal benefits to survivor's benefits, and then from survivor's benefits to retirement benefits.

At age 70, or perhaps earlier, delayed retirement credits may have increased her retirement benefits to the point that they are greater than the survivor's benefits. Then she can switch from survivor's benefits to retirement benefits. Or she can claim benefits in the reverse order—her retirement benefits first and the survivor's benefits later—depending on which order ultimately gives her the highest benefit.

You can see that rights to receive benefits on the basis of an ex-spouse's earnings history survive not only divorce but also death. If you're divorced and your ex-spouse passes away, review the surviving spouse options in chapter 6. You may be able to increase your lifetime benefits by claiming on the record of the ex-spouse, especially if you can coordinate the timing of the spousal benefits with the timing of your own retirement benefits.

The Age Game

The rules for claiming spousal benefits as a former spouse have the potential to put some people in unfortunate situations. A divorced spouse has an advantage over a current spouse, in that the former spouse can claim spousal benefits on the other former spouse's earnings history without having to wait for the other former spouse to claim benefits, provided they've been divorced at least two years.

But for a former spouse to claim spousal benefits, each of the former spouses must be at least age 62. Also, the former spouse won't receive full spousal benefits unless he or she has reached full retirement age at the time of the claim. Claiming before FRA results in a reduction of benefits.

Suppose John and Mary were married for more than ten years and have been divorced for two years. John had much higher earnings during his career, so Mary would like to claim benefits based on John's record. But Mary is 62 and John is 57. Mary can't claim any spousal benefits on John's earnings record for another five years, when John turns 62. At that point Mary will be 67, older than her FRA, so she'll receive the full spousal benefit.

Mary could claim her own retirement benefits beginning at age 62 and then switch to the spousal benefit when John finally turns 62. But if she does that she will be beginning her retirement benefits before full retirement age, and she'll receive 30 percent less than her full retirement benefit. And even when she switches to the spousal benefit, it will also be reduced because she claimed her retirement benefits early.

Now suppose the ages are reversed. John is 62 and Mary is 57. Mary can't claim the spousal benefits for another five years, when she turns 62. If she claims the benefits at that time, she won't receive the full spousal benefit, which is one-half of John's benefits at full retirement age. Instead, the spousal benefit will be reduced 30 percent because she is claiming so early. For Mary to claim full retirement benefits, she would have to wait until her FRA, which is age 67. By then, John will almost be ready to claim the maximum benefit at age 70, if he hasn't claimed benefits already. But that won't matter to Mary. As a former spouse she will receive no more than half of John's full retirement benefit, regardless of when he claims his benefits and how much he receives.

The Multiple-Ex-Spouse Daisy Chain of Benefits

If you have read the chapter closely to this point, some questions may have been raised in your mind. You have realized that several people may claim benefits based on the earnings history of one person. The person who had the work history, of course, can claim retirement benefits. In addition, the current spouse of that person may be eligible to claim spousal benefits. Plus, a former spouse of the person may also qualify to claim spousal benefits based on the work history. In fact, as far as the Social Security rules are concerned, an unlimited number of ex-spouses can claim benefits based on that one person's work history. Likewise, if the worker passes away first, however many surviving spouses and ex-spouses he or she had may qualify for survivor's benefits based on the same earnings record.

You might ask, what about the flip side of that scenario? On how many ex-spouse's earnings records might one person file claims for benefits? The number probably is higher than you would think. In fact, there is no numerical limit in the Social Security rules on how many former spouses you can base your claims upon. There are requirements that serve as practical limits: you must have been married to each ex-spouse for at least ten years and not be remarried at the time you claim the benefits. In addition, both you and the former spouse must be at least age 62 when you file the claim for benefits.

As we have seen, Social Security will pay you only one benefit at a time. But if you qualify for different types of benefits or for benefits on the basis of different people's earnings histories, Social Security will calculate each benefit and pay you the higher one. And if you later qualify for a different, higher benefit, you can switch to that benefit.

In addition, while you cannot file a claim under an ex-spouse's earnings history if you are remarried at the time the claim is filed, you can file a claim based on an ex-spouse's earnings history if you are unmarried at the time of the claim—even if you remarried after you and the first spouse divorced, provided you divorced the second spouse before filing the benefit claim.

Suppose Phil Ander now is age 62. He has had more spouses than most people have had jobs and now is divorced from each of those women. As Phil considers filing to claim Social Security benefits, he realizes that each of these women was more successful in her career or business than he was and thus is likely to qualify for far more in Social Security retirement benefits than he is. In fact, he suspects that spousal benefits equal to half any of their FRA benefits will exceed his own earned retirement benefits.

These ex-spouses are Paula, now age 65, Pam, age 58, and Pat, 52. Their relative earnings success is the inverse of their ages. Paula had the lowest earnings of the group, Pam's income was higher, and Pat's was highest of all.

Phil files for benefits at age 62, making sure the Social Security Administration knows that Paula was his ex-spouse, that they were married for more than ten years before divorcing, and that Phil currently is unmarried. Phil is granted spousal benefits based on Paula's earnings history. He receives one-half of Paula's full retirement benefit, less 30 percent because Phil claimed at age 62 instead of his full retirement age.

Time passes, and Pam, ex-spouse number two, turns 62. Phil files a new claim for benefits based on Pam's earnings history. Again, he makes it clear that they were married for more than ten years before divorcing and that he is unmarried. Because Pam's highest thirty-five years of earnings results in a higher full retirement benefit than Paula's, Phil is granted an increase in spousal benefits based on Pam's earnings history.

Here's a twist. Phil's spousal benefit based on Paula's earnings history was reduced by 30 percent because he claimed it at age 62. He's still a little shy of his full retirement age at the time of his second claim, so his benefit based on Pam's earnings history will be reduced. But it won't be reduced by 30 percent. The fact that he began his first spousal benefits at age 62 won't be held against him. Instead, his benefits based on Pam's earnings will be reduced only by the short period he claimed benefits before his full retirement age. This time his benefits are reduced by only about 10 percent.

Eventually Pat, ex-spouse number three, turns 62. Phil again files for benefits, this time based on Pat's earnings record. Again, he qualifies for those spousal benefits because he still is unmarried. Also, at this point he's older than his FRA, so there's no reduction in his benefits. He receives a full 50 percent of Pat's full retirement benefit, though she has no intention of claiming her benefit for years.

Phil may not be done maximizing his Social Security benefits. Suppose he outlives Paula. Though her earned retirement benefits at full retirement age were the lowest of the ex-spouses, she waited until age 70 to claim her benefits. It turns out that her benefits at age 70 were higher than Pat's full retirement benefits. Phil learns that Paula passed away and files for survivor benefits. Unlike spousal benefits to ex-spouses, survivor's benefits to ex-spouses are increased by delayed retirement credits. As a survivor, Phil is entitled to whatever benefit amount Paula was receiving at her death, since she claimed after full retirement age. So he receives a substantial upgrade from one-half of Pat's full retirement benefit to the full amount of the larger benefit Paula was receiving at her passing as a result of her delayed claim. Again, Phil receives only one benefit at a time, but he receives the highest of all the benefits for which he's qualified. As he becomes newly qualified for higher benefits, he can apply for those to replace his existing benefit.

If Phil outlives Pam and Pat, he can continue this practice of applying for higher benefits as each wife passes away. He also can look around for someone to marry who's receiving a higher benefit than any of his ex-wives. Once Phil is married to that person for at least nine months, he becomes eligible for a survivor's benefit equal to the benefit that person was receiving.

The tale is a comprehensive example of how the rules work. Phil Ander may not be an example you want to follow, but his story shows the circumstances in which you would receive the maximum benefits you're allowed.

CHAPTER 8

When Your Social Security Benefits Will Be Taxed

A t the beginning of the program, Social Security benefits were free of federal income taxes. Most states with income taxes also exempted the benefits. That's not the case anymore.

Congress first subjected some Social Security benefits to income taxes in the 1986 tax law, which provided that when total income exceeded a certain level, a portion of the benefits would be included in gross income. Then, in 1993, Congress provided that higher-income beneficiaries would have a larger percentage of their benefits subject to federal income taxes. The higher your income, the higher the percentage of your Social Security benefits subject to income taxes, until a maximum of 85 percent of the benefits are included in gross income.

Today about 40 percent of Social Security beneficiaries pay federal income taxes on a portion of their benefits. The percentage steadily increases each year, however, because the income thresholds at which the benefits are taxed are not indexed for inflation. As inflation steadily increases incomes, more people earn enough to exceed the taxation threshold and pay taxes on some of their benefits. It's a built-in tax increase on Social Security beneficiaries caused by inflationary increases in income. In time, a portion of almost all Social Security benefits will be taxed under laws that were originally intended to affect only upper-income beneficiaries.

This chapter explains when Social Security benefits might be taxed by the IRS. I also lay out some strategies that can help reduce or eliminate the tax.

Preliminary Calculations

Determining the amount of your Social Security benefits that will be taxed isn't simple or straightforward. In fact, the computation is fairly complicated, even for the tax code. Most people are better off using tax preparation software or a professional tax return preparer if their benefits might be subject to federal income taxes.

Determining the amount of your Social Security benefits that must be included in gross income is a multistep process. The first step is a fairly straightforward calculation to determine whether your income is in the range in which your benefits might be taxed. Doing this calculation saves someone from going through the full tax calculation only to find out that none of his or her benefits is taxed.

This initial calculation starts with the gross income, also known as total income, from your federal income tax return. On the latest Form 1040, this number is on line 7b. It's the sum of all your income that isn't tax-exempt. Your Social Security benefits are not yet included in the calculation at this point.

But now you add one-half of your Social Security benefits and all of your tax-exempt interest (which is interest from bonds issued by state and local governments) to your gross income. If you have already claimed Social Security benefits, then early in the year the SSA should send you a Form SSA-1099 listing the total benefits you received the previous year. Your broker or the government issuing the bonds should send you a Form 1099-INT listing the amount of tax-exempt interest you were paid the previous year.

You also add some other types of income that are exempt from taxes: interest on qualified U.S. savings bonds, employer-provided adoption benefits, foreign-earned income, the foreign housing exclusion, and income earned by residents of American Samoa or Puerto Rico.

Once you calculate the total, subtract what's called the "base amount" from it. The base amount depends on your filing status. For a taxpayer who is single, a head of household, or a qualified widow or widower, the base amount is $25,000. It also is $25,000 for a taxpayer who is married and filing separately, and lived apart from the other spouse for all of the tax year. For taxpayers who are married but filing separately, and did not live apart the entire year, the base amount is zero dollars. Taxpayers who are married filing jointly have a base amount of $32,000.

If the result of the subtraction is zero dollars or less, none of your benefits are taxable. In other words, if your total income plus the additions is less than your base amount, none of your Social Security benefits are taxable.

Next Steps

But if your total income plus additions exceeds the base amount, some of your benefits might be taxable. You have to make the full calculation of the amount of taxable Social Security benefits.

You can do this computation by completing Worksheet A in IRS Publication 915, which is free on the IRS website www.irs.gov. You also can use the IRS's Interactive Tax Tool on its website at this link: www.irs.gov/help/ita.

At first you will be computing the amount of Social Security benefits that must be added to your gross income, or total income, on Form 1040. That's the part of your benefits that (along with your other income, less any deductions) may be subject to your regular income tax rate. Only after you determine that percentage—which can go no higher than 85 percent of your benefits—can you compute the actual tax on your benefits.

The calculations begin with your adjusted gross income (AGI) from line 8b of your Form 1040. It's your gross income, or total income, minus certain adjustments or deductions you may have, such as deductible IRA contributions and self-employed medical insurance premiums.

Then you add certain types of income that aren't subject to income taxes. These are the same types of income that we added to gross income in the initial calculation: tax-exempt interest, interest on qualified U.S. savings bonds, employer-provided adoption benefits, foreign-earned income, foreign housing exclusion, and income earned by residents of American Samoa or Puerto Rico. The result is known as modified adjusted gross income (MAGI) or provisional income.

From your MAGI you subtract the appropriate base amount listed earlier. (The most common base amounts are $25,000 for single taxpayers and $32,000 for married taxpayers filing jointly.)

Then, from that result, you subtract another amount, $12,000 for married taxpayers filing jointly or $9,000 for other taxpayers. When the difference is zero or less, none of your benefits are taxable. But when the difference is greater than zero, part of your benefits will be included in gross income and subject to federal income taxes. At this point, the calculation becomes very difficult to explain. If your MAGI minus that $12,000 or $9,000 is greater than zero, you know that a portion of your benefits will be taxable. At that point, you use tax preparation software or a professional tax return preparer to compute your taxes. You also can use Worksheet 1 in IRS Publication 915.

In general, when MAGI is between $32,000 and $44,000 for married taxpayers filing jointly or between $25,000 and $34,000 for single taxpayers, up to 50 percent of benefits will be included in gross income. Up to 85 percent of benefits will be included in gross income when MAGI exceeds $44,000 for married taxpayers filing jointly or $34,000 for single taxpayers. But the percentage of benefits included in gross income is on a sliding scale. You don't include the full 50 percent of benefits in gross income simply because you're married filing jointly and your MAGI is above $32,000. You only include at least 50 percent of benefits in gross income when your MAGI equals $44,000.

These basic rules for taxes on Social Security benefits should at least give you a good idea whether a portion of your benefits will be included in your gross income for purposes of taxation.

Taxes on U.S. Citizens Abroad

The U.S. Department of State negotiates various agreements with other countries regarding Social Security. Those agreements can reduce federal income taxes on Social Security benefits for some U.S. citizens who reside in other countries.

The latest agreements are as follows:

U.S. citizens who are residents of the following countries are exempt from U.S. tax on their benefits.

- Canada
- Egypt
- Germany
- Ireland
- Israel
- Italy (you must be a citizen of Italy for the exemption to apply)

- Romania
- The United Kingdom

These agreements can change over time, so you always should check with the government on their latest status.

Be Sure to Prepay Your Taxes

You need to prepay federal income taxes during the year if you want to avoid a penalty for failing to pay estimated taxes. Most people are used to having taxes withheld from their employment income during their working lives. Thus, it often comes as a surprise to learn during the first year or two of retirement that taxes aren't being withheld and have to be prepaid to avoid penalties. The SSA doesn't withhold income taxes on Social Security benefit payments unless you specifically request withholding.

You can find the details of how much to pay and how to pay estimated taxes in Publication 505, "Tax Withholding and Estimated Tax," which also is available free on the IRS website. When your prepayments by withholding, or estimated taxes, or both exceed the minimum required, you avoid penalties for underpayment of estimated income taxes. If your state has an income tax, it also will have estimated tax requirements. Check with the state Department of Taxation for its requirements.

How the Tax on Social Security Benefits
Increases Marginal Tax Rates

Social Security beneficiaries can face some of the highest marginal tax rates among taxpayers. The marginal tax rate is the tax rate on your last dollar of income. For most taxpayers, the marginal tax rate is the same as the rate for their tax bracket. But other taxpayers face what I call "Stealth Taxes." They have tax breaks that phase out as income rises. For them, the marginal tax rate is higher.

You see, when your Social Security benefits are taxed, more than one dollar of income is taxed for each dollar your income increases. Suppose you receive Social Security retirement benefits, and at your income level you must include $1,000 of your benefits in your gross income. Then suppose your other income unexpectedly increases by $1.00. You include that dollar in gross income and pay taxes on it. But adding that additional income also causes more of your Social Security benefits to be included in your gross income. Let's say that you have to include another $0.25 of benefits in your gross income because of the additional dollar of income. Your gross income increases by $1.25 because you earned that extra dollar of income.

If your tax rate is 25 percent, you would now owe 25 percent of an additional $1.25, not just 25 percent of the actual $1.00 increase in your income. The tax on the extra dollar is $0.3125 instead of $0.25. Your marginal tax rate has just jumped to 31.25 percent. Higher income taxpayers, especially those in states with high income taxes that don't exempt Social Security from income, face a much higher marginal tax rate. The marginal tax rate can exceed 50 percent, and in a few instances is around 90 percent.

The tax on Social Security benefits has a multiplier effect. The more income you earn during the year, the greater the amount of your Social Security benefits included in your gross income. The increase can even push you into a higher tax bracket or increase other taxes, such as the Medicare premium surtax.

You need to consider all the effects of the taxation of Social Security benefits, and those effects can be quite complex.

For example, you may be planning a stock sale that would incur a long-term capital gains tax. Before deciding to go ahead with the sale, you need to compute more than the tax on the sale. You also need to determine whether the sale will increase the amount of your Social Security benefits that will be included in your gross income for that year. Only then will you know the true tax on that stock sale.

The tax on Social Security benefits is progressive. In other words, as your income increases, the tax rate increases. The tax is *very* progressive, as William Meyer and William Reichenstein have demonstrated. The duo determined that when wealth (not income) rises from $200,000 to $900,000, the percentage of Social Security benefits subject to federal income taxes rises from 2.1 percent to 83.0 percent. That's over the course of a 30-year retirement. (The maximum amount of benefits that can be taxed under the law is 85 percent.) Their calculation assumes that the retiree distributes 4 percent of the balance of his or her retirement accounts each year and owes taxes on them.

Most of the increase occurs between total assets of $200,000 and $600,000. As wealth rises in this range, each additional dollar distribution from a retirement account such as a 401(k) or traditional IRA causes an additional $0.50 or $0.85 of Social Security benefits to be included in gross income.

Meyer and Reichenstein make a strong argument for delaying Social Security as long as possible, especially if your net worth is in the $200,000–$600,000 range. If you have assets in that range, you will be able to retain far more after-tax wealth over your lifetime by delaying Social Security benefits, even if you retire at age 62 and withdraw money from 401(k) or other retirement savings to pay expenses between ages 62 and 70. Because delaying the benefits to age 70 increases the amount of Social Security benefits, it ultimately also reduces the amount of distributions from your 401(k) distributions or other sources of income that will be needed to finance retirement. And that reduction in other sources of income you'll need to draw will also reduce the amount of your Social Security benefits that are taxed and keep your marginal tax rate down. In other words, you will not only receive a higher gross amount of benefits, but also keep more of those benefits because the taxes are lower.[1]

Tax Planning in the Social Security Benefits Tax Zone

If your Social Security benefits may be taxed, you need to review tax-planning options. Tax planning is especially important when you're in the income range that carries a high marginal tax rate on each additional dollar of income. It can be upsetting to realize only after completing your income tax return that some actions you took during the year significantly increased the amount of your Social Security benefits that were taxed and that different actions could have reduced the amount of benefits taxed.

Tax-planning strategies are most important for people whose income is approaching the level at which benefits are taxed up to the amount of MAGI at which the maximum amount of benefits are included in gross income. At that point, close to the maximum percentage of benefits is taxed. This is the Social Security Benefits Tax Zone. People with lower incomes only need to worry about avoiding any sudden increases in income, such as large asset sales, that would trigger the tax. And people with higher incomes can't do much to reduce the tax burden on their benefits. If your income is high enough that close to 85 percent of your benefits are included in gross income, you may be able to reduce that percentage a little bit, but not substantially. But there are a lot of people whose income is in the middle, and they may be able to reduce the amount of their benefits that is taxed substantially, even if they can't eliminate taxes on their benefits altogether.

Tax-Avoidance Strategies That *Don't* Work

Before considering strategies that can effectively reduce the amount of your benefits that are taxed, let's first take a look at some strategies that *don't* work. Many people assume one or more of these widely recommended strategies will reduce their taxes. But they don't work. I'll explain why.

First of all, let me identify some misunderstandings about how married couples' benefits are taxed. The amount of Social Security benefits that are taxed is based on the joint income of the couple, even if only one spouse is receiving benefits. It's a tough rule, but that's the way the tax code is written. Thus, the income earned by a spouse who is still working and not receiving Social Security benefits can trigger income taxes on the benefits of the other spouse who is not working and is receiving benefits.

The income level at which the benefits are taxed for married couples filing jointly is higher than the level for single taxpayers, but the income level for couples is less than twice the trigger level for individuals, so the two situations aren't equalized. You can say this is a form of marriage penalty. Some married couples will pay more taxes on their benefits than they would as two single taxpayers.

A married couple can't avoid or reduce this tax by filing separate returns. In fact, filing separate returns will increase the amount of benefits that are taxed. That's because Social Security benefits for a married couple filing jointly aren't included in gross income until their MAGI exceeds $34,000. But for a married couple that didn't live apart for the entire year but files separately, benefits are included in gross income when MAGI exceeds $0. Unless there are other compelling reasons to file separate returns, a married couple in which at least one spouse is receiving benefits shouldn't file separate returns if they haven't lived apart the entire year.

Other strategies that you'll see widely recommended are for self-employed taxpayers. One is to form a corporation and have most of your income earned by the corporation, then pay yourself a salary low enough to keep your Social Security benefits from being taxed.

But if the IRS or SSA found out that you're attempting to use this strategy, they'll prevent it. The tax law requires a corporation to pay a reasonable salary to owners who also are employees. Usually the rule is used to prevent a corporation from taking a deduction for an excessively high salary. But it also can be used to keep a business owner from avoiding taxes by taking an artificially low salary.

Tax-exempt income is another misunderstood area. Certain types of tax-exempt income may reduce regular income taxes, but won't reduce the amount of Social Security benefits included in gross income—because these types of income are added to regular AGI to determine MAGI, and the level of MAGI determines how much of your benefits are taxed.

The most common point of confusion here is about the interest on tax-exempt bonds. This interest is exempt from income tax, so it's excluded from gross income. But tax-exempt interest is added to arrive at MAGI. That means that tax-exempt interest can be taxed in an indirect way, because the amount of tax-exempt interest is used to determine the amount of Social Security benefits that are included in gross income. The bottom line is that if you earn a lot of tax-exempt interest, it may cause a portion of your Social Security benefits to be included in gross income. The same applies to the other kinds of tax-exempt income that are excluded from your gross income but are added to arrive at MAGI.

That doesn't mean you should avoid tax-exempt interest. There is a different way in which shifting from taxable to tax-exempt investments can reduce the amount of your benefits that are taxed. Because of the tax advantage of tax-exempt bonds, the interest rate on them is usually lower than the interest rate on taxable bonds. The difference essentially equalizes the after-tax income from tax-exempt and taxable bonds. In other words, they have the same after-tax interest rate.

But because the gross amount of interest earned on a tax-exempt bond is less than that on a taxable bond, shifting your investments from taxable bonds to tax-exempt bonds can reduce your MAGI and thus the amount of your Social Security benefits included in gross income. You probably don't want to make such a drastic change in your investment portfolio solely to reduce taxes, but this tax advantage is something to consider when reviewing investment options.

One widely recommended strategy that won't work to reduce the amount of Social Security benefits included in your gross income is for you to increase your itemized deductions. The major itemized deductions are for mortgage interest, state and local taxes, and charitable contributions. Increasing your itemized deductions will reduce your income tax. But your deductions are subtracted from your adjusted gross income, and it is your adjusted gross income—before the itemized deductions are subtracted—that is used to figure your MAGI. So you can maximize your itemized deductions and it won't have any effect on the amount of Social Security benefits that are taxed.

You may hear about other strategies designed to reduce the income taxes on Social Security benefits. Be wary of them. If it isn't one of the strategies I discuss below, it probably doesn't really work.

How You *Can* Beat the Tax on Social Security Benefits

Since the amount of Social Security benefits included in gross income is based on MAGI, any actions that reduce your MAGI reduce the taxes on Social Security benefits. That means most of the strategies that reduce gross income and AGI also reduce taxes on Social Security benefits. (The exceptions are the types of tax-exempt income that are added to AGI to arrive at MAGI. As I explained earlier, these types of income are tax-exempt interest, interest on qualified U.S. savings bonds, employer-provided adoption benefits, foreign-earned income, foreign housing exclusion, and income earned by residents of American Samoa or Puerto Rico.)

Below are strategies that will reduce not only your gross income but also your MAGI, and therefore the amount of your Social Security benefits included in taxable income and your taxes. I highlight the strategies that are most likely to be available to someone in or near retirement.

Convert a traditional IRA to a Roth IRA. Distributions from a traditional IRA or 401(k) are included in gross income and increase MAGI. But distributions from a Roth IRA are tax-free and aren't included in MAGI. The more income you can take from a Roth IRA instead of a traditional IRA, the lower the taxes will be on your Social Security benefits.

You can convert a traditional IRA to a Roth IRA and reduce future MAGI. The amount you convert has to be included in gross income as though it were distributed to you. Your income taxes will be higher in the year of the conversion, and the taxes on your Social Security benefits will be higher if you're receiving benefits that year. But your future taxes on Social Security benefits and overall income taxes will be lower.

Many factors have to be considered before you decide to convert an IRA. I go into the details in the revised 2016 edition of *The New Rules of Retirement*.

Minimize distributions from traditional IRAs, pensions, and annuities. Many retirees hold their investments in different types of vehicles or accounts, each of which is likely to be treated differently for tax purposes. When you need cash to pay expenses, you often have a choice about which investment to take it from. You should pay careful attention to the tax effects of your decision about where to take money from.

For example, you may have a stock or mutual fund in a taxable account. Selling some shares of that investment might incur some capital gains taxes, but the amount included in MAGI will be less than the amount realized on the sale. Your MAGI will include only the amount of your taxable gain on the sale. But if you take that same amount of money from a traditional IRA, the full amount will be included in MAGI. You reduce the amount of MAGI, and therefore the amount of Social Security benefits that are included in your gross income and taxed, by taking a capital gain instead of a distribution from the traditional IRA.

Manage taxable investment accounts. Give careful thought to tax implications before making changes in your taxable investment accounts. These transactions will affect your gross income and therefore your MAGI.

Before selling appreciated investments, for example, estimate your MAGI for the year and consider how much the sale might increase the MAGI and thus the amount of your benefits that are included in gross income. If there's not an urgent reason to sell an investment now, you may want to delay taking some of the gains until next year.

Another strategy is to look for investments that have paper losses. When you're planning to take some gains or already have taken gains during the year, you might be able to offset some or all of those gains by recognizing some capital losses. This will reduce your MAGI and the amount of your benefits that are taxed.

If you own mutual funds, be aware that mutual funds often make distributions of capital gains and other income near the end of the year. It's not unusual for large, year-end distributions from mutual funds to increase MAGI and trigger additional taxes on Social Security benefits.

Consider deferred annuities. Let's suppose you have a fairly substantial portfolio of investments in a taxable investment account. This portfolio is generating interest, dividends, capital gains, and perhaps other income. The income exceeds your spending needs. You're paying taxes on the income, and the income is high enough to cause most of your Social Security benefits to be included in gross income.

A strategy to consider is to use some of that portfolio to purchase a deferred annuity. The income earned in the annuity will be tax-deferred until it is distributed to you. By shifting some of your money to an annuity, a portion of the income that was being taxed to you won't be taxed for a while. That will reduce your MAGI. Eventually, you'll probably take distributions from the annuity, and those distributions will be included in gross income at that time. But in the meantime, the annuity will reduce the amount of taxes on your Social Security benefits.

This is another strategy you won't want to decide on simply to reduce taxes on Social Security benefits. There are many factors—including the many different kinds of annuities—to consider before purchasing one. But reducing taxes on Social Security benefits might be one factor in favor of putting some money in an annuity.

Plan with family members. This is another strategy for you to consider if your income exceeds the amount needed to support your standard of living. You probably expect to have an estate to leave to your children or other loved ones. In this situation, consider giving some of the income-producing assets to the eventual heirs now instead of waiting to give them through your estate. The people you love will benefit from having the assets now, and you'll get to see how the gifts help them. In addition, the income generated by the investments will be off your income tax return. Your MAGI will be lower, so less of your Social Security benefits will be taxed.

In addition, the family members may be in lower tax brackets than you are. In that case, giving them the income-producing assets or appreciated assets to sell will reduce the family's tax burden and increase its after-tax wealth. Of course, give away property only if the gift won't reduce your standard of living. And don't forget that you may have to pay gift taxes. If the value of the assets you give to anyone over the course of a year exceeds $15,000 (in 2020), you are required to file a gift tax return.

Generate business losses. Losses from businesses, including part-time businesses, can reduce gross income and MAGI. Of course, you don't want to turn a profitable retirement business into a money-loser or throw money at an activity solely to reduce taxes on Social Security benefits.

But you may find it beneficial to turn a hobby into a business that generates a tax loss. The losses can be deductible if you make a profit in at least three out of any five consecutive years. Or you can never earn a profit and still deduct the losses if you are running the activity in a professional manner with the intention of making a profit.

The tax rules on deducting business losses are tricky. Consult with a tax advisor before deciding to pursue this strategy.

Don't Forget about State Income Taxes

Most states exempt all or a portion of Social Security benefits from their income taxes. In fact, thirty-seven states either have no income tax or exempt Social Security benefits from their income taxes. That leaves thirteen states that impose some level of taxes on the Social Security benefits of their residents.

The states that tax Social Security benefits are Colorado, Connecticut, Kansas, Minnesota, Missouri, Montana, Nebraska, New Mexico, North Dakota, Rhode Island, Utah, Vermont, and West Virginia.

Six of those states tax Social Security benefits the same way the federal government does. These are Minnesota, Nebraska, North Dakota, Rhode Island, Vermont, and West Virginia. They are known among tax experts as piggyback states, because their tax codes largely mirror the federal income tax code.

The other eight states determine the amount of taxes on Social Security benefits using their own formulas. These states are Colorado, Connecticut, Kansas, Missouri, Montana, New Mexico, and Utah.

The rules in these eight states vary considerably. For example, the Social Security benefits of a Connecticut taxpayer who is married and files jointly are fully exempt if the taxpayer's adjusted gross income is $60,000 or less. In Kansas, the AGI exemption level is $75,000. In Missouri the AGI limit is $100,000. In the other states, the amount of benefits taxed varies based on age and income levels.

CHAPTER 9

How Social Security Is Different for Some Government Employees and Other Non-Covered Workers

The salaries and wages of some workers are exempt from Social Security taxes. The employer doesn't have to withhold taxes from the employee's wages and pay them over to the IRS, and also doesn't have to pay the employer's ordinary share of those taxes.

A lot of people may be surprised by that fact because they've always had Social Security taxes (also known as FICA contributions) withheld from their pay, perhaps dating back to their first part-time and summer jobs in high school. But some employers are exempt from the Social Security withholding requirements.

Exempt employers include many state and local governments, non-profit organizations, and non-U.S. employers. In the early days of Social Security, state and local governments were allowed to choose to be exempt from the program. Many made that election. Non-U.S. employers aren't subject to U.S. laws, including the requirement to withhold Social Security from U.S. citizens who are their employees. Work for any of these employers is known as non-covered work, because their employees aren't covered by the Social Security program. But to opt out of Social Security, employers are required to provide alternative pensions to their workers. These pensions are called non-covered pensions.

A number of people work part of their careers in non-covered jobs and part of their careers in jobs covered by Social Security. This wasn't a problem for the workers, but—Congress discovered, after diving into the intricacies of the system—it was a potential problem for Social Security. People who had both covered and non-covered jobs during their careers could receive Social Security benefits that were higher than intended—and higher than would be received by workers who had identical earnings records but who had worked all their careers in covered jobs. (Below, I'll explain how this unintended effect can occur.)

So Congress enacted two specific provisions to adjust Social Security benefits for workers who have both covered and non-covered work during their careers. The windfall elimination provision adjusts the Social Security benefits of the worker. The government pension offset adjusts the Social Security spousal and survivor benefits of people who worked at least part of their careers in non-covered work and were married to someone who worked in covered jobs.

How the Windfalls Are Eliminated

Windfall is somewhat of a loaded term. Many people subject to the windfall elimination provision (WEP) don't believe they were at risk of receiving windfalls. But Congress and its analysts disagree.

Here's how some Social Security beneficiaries used to get what Congress considered a windfall. You may recall from chapter 4 that the calculation of Social Security benefits is progressive. A person with a lower level of career earnings receives a higher percentage of his or her annual earnings in Social Security benefits than a higher-income worker. The percentage of your working years' earnings that you receive as retirement benefits is called the replacement ratio.

Workers near the lower end of the income scale have replacement ratios of 80 percent to 90 percent. Their Social Security retirement benefits are a high percentage of their pre-retirement earnings. The average worker has a replacement ratio of about 40 percent. Higher-income workers can have replacement ratios of 20 percent or less.

But the progressive nature of Social Security created an unintended result—a windfall—for retirees who had earned a fair amount of money at non-covered jobs and a relatively low amount at covered work but still enough at covered work to qualify for Social Security retirement benefits. Before the WEP, the Social Security retirement benefits were calculated taking into account only the earnings record of the covered work. Thus the retiree would appear to be a relatively low earner, and the Social Security benefits formula would mandate a high replacement ratio of their covered earnings, higher than warranted considering that retiree had been paid a high salary at non-covered work and earned a non-covered pension in lieu of some Social Security benefits.

This situation wasn't addressed for many decades—until Congress made a change in 1983 by creating the WEP, which adjusts the retirement benefits formula to eliminate the progressivity benefit for people who are receiving pensions from non-covered work. The SSA estimates the WEP applies to about 2.5 percent, or 1.5 million, of beneficiaries.

Recall from chapter 4 that Social Security benefits are calculated by applying three different percentages to three different portions of a person's lifetime average indexed monthly earnings (AIME). The results then are added to obtain the worker's monthly full retirement benefit (FRB) or primary insurance amount (PIA) at full retirement age (FRA). The income levels at which the different percentages are used change each year because of inflation indexing. For most beneficiaries in 2015, the PIA equaled the sum of:

- 90 percent of the first $826 of AIME, plus
- 32 percent of AIME over $826 and through $4,980, plus
- 15 percent of AIME over $4,980

That was the regular computation. But for everyone subject to the WEP, a special WEP PIA is computed. The WEP PIA replicates the regular PIA but scales down the first percentage from 90 percent to 40 percent in increments of five percentage points for workers with less than 30 years of coverage (YOCs). Thus, workers with thirty or more years of coverage have a first PIA factor of 90 percent, workers with twenty-one to twenty-nine covered years have a first PIA factor between 45 and 85 percent, and workers with twenty years of coverage have a first PIA factor of 40 percent.

There are additional controls and limits put on the WEP, so the reduction may not be this great in every case. For example, the Social Security benefits from covered work can't be reduced by more than one-half of the non-covered pension being received. This is called the WEP guarantee.

I won't go into every detail, but the general principle is clear. The fewer years of covered work a person has, the greater the WEP effect is and the more retirement benefits are reduced.

Suppose a person worked twenty years in covered jobs. Using the regular benefits calculation, the person's FRB would be $1,089. But the person also worked in non-covered jobs and receives a monthly pension of $800 from non-covered work. Applying the WEP formula reduces the PIA to $676, a substantial reduction of $413. But the WEP guarantee says the Social Security PIA can't be reduced by more than half of the non-covered pension, or $400 in this case. So, the WEP reduction is $400 instead of $413, and the person's PIA is $689 instead of $676.

The WEP doesn't apply at all to a worker who has thirty or more years of "substantial earnings." This is a technical term. The amount that qualifies as substantial earnings changes each year. For 2020, the amount was $25,575. You can see a chart setting out the amount of substantial earnings for each year on the Social Security website at https://www.ssa.gov/pubs/EN-05-10045.pdf.

In addition, there's a maximum amount by which WEP can reduce monthly benefits, because the WEP applies only to the first level of earnings, reducing the multiplier for that level from 90 percent to no less than 40 percent. And, as we have seen, the maximum reduction depends on the number of years of substantial earnings a worker had. The maximum monthly reduction in 2019 for a worker with twenty years or fewer of substantial earnings worked out to be $463. The reduction can be higher for someone who starts Social Security benefits after full retirement age, because delayed retirement credits are applied only after your PIA has been reduced by WEP. You can find a chart of the maximum monthly reduction for each year at this link: https://www.ssa.gov/planners/retire/wep-chart.html.

The WEP also affects many benefits that are paid to others on your earnings history, including spousal benefits, children's benefits, and benefits for an ex-spouse. But WEP won't reduce survivor's benefits.

The WEP benefit is complicated. SSA offers two online calculators on its website to estimate the effect of WEP on your benefits. There is a WEP Online Calculator that is easy to use but not as robust as it could be. You can download the Detailed Calculator, which can give more robust calculations and accurate results. Both calculators are free. Links to them are available on this page on the Social Security website: https://www.ssa.gov/planners/retire/wep.html.

Workers who had non-covered work at a non-U.S. employer generally are covered by WEP, but that's not always the case. The U.S.

enters into agreements with other countries known as "totalization agreements." The details of these agreements vary. Sometimes each country agrees to give credit under its national retirement system to citizens of the other country who performed covered or non-covered work in the non-citizenship country. Sometimes the totalization agreement will prevent WEP from applying to your Social Security benefits and sometimes it won't.

On its website, SSA maintains a list of countries with which the U.S. has totalization agreements. There currently are thirty such agreements. You can learn some details of the agreements starting at the International Programs page on SSA's website at: https://www.ssa.gov/international.

How Others Can Be Affected by Your Non-Covered Employment

The WEP applies to the benefit calculation for a worker who spent time in non-covered jobs. A Social Security windfall benefit also is possible when someone who will receive a non-covered pension qualifies for Social Security benefits under someone else's work history as a spouse or surviving spouse.

First, let's repeat a couple of basic rules. When someone qualifies for two types of benefits under Social Security, he or she is paid only one benefit, the higher of the two. For example, if someone qualifies for retirement benefits under his or her own work record and also qualifies for spousal benefits based on the work history of another covered worker, that person will receive only the higher of the spousal benefits and his or her own retirement benefit.

Now suppose a person who will receive a non-covered pension is married to someone who worked only at covered jobs. If no adjustment is made to the benefit formula, that person will receive both the full pension from the non-covered job and also the full spousal benefit.

That's because the person doesn't qualify for Social Security retirement benefits. He or she qualifies for only one Social Security benefit and so will receive that benefit in full.

Congress decided this was another unintended windfall. There should be some adjustment when a person with a non-covered pension also qualifies for a spousal or survivor's benefit under Social Security. The person should receive only one benefit, not two, just like a person with only covered benefits.

The Government Pension Offset (GPO) was created in 1977 to address this situation. Initially, the GPO reduced the spousal or survivor benefit dollar for dollar by the non-covered pension amount. In 1983 the GPO was amended to reduce the Social Security benefit by only two-thirds of the amount of the non-covered pension.

For example, if you receive a monthly non-covered pension of $600, your Social Security spousal or survivor benefit is reduced by two-thirds of that pension, or $400. So if you are eligible for a $500 spousal benefit, you will receive $100 per month from Social Security.

When two-thirds of your non-covered pension exceeds the Social Security benefits you're eligible for, the Social Security benefits could be reduced to zero.

You don't avoid the GPO by taking the non-covered pension in a lump sum. If you take the non-covered pension as a lump sum instead of an annuity, the SSA will calculate the monthly pension benefit you would have received from the pension and use that amount to adjust your Social Security benefits.

The effect of the GPO declines over time when your non-covered pension is fixed, rather than being indexed for inflation. Social Security benefits are indexed for inflation, so they'll increase most years. Thus, over time, the difference between the pension and your Social Security will decrease. And as a result, the reduction in your Social

Security benefits caused by the GPO will be smaller each year. Many state and local government pensions are indexed for inflation. But for non-covered pensions that aren't inflation-indexed, the effect of GPO declines over time.

The GPO doesn't apply if you receive a government pension that isn't based on the amount of your earnings.

There are other exceptions to the GPO, but they apply mainly to people who ceased employment during or before 2004. For a complete list of exceptions to the GPO, see this page on the Social Security website: https://www.ssa.gov/pubs/EN-05-10007.pdf.

Social Security estimated that in 2014 the GPO applied to about 9.7 percent, or 630,000, of spousal and survivor beneficiaries. About three-quarters of those affected by the GPO had their Social Security survivor or spousal benefits reduced to zero. That's because the average monthly pension of non-covered workers was $2,250, well above the average Social Security benefit.

Strategies to Consider

We have seen that you may want to delay claiming Social Security retirement benefits and possibly also work at a covered job to boost those benefits, in the case that your non-covered pension starts at an early age, as many of them do. But if you are subject to either the WEP or GPO, you may also want to consider taking your Social Security benefits as early as you're eligible for them and delaying the start of the non-covered pension.

The WEP and GPO take effect only when you are collecting a non-covered pension—not when you're eligible for one. The reductions in Social Security benefits don't take effect until you start actually receiving the non-covered pension. Until then you can receive whatever Social Security benefits you're eligible for without the WEP or GPO reductions. Another potential advantage of this strategy is that many non-covered pensions increase when you delay the beginning date. So, you may receive a double benefit by delaying the non-covered pension.

But there are a couple of points to consider before opting for this strategy.

One point is that the strategy might not make sense if the non-covered pension isn't increased by delaying the starting date. Especially if the pension from your non-covered employment is greater than the Social Security benefit, you will probably increase lifetime income by claiming the pension as soon as you qualify for its maximum level.

The second point is that when you take a Social Security benefit early its amount is reduced and the amount paid to anyone who qualifies for benefits based on your work history also is likely to be reduced. If others will receive benefits based on your covered work history and you want those benefits maximized, don't take any of your Social Security benefits early.

An alternative strategy is the opposite: delay claiming Social Security benefits as long as possible, preferably to age 70. You might especially want to do this if your spouse is younger than you and spousal or survivor's benefits based on your work history are likely to be higher than his or her earned retirement benefit.

The survivor's benefit isn't affected by WEP. It makes sense for you to maximize the Social Security survivor's benefit by delaying your claim for Social Security benefits as long as possible. Increasing the survivor's benefit is likely to be more beneficial to your spouse than the additional Social Security benefits you'll receive after WEP by claiming earlier.

Another strategy is to increase your years of covered earnings. Under the WEP formula, the more years of covered earnings you have, the smaller the effect of the WEP. Many workers who qualify for non-covered pensions are able to retire on the full pension well before Social Security's full retirement age. In that case, you may find it beneficial to retire from the job with the non-covered pension and work a few more years at a covered job. Increasing your total years of covered employment from ten to twenty years causes a substantial reduction in WEP, and WEP is eliminated when you have thirty years or more of covered employment.

There are a lot of variables to consider when either the WEP or GPO is involved, so developing universally applicable strategies is difficult. But there are some general points that it's important to understand. First, if you receive a non-covered pension and also worked in covered jobs long enough to qualify for Social Security benefits, the amount you receive from Social Security is likely to be reduced.

But, second, the most important consideration may not be the amount of net Social Security benefits that you receive. You should also consider the effect of your Social Security timing decision on your spouse and anyone else who might receive benefits based on your work history. Claiming your Social Security benefits at a later date may increase their benefits in the future, and that increase may be more significant than the reduction that the application of WEP will make in your own Social Security retirement benefit.

CHAPTER 10

Should You Take a Lump Sum?

L et's be clear about one point at the outset of this chapter. You don't have a Social Security account like a 401(k) or investment account. The Social Security taxes deducted from your salary or that were part of your self employment taxes weren't set aside in your name and invested. You can't withdraw your Social Security benefits in a lump sum.

The amount of your Social Security benefits is determined by formulas, as I have explained. For the most part, the benefits—whether they're retirement, spousal, survivor, disability, or other benefits—are paid monthly.

Yet there are a few narrow exceptions to this rule, in which Social Security benefits can be received in a lump sum.

The most important exception allows some beneficiaries to receive a lump sum of retirement benefits, for up to six months of benefits. The lump sum is selected—or deselected—when the claim for retirement benefits is first made. Not many people know about this option until they apply for retirement benefits over the telephone or at a Social Security Administration office. Then they are told about the option and in some cases, as we saw in the example of Jess in chapter 1, are encouraged to take it without being warned of all the consequences.

The lump sum benefit is a nice option that can be useful for someone who has an unexpected expense near the claiming date or has a debt to retire. Too often, though, people are surprised and confused by the option and don't take the time to analyze the choice carefully—with the result that they don't receive the best benefit package for them and come to regret their decision.

The Lump Sum Retirement Option

Though few people know about it, the lump sum option for retirement benefits isn't new. The Social Security rules give someone who is claiming retirement benefits at full retirement age (FRA) or later the option to take a portion of his or her benefits in a lump sum. People who claim benefits before FRA aren't eligible for the lump sum.

Social Security reps are required to tell eligible applicants about the choice and fully explain it. Unfortunately, because the choice is offered late in the claiming process and is unexpected, I believe many people don't really understand it. Some of my *Retirement Watch* readers have told me that their Social Security reps tilted the options in favor of taking the lump sum by telling them that it is a valuable benefit of the program and that most people take it. I've heard some people say they understood it as free money, instead of what it really is. I've also read anecdotes indicating that SSA reps even pressure applicants to select the lump sum.

Here are the details of how the lump sum retirement benefit option works and how it should be analyzed.

As I have explained, the lump sum option is available only to people who wait until at least FRA (age 66 for those born in 1943–1954, and over age 66 on a sliding scale for those born after 1954) to claim their retirement benefits. At that point, those who qualify can choose to receive a lump sum payment equal to up to six months of retirement benefits. But if you do, it will come at a cost.

What the Lump Sum Costs You

Here's the catch. The lump sum is a retroactive payment of benefits. When you select the lump sum option, SSA will treat you as having claimed and begun your benefits six months earlier than you did. You'll receive a payment equal to six months of benefits, but the amount won't be based on the level of benefits that would have been paid on the date you actually applied for benefits or initially wanted them to begin. The payment will be based on the level of monthly benefits if you had begun them six months earlier.

In addition, your monthly benefit going forward will be the amount you would have been paid if you had claimed benefits six months earlier. Suppose you waited until age 70 to apply for benefits because you wanted to be paid the maximum amount of benefits. Then suppose that when you apply to claim your benefits at age 70, you elect the lump sum option. When your monthly benefits begin, your payments will be for the amount you were due at age 69 and six months, not at age 70. And that reduction in your expected benefits will apply going forward, for the rest of your life.

The cost to taking the lump sum is that your beginning benefit date and the amount of your monthly benefit are rolled back six months.

For example, say that Tom contacts Social Security and says he wants to begin retirement benefits at age 70, receiving the maximum allowable benefit. Under his earnings history, he is due $3,000 per month. But also say that, after hearing about the lump sum option, he chooses it. Tom receives a lump sum of $17,310 (six months of

the monthly benefits that were due to him at age 69 and a half). And
now the official starting age for his benefits is 69 and a half instead
of 70, and his monthly benefits will be based on that earlier age. So
he'll receive only $2,885 per month, instead of the $3,000 he
expected. His payment will be 4 percent less than his maximum
benefits for age 70. That reduction in benefits will continue for the
rest of Tom's life.

Remember, for every year after FRA that you delay your benefits,
you increase them by 8 percent. So for each six months that you *don't*
delay claiming benefits you lose a 4 percent increase.

In Tom's case, when his claiming date was rolled back six months
because he accepted the lump sum payment, he lost a 4 percent increase
in his retirement benefits.

How to Decide about a Lump Sum

Was this a good deal for Tom?

The answer to that question depends on several factors. One factor
is how long Tom lives. Because he took the lump sum, Tom's monthly
benefit is $115 less. If he had decided not to take the lump sum, it
would have taken about twelve and a half years for that extra $115
per month to equal the lump sum he received. So, if Tom lives into his
mid-eighties, the higher monthly benefit probably would have been
the better move. If he doesn't live that long, taking the lump sum would
have been better.

Of course, what Tom would do with the lump sum is another
important consideration. Using the lump sum to pay debt, especially
high-interest debt, might be more valuable than the 4 percent increase
in benefits. Or if he invests the lump sum and earns a high return, he'll
end up with more money than if he had taken the higher monthly
benefit. An important consideration, though, is that the increase in

Social Security benefits from waiting six months is guaranteed, while investment returns in the markets aren't.

If Tom is married, that fact should also factor into his decision. As we have learned, when one spouse dies the household no longer receives two Social Security benefits. As a general rule, the surviving spouse receives only the higher of his or her earned benefits or what the other spouse was receiving at death. If Tom was the higher-earning spouse, it might make sense for him to maximize his monthly benefit so that whichever spouse survives has the highest possible monthly benefit for life. (See chapter 6 for details on survivor's benefits.)

The right choice depends on your longevity, what you would do with the lump sum, and your spouse's needs. Yet, the Social Security reps don't present the choice this way when discussing it with people who are claiming their benefits, according to the anecdotes I've heard.

As I have pointed out, Social Security should be viewed basically as an insurance program. It exists to insure you against the risks that come from living a long life, long-term inflation, and market fluctuations that can make investments risky. Social Security benefits are guaranteed for life, no matter how long you and your and your spouse live. They also are indexed for inflation, so the purchasing power of the benefits is at least partially preserved. For married couples, Social Security also provides a form of life insurance by guaranteeing that the surviving spouse, regardless of lifetime earnings, will receive the survivor's benefit based on the record of the higher-earning spouse.

The lump sum option is for people who want as much money as they can get now and aren't too concerned about the long-term consequences of that decision. The lump sum can be a good option for someone who will use it to pay debt or invest wisely. But remember the caveats. You can't always be assured your investments will return more than higher Social Security benefits would. And the returns aren't guaranteed.

The best choice for you depends on your preferences and factors such as life expectancy and what you would do with the lump sum. Be sure that you fully understand the choice that's being offered and the consequences of each option.

The Other Lump Sum Benefits

There are a few other Social Security benefits that are sometimes paid in a lump sum.

Disability benefits are sometimes paid in a lump sum. But the lump sum is a payment of retroactive benefits that doesn't affect the amount of future monthly payments.

When someone becomes disabled, he or she applies for Social Security disability benefits. The SSA will investigate the claim. It might ask for additional documentation of the disability. Sometimes it will deny the claim and the applicant will appeal the claim through SSA and sometimes in the courts.

If the applicant eventually is deemed eligible for disability benefits, the benefits are payable as of the date the application was made. For the time that passed between the application date and when the eligibility for benefits was confirmed, SSA will compute the benefits that should have been paid during that period and pay them in a lump sum. Thereafter, the disability benefits will be paid monthly.

There's no option for the beneficiary to select. Once the SSA rules that the beneficiary qualifies for disability benefits, a lump sum will be paid equal to the sum of the monthly benefits for the period from the date of the application until the date the benefits were approved. Details of disability benefits are in chapter 19.

The other lump sum is the lump sum death benefit. This is a relatively small, fixed amount of $255. The payment usually is made to the surviving spouse if he or she was living with the deceased or was receiving benefits based on the deceased's earnings record. It also can be paid to a child who was receiving benefits based on the deceased worker's earnings history or is eligible to receive benefits upon the death of the worker.

The lump sum death benefit is generally referred to as the funeral benefit. But these days the amount isn't enough to pay for a funeral or a cremation. There's no option for the beneficiary to select. After SSA approves the application, the benefits are paid in a lump sum.

Another time you could receive a lump sum benefit is when, if you received benefits for a while, you asked for them to be suspended, and you have asked for the suspended benefits to be resumed. At that point you have the option of being paid all the suspended monthly benefits in a lump sum. You'll learn more about this option in chapter 11.

CHAPTER 11

Can You Change Your Mind?

No doubt some readers of the first ten chapters of this book have been saying to themselves, "I wish I had known that before." Their next thought may be to wonder whether it's possible to change actions already taken on Social Security benefits.

It's not surprising that there are people who'd like a redo or mulligan on their Social Security decisions. As I have explained, Social Security's rules were written primarily by lawyers and Ph.D.s., and they often aren't intuitive or easy to understand. When making decisions about benefits, people have to balance the short-term and long-term benefits. Many people make decisions about their benefits without a careful examination of the long-term consequences. It's not unusual for people to wish they had made different decisions in hindsight.

Social Security decisions are generally once-in-a-lifetime choices. After the decision is made and an action taken, it's locked in. But that's not always the case. There are a few instances when a decision about Social Security benefits can be changed or modified.

It's important to know when a Social Security decision can be changed. A modification can increase your monthly income for the rest of your life, perhaps by a substantial amount. In this chapter I review the times when it might be possible to change a decision about Social Security benefits.

Withdrawing Your Application

For many decades a beneficiary could change the decision about retirement benefits at almost any time before age 70. After beginning retirement benefits, the beneficiary could decide the initial decision was a mistake. A person who began benefits at age 62 could decide just before age 70 that it would have been wiser to delay the benefits until age 70. The beneficiary could notify the SSA of the change of mind, and the higher level of benefits would begin at age 70.

The only catch was that the beneficiary had to repay all the benefits that had been received to date. A beneficiary who had received benefits for five years before deciding a later starting date could reset the benefit decision, but he or she would have to repay the five years of benefits to SSA in a lump sum. The good news was that no interest was due. The beneficiary had use of the benefits for five years and Social Security didn't have the money to invest or pay other benefits, yet the beneficiary wasn't charged for use of the money.

The SSA decided this policy was too generous. It was possible for a person who didn't need the benefits for survival to begin benefits at age 62 and invest all the benefits as they were received. Just before age 70, the person could repay the benefits, keep the investment earnings, and begin maximum monthly benefits at age 70.

The current rule is that you still can decide to change the starting date of your Social Security retirement benefits, but you have to act to make the change within twelve months of the initial start date of your benefits. Once the twelve-month window passes, you no longer can change the starting date of your retirement benefits.

Social Security refers to changing the starting date of your benefits as withdrawing your application. You applied to claim your retirement benefits, and if you decide to start the benefits at a later date after all, you withdraw the initial application for benefits. The benefits will stop after the application to withdraw your initial application is approved. You can reapply for benefits in the future, and the application will be treated as though you never applied for benefits.

Even after you withdraw your claim for benefits and the withdrawal is approved, you have yet another opportunity to change your mind. Once the application for withdrawal is approved, you have sixty days to cancel the approved withdrawal. That means you can begin your benefits, apply to withdraw the application to begin benefits, and then cancel the approved application to withdraw.

You withdraw an application for Social Security benefits by filing Form SSA-521. On the form you state why you want to withdraw the application.

Just as under the old rule, for your application to withdraw benefits to be approved, you have to repay all the benefits you and your family received. Notice that the decision to withdraw the benefit application can affect other people. Any benefits received by any person based on your earnings history and initial claim for benefits must be repaid in order for your application to be approved. The other person's benefits will stop when your benefits stop. If your spouse received spousal benefits based on your work history and application to begin benefits, your benefits and the spousal benefits must be repaid. There also are instances when children receive benefits based on a parent's earnings history and application, and those benefits might have to be repaid.

Here's a key point many people overlook when withdrawing the application for benefits. Money is often deducted or withheld from

Social Security benefits. Frequently, premiums for Medicare Parts B, C, and D are deducted. Some people have federal or state income taxes, or both, withheld from their benefits. Sometimes creditors have a portion of Social Security benefits garnished. For the withdrawal application to be approved, you must repay the gross amount of the benefits received. You have to repay the net amount you received plus any amounts that were deducted or withheld from the benefits.

As under the old rules, no interest is due. A beneficiary has to repay only the gross amount of benefits that were paid.

An application to withdraw can be used only once during a lifetime. That's not a major restriction, since the application to withdraw must be used within twelve months of applying for benefits. Even so, you can't keep applying for and withdrawing the application for benefits. The second application to claim retirement benefits will be final.

An approved withdrawal of an initial claim for benefits effectively wipes the slate clean. The person is treated as though retirement benefits had never been claimed or paid. If he later applies for retirement benefits to begin at full retirement age, the full retirement benefit will be paid. If the person waits until age 70 to begin benefits again, the age-70 benefits with maximum delayed retirement credits will be paid. There is no penalty for the earlier false start.

You still can make a change to a different type of benefit if you later qualify for one, such as a spousal or survivor's benefit. You can also make a partial change by suspending your benefits.

Suspending Your Benefits

Withdrawing an application for benefits is not the only thing you can do if you change your mind. A beneficiary who is receiving Social Security benefits can ask the SSA to suspend them. Suspended benefits are just what the term implies. If a person who has been receiving monthly Social Security retirement benefits asks the SSA to stop the benefit payments, the SSA will stop paying the benefits.

There's a one-month lag in benefit payments. The SSA pays benefits the month after they are due. June's benefits are paid at the start of July. This affects the timing of a suspension of benefits. When someone requests that suspension start immediately, suspension of benefits will take effect the month after the month in which the request is made.

Benefits can't be suspended until the beneficiary reaches full retirement age. Suppose Elaine began retirement benefits at age 62. At age 63 and a half, Elaine decides that was a mistake. She realizes that it would have been better for her to delay receiving the benefits so she could receive a higher amount later.

It's too late for Elaine to withdraw her application for benefits, because more than twelve months have passed since the benefits began. Elaine's next opportunity to make a change is at FRA. At that point she can ask for her benefits to be suspended. She will receive monthly benefits until she requests suspension of her benefits, and she can't do that before she reaches FRA.

A suspension of benefits can last for any length of time until age 70. A beneficiary can ask for the benefits to be suspended for a few months, a few years, or indefinitely. If the beneficiary doesn't ask for the suspension to end, SSA automatically will restart benefits the month the beneficiary reaches age 70.

Suspension of benefits is an informal process. There is no official SSA form to apply to have your benefits suspended. In fact, you don't even have to make your request in writing. A request for suspension can be made orally, either on the telephone or at an SSA office. It can be made in writing, in any format the beneficiary chooses to use, as long as the meaning is clear.

When Suspending Benefits Can Be a Good Idea

There are several potential advantages to suspending benefits.

A person who initially retired might go back to work and no longer need the monthly benefits to meet expenses. Or someone who was working at a relatively low income before the benefits were claimed might receive an income boost from working longer hours or changing jobs. Or a Social Security beneficiary who is working might want to avoid paying income taxes on the benefits (see chapter 8) or losing benefits by exceeding the earned income limit (see chapter 5).

Another reason to suspend benefits, whether the beneficiary is working or not, is to accrue higher Social Security benefit payments in the future by earning more delayed retirement credits. If the beneficiary has sufficient income and assets other than the Social Security benefits to support his or her standard of living, he or she might decide it was a mistake to claim Social Security benefits at the earlier age. Higher monthly payments beginning at a later date and guaranteed to last for life might be more attractive than they were a few years earlier.

Unlike the withdrawal of the benefit application, suspending benefits doesn't wipe the slate clean. The beneficiary's record won't be treated as though benefits had never been claimed or paid. Instead, the beneficiary will receive delayed retirement credits only for the period of time the benefits were suspended.

And remember, benefits can't be suspended until full retirement age. If someone with a full retirement age of 66 begins benefits at age 62 and misses the twelve-month window for withdrawing the benefit application, then he or she has to wait until full retirement age to suspend the benefits. And the beneficiary will forever receive less than the full retirement benefit, because benefits were claimed for four years before full retirement age, and so during that time no delayed retirement credits were earned.

The beneficiary, however, will receive delayed retirement credits for the period the benefits were suspended beginning at full retirement age. Potentially, the benefits can be suspended from full retirement age through age 70, giving the beneficiary a substantial increase in the benefits. It won't be as high as the amount that would have been paid if the beneficiary hadn't claimed at all until age 70, or had withdrawn the application in the first twelve months, but it will be substantially higher (about 32 percent higher) than the benefits that were being paid when they were suspended.

The process for restarting benefits is as informal as for suspending them. The SSA can be notified either orally or in writing. No particular form is required. You can notify SSA to restart the benefits as soon as possible, which will mean a delay of about a month, or you can name a month in the future when you want the suspension to end.

Suspension Followed by a Lump Sum Benefit

Another option is to ask that benefits be restarted and also request a lump sum payment of all or part of the benefits that weren't paid during the suspension period. By requesting the lump sum of retroactive benefits, though, you lose one of the potential advantages of the suspension. You won't receive the delayed retirement credits for the months of the suspension for which you received the benefits in a lump sum. If you claim all of the suspended benefits in a lump sum, when your monthly benefit starts up again it will be the same amount as before the suspension. If you receive only some of the suspended benefits in a lump sum, when monthly benefits begin you'll receive delayed retirement credits only for the months benefits were suspended and not paid in the lump sum.

The lump sum could be a good choice if your circumstances changed. You might have incurred debts or expenses that need to be paid. Or the higher monthly lifetime benefit may no longer be as important to you as when the benefits were suspended.

When a beneficiary suspends Social Security benefits, payments also will be suspended for anyone who is receiving benefits on that person's record. As we have seen, a spouse will stop receiving spousal benefits when the spouse on whose earnings record the spousal benefits were based asks for his or her benefits to be suspended. Both benefits will resume when the suspension ends for the worker's benefits. (This rule doesn't apply to former spouses. Divorced spouses can receive benefits regardless of the benefit status of the other former spouse. See chapter 7 for details about divorce and Social Security benefits.)

For example, Greg claimed his retirement benefits at age 63. At that same time his wife Megan claimed spousal benefits, because her spousal benefits based on Greg's earnings record were higher than her earned retirement benefits. After a while, Greg decided that he would rather have a higher benefit later in life instead of the lower monthly benefit now. When Greg reaches FRA he asks for his retirement benefits to be suspended. Megan's benefits are automatically suspended, because she was receiving benefits based on Greg's work record and benefit application.

You might have read about a strategy known as "claim and suspend," in which one spouse claims benefits and immediately suspends them. That way, the other spouse could begin collecting a spousal benefit based on the first spouse's work history. Meanwhile, the spouse whose benefits were suspended would continue to earn credits for delaying retirement benefits and could begin maximum benefits at age 70. But Congress changed the law in 2015, and this strategy no longer is available, except to people who were born on or before January 1, 1954. Now, when a person suspends his or her benefits, anyone who was receiving benefits based on that person's work history (except a divorced spouse) also has benefits suspended.

Implications for Medicare

There is some interplay between Social Security and Medicare, and you should be aware of how the two programs can affect each other before you suspend Social Security benefits or withdraw your application for those benefits.

Most Americans are eligible for Medicare at age 65. When you're receiving Social Security benefits at age 65, the SSA will automatically enroll you in Medicare. If you're not yet receiving benefits at that age, you must enroll in Medicare on your own.

Medicare premiums are often deducted from Social Security benefits at the request of the beneficiary. When Social Security benefits are suspended or the application for benefits is withdrawn, Medicare premiums can no longer be deducted, because there won't be any benefits from which to deduct the premiums. The Medicare beneficiary must arrange to pay the premium directly. After benefits are suspended, the beneficiary will be billed individually for the Medicare premiums and will be responsible for paying them monthly. Failure to pay the premiums could result in the loss of Medicare benefits.

Also, when an application for Social Security benefits is withdrawn and the applicant is enrolled in Medicare, the applicant must make clear whether or not the application also is to withdraw from Medicare. You don't want to inadvertently withdraw from Medicare, because there are serious consequences. Withdrawing from Medicare means the beneficiary has to repay any benefits received under the Part A hospitalization program. In addition, withdrawing from Medicare and re-enrolling later can mean that you have to pay higher lifetime premiums as a penalty for not enrolling in Medicare when you are first eligible.

Switching Benefits

A beneficiary may be eligible for more than one type of Social Security benefit. As we have seen, the beneficiary will usually be deemed to have applied for all the different benefits but will be paid only one of them, the one with the highest monthly benefit.

It also can happen that a beneficiary is eligible for only one type of benefit but later becomes eligible for another. In these cases, Social Security will sometimes automatically switch the beneficiary to the higher benefit. Sometimes the SSA will notify beneficiaries by letter that they might be qualified for a higher benefit and should consider applying for that benefit. Often, however, it is up to the beneficiary to realize that a higher benefit is available and apply for that benefit.

In these cases, there's no penalty for changing from one benefit to a higher benefit for which one is newly eligible. It's even possible that after processing the application the SSA will determine that the beneficiary was eligible for the higher benefit months earlier and will pay the higher benefit for the earlier months in a lump sum.

The most likely circumstances in which a person will be newly eligible for a higher benefit is after the death of a spouse. A married person might be receiving retirement benefits or spousal benefits. But if the other spouse dies, the surviving spouse generally is entitled to the higher of the benefits that he or she was receiving and the benefit that the deceased spouse was receiving at death or would have been entitled to at full retirement age. The surviving spouse can switch to survivor's benefits if they are higher, and there won't be any penalty for the change. (See chapter 6 for more details about survivor's benefits.)

A married person also may be entitled to a change in benefits. Suppose the spouse with lower earnings during his or her career begins retirement benefits at age 62. Later, the higher-earning spouse claims his or her retirement benefit. At that point the lower-earning spouse then is eligible for spousal benefits equal to one-half of the retirement benefits of the other spouse, minus a reduction for claiming his or her retirement benefits early. There won't be any additional reduction or penalty for changing benefits.

Divorced spouses are also likely to become newly entitled to a higher benefit over time. A divorced person could begin receiving spousal benefits based on the earnings record of a former spouse. Later, the beneficiary might switch to his or her own earned retirement benefit or to a survivor's benefit following the death of the former spouse.

These situations show why it is important to know all the different types of benefits for which you may become eligible and track your eligibility throughout life. You can't depend on Social Security to tell you when you might be eligible for a higher benefit, though the SSA does try to do that. As you near age 62, know the different types of benefits potentially available to you. Keep track of them through the years in case you are eligible to switch to a higher benefit at some time during your life. Many people are eligible for benefits they aren't aware of, and they end up leaving a lot of money on the table.

How the Right Social Security Decision Will Make Your Nest Egg Last Years Longer

D o you want your retirement nest egg to last as long as possible? Do you want to avoid running out of money in retirement? Most retirees and pre-retirees answer affirmatively to both of those questions. Assuming you're in that number, you should give special consideration to when you decide to claim Social Security retirement benefits.

Retirement decisions shouldn't be made in isolation. A decision about one aspect of your retirement finances often has consequences in other areas. For example, maximizing lifetime Social Security benefits means you won't need as much cash from your investment portfolio to fund retirement expenses. Your nest egg will last longer. Or you can afford to take less risk with your nest egg and earn a lower rate of return on the portfolio in safer investments.

As I explained in chapter 2, one of the greatest risks for retirees is what economists call "longevity risk." Living a long time is a risk, because the expenses during those additional years of life increase the possibility that you may outlive your financial resources. So you need to estimate life expectancy to make good retirement-planning decisions. A key point is that most people significantly understate their life expectancies and therefore downplay their longevity risk. And when you underestimate your longevity, you are more likely to run out of money in retirement.

One way to avoid running out of money in retirement is to have guaranteed lifetime income. An income that is guaranteed for life, no matter how long you live, is the safest and surest way to ensure that you don't exhaust your financial resources. Social Security benefits are guaranteed for life, and they have the additional benefit of being indexed for inflation. Most other sources of guaranteed lifetime income, such as commercial annuities, aren't adjusted for inflation. You receive the same amount of income each year, but its purchasing power declines because of inflation. Social Security benefits, on the other hand, increase with the Consumer Price Index (CPI).

You also can protect against the risk of running out of money in retirement by starting retirement with a large investment portfolio to ensure it is never depleted. Another way is for your investment returns during retirement to be above average—or at least high enough to support your level of spending. But not everyone is able to accrue a very large nest egg. And investment results aren't guaranteed.

Someone who retired in 1982 and invested his or her nest egg in a diversified portfolio likely had a high rate of return on the portfolio. That person's retirement assets likely increased during retirement even as money was being spent each year.

But results from an investment portfolio aren't guaranteed. The average long-term returns from the markets are sufficient to finance the retirements of most people who save a reasonable amount during their careers. The same average long-term returns, however, don't occur each year. The averages are made up of annual returns that differ quite a bit from the averages. A bear market or a period of below-average returns could coincide with the beginning of retirement. Instead of earning positive returns during the first years of retirement, the retiree could be spending principal and watching the nest egg steadily decline because of spending and investment losses. The risk that the early years of retirement might coincide with a period of below-average or negative investment returns is called the "sequence of returns" risk.

Guaranteed lifetime income reduces both longevity risk and sequence of returns risk. For most people, Social Security is the primary means of reducing these risks. Even if the rest of your nest egg has been spent, Social Security benefits will still give you a minimum level of income for no matter how long you live.

In many cases, the longer a person lives the more important Social Security benefits become. Those benefits become a higher and higher percentage of annual income, both because other assets are being spent and because other forms of guaranteed lifetime income aren't indexed for inflation.

The importance of guaranteed lifetime income—including Social Security—in avoiding running out of money in retirement has been established in several studies.

Guaranteed Income Increases Retirement Spending

One of the first questions to be considered in retirement planning is how much the retiree can safely spend each year without running out of money. Financial planners call this number the safe spending rate or safe withdrawal rate. For details on this complicated issue, you can consult the revised 2016 edition of my book *The New Rules of Retirement*.

One important consideration is your level of guaranteed income, including Social Security benefits. The higher the level of guaranteed income, the higher the safe spending rate, according to a study by David M. Blanchett in the April 2017 *Journal of Financial Planning*.

According to Blanchett's study, the amount of guaranteed income is the most significant factor that should be considered in determining the safe spending rate. (As we all understand intuitively, a household with $100,000 in guaranteed income can afford to draw down an investment portfolio at a higher rate than a household with only $10,000 of guaranteed income.) Blanchett considered the effects of investment returns, asset allocation, and adjusting the withdrawals with changes in the portfolio's value. Blanchett assumed that the amount of the guaranteed income increases with the CPI, just as Social Security benefits and inflation-adjusted annuities do.

Blanchett found that the safe spending rate is about 6 percent of the portfolio's initial value when 95 percent of a household's wealth is in guaranteed income. The safe spending rate declines to 2 percent of the investment portfolio when only 5 percent of the wealth is in guaranteed income. In fact, through a range of scenarios that used different economic and investment assumptions, Blanchett concluded that the level of guaranteed income could change the safe spending rate by about four percentage points, from 6 percent when 95 percent of wealth was in guaranteed income to 2 percent when only 5 percent of wealth was in guaranteed income. None of the other factors and assumptions changed the safe spending rate as much.[1]

Another study looked specifically at how the amount of Social Security benefits influenced a portfolio's longevity. The study published, in the April 2012 *Financial Planning Journal* and written by William Meyer and William Reichenstein, examined the effects on spending and portfolio longevity when individuals claimed their Social Security retirement benefits at different ages. The study looked at how much a retiree could spend during his or her lifetime and how long a portfolio would last under the different Social Security–claiming strategies.

The longer a retiree delays the start of Social Security benefits, the longer a portfolio will last, according to the study. If the Social

Security–claiming date is delayed to age 70, the portfolio will last ten years longer than if benefits were claimed at 62. Claiming at ages later than 62 but earlier than 70 extend the longevity of the portfolio, but by shorter periods.[2]

This finding seems counterintuitive to many people. The study assumes that a person stops earning income from employment at age 62, regardless of when Social Security benefits begin. Thus the retiree's investment portfolio is used to fund living expenses during the years before Social Security benefits begin, and it steadily declines during those years. Most people assume that spending down the retirement nest egg so early will create solvency problems later in retirement. So they want to take Social Security as early possible and delay drawing down their portfolios.

Yet once Social Security benefits begin, the benefits replace the funds you had been taking out of your portfolio to pay expenses. Less money now needs to be withdrawn from your investments each year. So the value of your portfolio value will either stabilize or at least decline much more slowly than it was declining before you began receiving your Social Security benefits. At this point the late-claimer's portfolio can begin to "catch up" with the portfolio of the early-claimer. The study demonstrates that the portfolios of the late-claimers and early-claimers have about the same values after about seventeen years, or at about age 79 for someone who retired at 62. That's the crossover date when there's no difference in the results despite the different Social Security–claiming decisions.

But the results of the portfolios are very different after that. After the crossover date, the portfolios of the late-claimers decline much more slowly than the portfolios of those who claimed early. An important assumption of this study is that the people who claim benefits after age 62 draw all their income from the portfolios in the initial years, but once Social Security benefits begin the amount withdrawn from the portfolios each year declines by an amount equal to the Social Security benefits. In other words, the Social Security benefits aren't used to increase spending but are used to reduce the amount of annual withdrawals from the portfolios.

(The Social Security–claiming decision is less important to portfolio longevity the more wealth a person has. Higher wealth usually means the person had a higher lifetime income, and that means less of the person's employment income is replaced by Social Security than is the case for a lower-earning person. Also, a higher portfolio value means that, at any level of Social Security benefits, the portfolio provides a much higher percentage of the annual income than Social Security does.)

Someone with a portfolio of $250,000 would see the portfolio last four years longer as a result of claiming Social Security at 64 instead of 62. That's four extra years of life for the portfolio solely from waiting two years to begin Social Security benefits. (That effect was not as large for a retiree with larger assets. Someone with a portfolio of $1 million or more would see the portfolio's longevity increase by only one year if he claimed Social Security at 64 instead of 62.)

The study also found that delaying Social Security benefits gives the retiree an option. Instead of having the portfolio last longer, the retiree can increase the amount of real (adjusted for inflation) spending during retirement. Mayer and Reichenstein concluded that even a retiree who wants to ensure the portfolio lasts at least 30 years could spend $36,150 in real dollars annually if he claimed his Social Security at 62. Delaying benefits to 70 allows annual real spending to increase to $39,750 each year for thirty years. That's a $3,600 increase in annual spending made possible by waiting a few years to claim Social Security benefits.

Many people don't understand the power of delaying Social Security benefits. The longer you live, the more beneficial and powerful delaying benefits is. The benefit amount increases each month you wait to claim benefits. The amount of the increase varies during the waiting period. The range of annual benefit increases between ages 62 and 70, and varies from 6.34 percent to 8.34 percent. From full retirement age to 70, benefits increase by 8 percent annually.

These increases are real. That is, they are adjusted for inflation. You receive a nominal increase in benefits for the delay, and your benefits are also adjusted annually for inflation, and those increases compound over time.

Of course, the longer you live, the more significant the gain from delaying benefits. Meyer and Reichenstein calculate that if someone lives to age 92, the monthly Social Security benefit is about 29 percent higher for a person who waited until age 70 to begin benefits than if he or she had initiated benefits at age 62. That's about a 30 percent higher monthly income every month for the rest of the person's life.

The statistics show that most people don't see the value of waiting for their Social Security benefits. Most people claim benefits soon after they are eligible to, and very few wait to age 70 to claim the maximum benefit. A careful consideration of the long-term advantages of claiming Social Security retirement benefits should convince more people to delay receiving benefits. Claiming Social Security benefits later can cause the financial assets used to fund retirement spending to last longer. Unless there is any reason to believe there's a high probability that both you and your spouse won't live at least to life expectancy, you should give strong consideration to delaying benefits. The less wealth a person has, the greater the value of the higher benefits, and thus the more important it is to consider delaying the claim.

CHAPTER 13

How to Fund a Social Security Delay and When Not to Delay

Some people find the arguments in favor of delaying a claim for retirement benefits compelling, and yet they still claim benefits soon after they are eligible to. The most common reason given for not delaying the claim for benefits is, *I would love to increase my Social Security retirement benefits by 50 percent or more by delaying them, but I can't afford to.* Their need for the money is why most Americans claim their Social Security benefits well before age 70 and the vast majority well before full retirement age (FRA).

Most people claim their retirement benefits when they stop working. They want Social Security to help replace the incomes they were receiving from their jobs. And often they believe that they need to claim Social Security early to limit spending from their retirement savings. Most people list running out of money in retirement as one of their greatest fears. They believe that limiting the amount of money they withdraw from their nest eggs reduces the risk of running out of money in retirement. They claim Social Security benefits early to reduce the amount of money they will have to withdraw from their nest eggs.

Yet, as we saw in chapter 12, a careful study of the numbers and the various probable scenarios shows that taking Social Security early *increases* the probability of running out of money later in retirement and also reduces the total amount you are able to spend in retirement. Most people should delay Social Security benefits as long as possible. It will be worth it to work to create a retirement plan that will allow you to delay claiming Social Security benefits.

Financial advisors generally refer to such as plan as "building a bridge to Social Security."

I have already explained some good reasons for such a plan in earlier chapters. To recap: Social Security benefits increase each month you delay receiving them. The increase is fairly substantial as the period of delay increases. The rate of increase is higher than the after-tax return most people earn on their investments. Unlike investment market returns, the increase in Social Security benefits is guaranteed. The increase in benefits also is indexed for inflation.

Further, the increase in Social Security benefits is tax-free. When you earn money in the markets, the investment return is taxed. Even if the money is in a traditional 401(k) or IRA, the taxes are only deferred. To match the benefit from delaying Social Security benefits, the investment account has to earn a higher pre-tax return than the percentage increase from delaying Social Security, which is 8 percent annually after FRA.

So, as we have seen, the advantages of delaying Social Security benefits are substantial. Yet few Americans reap those benefits.

The exact percentage changes from year to year, but on average only 4 to 5 percent of each age group waits until age 70 to claim the maximum Social Security benefit. About 35 percent of Social Security beneficiaries claim their benefits at age 62, the earliest possible age to begin retirement benefits. The median claiming age in 2017 was 64 for men and 63 for women, according to a study from the Center for Retirement Research at Boston College.[1]

For some people, claiming Social Security benefits at an earlier age is the best strategy. When someone no longer can work because of health problems, the only alternative may be to claim benefits. A person who no longer is employed and doesn't have adequate savings to fund an early retirement often has to claim benefits before FRA. When someone has good reason to believe he or she won't live to average life expectancy, that's another good reason to claim retirement benefits early. In a married couple, it often makes sense for the spouse with lower career earnings to claim benefits early while the other spouse delays claiming benefits.

In many other situations, though, the best move is to delay Social Security benefits. The issue for many people is how to finance the delay.

The Advantages of Working Longer

Not everyone can choose his or her retirement date. Some people stop working because of health reasons. Other people lose their jobs and are unable to obtain comparable positions. Eventually they decide to stop seeking employment and apply for Social Security retirement benefits.

But many people are able to choose when to retire. While 65 is considered the traditional retirement age, for many decades Americans have on average retired at earlier and earlier ages. Until the financial crisis of 2007–2009, the average retirement age steadily declined. The average retirement age began to increase during that crisis, but it is still younger than 65.

It's understandable that a person would want to retire as soon as retirement appears to be financially feasible. Before retiring as early as you can, however, you should consider the benefits of working a little longer.

Working even one additional year can significantly increase retirement financial security, according to "The Power of Working Longer," a research paper by Jason Scott, John B. Shoven, and Sita Nataraj Slavov published by the Stanford Institute for Economic Policy Research.

According to this research, postponing retirement by only one year from 66 to 67 increases the sustainable retirement standard of living by about 8 percent, after adjusting for inflation. The advantage comes from several sources: higher Social Security benefits, an additional year of contributions to a 401(k) plan, and an additional year of compounded investment returns for the 401(k) plan.

Another thing the authors factored into the sustainable retirement standard of living was calculating the lifetime annuity that could be purchased with the 401(k) balance. Waiting a year to buy the annuity until the individual is a year older increases the lifetime payout, also increasing the retirement standard of living.

The gains from working longer than one additional year are even more powerful. When the primary earner in a married couple postpones retirement to age 65 instead of 62, the retirement standard of living increases by about 24 percent. When retirement is delayed from 65 to 70, the standard of living increases by another 41 percent, according to the study. Delay retirement five years after age 62, and the standard of living increases by 43 percent.

These gains from delaying retirement were calculated assuming the prospective retiree was a conservative investor, with an assumed rate of return on investments equal to the inflation rate. That's a very modest rate of return. Someone who earns an investment return even a little bit higher would see his or her retirement standard of living increase even more.

An important conclusion from the study is that the gains from working longer are far more substantial than the gains from increasing the savings rate before retirement. For example, the study calculated the advantages of increasing the savings rate by one percentage point for the thirty years preceding retirement. In other words, the individual saves 10 percent of income each year instead of 9 percent.

When the conservative investment return equal to the inflation rate is used, the increased savings is equivalent to working only an additional 3.3 months before retiring. That is equal to a 2.16 percent increase in the retirement standard of living. When the investment return is increased to 4 percent above the inflation rate, the additional savings is equivalent to working only an additional 4.9 months before retiring, or a 3.45 percent increase in the retirement standard of living.[2]

Remember, these are the results assuming the savings rate is higher for thirty years before retirement. When the savings rate is increased later in the career, the benefits from a higher savings rate are even less pronounced.

The bottom line is that working even a few years longer is a powerful way to increase your retirement standard of living and financial security. The advantages of delaying your Social Security benefits are more substantial than of saving more money for an extended period of time or of earning a higher rate of return on investments.

When You Don't Want to or Can't Work Longer

Working longer isn't always an option, and sometimes even when a person is able to work longer it isn't an attractive option. In those cases, delaying Social Security retirement benefits can still be a good idea. As we saw in chapter 12, delaying Social Security benefits causes a retirement nest egg to last longer, even if you have to begin drawing down your investment portfolio to pay retirement expenses from age 62 through the date you begin Social Security benefits. After Social Security benefits begin, you reduce the distributions from the nest egg by the same amount as the Social Security benefits.

In other words, even if you can't or don't want to work longer to fund a delay in claiming Social Security benefits, you should seriously consider using your retirement assets to fund retirement expenses until Social Security is claimed. Increase distributions from the retirement accounts by the amount that your Social Security benefits would be.

Here's one way to look at the decision.

Social Security benefits are essentially an annuity. You receive the benefits every month for the rest of your life no matter how long you live. But the monthly benefits are increased for inflation each year, while most private commercial annuities aren't. A commercial annuity indexed for inflation generally has an initial payment that is 25 percent to 33 percent lower than the payment from an annuity that is not indexed for inflation. The benefit of inflation indexing is substantial. In addition, the annuity you receive from Social Security increases by about 8 percent for each year you delay receiving it.

In effect, you're purchasing that higher annuity payout with the money from your retirement nest egg that you're using to fund living expenses while you delay your Social Security benefits. If you do the math, you can see that that's a bargain. You won't find an annuity available in the commercial annuity market that's nearly as good a buy.

These factors mean it makes a lot of financial sense to delay claiming Social Security benefits, even if it means drawing from an IRA, 401(k) account, or other investment account to pay your living expenses during the delay period. A study from the Center for Retirement Research at Boston College found that the advantages of "purchasing" that higher Social Security annuity are so substantial that it should be the first consideration of anyone who doesn't want to continue working.[3] For many people, drawing from retirement assets to allow a delay in Social Security benefits is the smartest move.

Here's an example of how the bridge funding could work.

Suppose Jeff would receive a $1,875 monthly Social Security retirement benefit at age 62, a $2,500 benefit at FRA, and a $3,300 benefit at 70. Jeff plans to spend about $60,000 annually in retirement and would like to stop working at 62. Adjusted for inflation, Jeff's eight years of Social Security benefits from age 62 to age 70 would total about $172,970.

Jeff can keep his investment portfolio invested as it is and withdraw the money he needs each year. Or he can segregate the money that he will need to spend in lieu of taking early Social Security and invest that money safely but earn a lower rate of return. When he turns 70 and his Social Security benefits begin, he will be able to reduce the amount that he is withdrawing from his nest egg.

In a study published in the *Journal of Financial Planning*, economist Wade Pfau found that even after taking the higher withdrawals to fund the Social Security delay, a retiree like Jeff would have a lower lifetime withdrawal rate from his portfolio if he delayed Social Security benefits. His lower lifetime withdrawal rate means his portfolio is likely to last longer. Pfau arrived at his results on the assumption that the assets to fund the Social Security delay are segregated from the rest of the portfolio and invested safely to earn a minimal rate of return. The results would be better if an average historic rate of return was assumed.

Jeff also could take the segregated money and use it to purchase an annuity that will pay him a fixed annual income for eight years. He can probably get a higher return from an annuity than from investing the money, particularly in investments that are safe. An annuity would ensure that Jeff has the equivalent of Social Security during these gap years. To learn how much you would need to invest in a fixed-term annuity to equal the Social Security benefits, take a look at websites such as www.immediateannuities.com, www.annuities.net, or www.annuities.direct.

A person concerned about running out of money in retirement would be well advised to use his nest egg to fund a delay in Social Security benefits instead of taking Social Security benefits earlier. Even if the portfolio were to be depleted over time, the Social Security benefits will still continue at the higher rate and will be indexed for inflation.

The bottom line here is that a delay in Social Security benefits should be considered an investment in an annuity. You're unlikely to find an investment that generates an after-tax return equal to a delay in Social Security, and you won't find one with an equivalent guaranteed return. When you have sufficient investment assets and want or need to stop working early, your best investment likely will be to delay Social Security benefits while using retirement savings to make up the income that would have been received from Social Security if you had claimed earlier.

Home Equity Can Build a Bridge

You may not have enough retirement savings accumulated to fund a delay in Social Security benefits. There's an alternative if you have substantial home equity. A reverse mortgage, also known as a home equity conversion mortgage, can supplement your income while you wait to claim Social Security.

A reverse mortgage is available to anyone age 62 or older who owns a home with little or no debt against it. Once the reverse mortgage is arranged, you receive money from the mortgage lender. No payments on the mortgage are due until you no longer use the home as a full-time residence, either because you have moved, or when you pass away. At that point the home will be sold, and the lender will be paid from the sale proceeds. Any sale proceeds that exceed the amount due on the loan are paid to you or your estate.

Reverse mortgages come in several forms. You can take a lump sum or receive fixed monthly payments. Or you can set the reverse mortgage up as a line of credit on which you draw only when you need cash. Under the line of credit, no interest is charged until you actually borrow money.

The line of credit reverse mortgage can work well for someone who would like to fund a delay in Social Security benefits. Each month, as you need money to pay living expenses, you draw on the line of credit. You don't borrow any more money than you need, and interest accumulates only on the money you actually borrow. In addition, once Social Security benefits commence, you can begin to pay down the reverse mortgage balance if your cash flow allows. That would free up the home equity either to be borrowed again when you have a need for cash or to be inherited by your loved ones.

There's a lot you need to know about reverse mortgages before taking one. You won't be able to borrow the full amount of your home equity. The younger you are, the less you'll be able to borrow. The value of your home and current interest rates also affect the amount you can borrow. Fees are charged before the loan is made, and some people find the amount of the fees to be daunting. Also, interest accumulates on the loan balance from the day you start borrowing. If you live a long time and never pay down any of the principal, the balance can be more than the value of your home. You won't have to pay the excess. Under a federally insured reverse mortgage, the federal government pays the difference to the lender. But your heirs won't inherit any of the home equity.

To learn more about reverse mortgages, go to www.benefits.gov/benefit/709. Or read Wade Pfau's book, *Reverse Mortgages: How to Use Reverse Mortgages to Secure Your Retirement*.[4]

Not everyone has accumulated a large enough nest egg or has sufficient home equity to make up the gap between retiring and a delayed claim for Social Security benefits. But for those who do, it's a smart move. More people than realize it have enough assets to fund a Social Security delay. You should take a fresh look at the numbers and possibly work with a financial planner who can help develop forecasts and show the effects under different scenarios.

CHAPTER 14

The Future of Social Security and What It Means to You

S ocial Security is going broke.

You've heard that, probably numerous times. There's some truth to that widely repeated claim. And yet it can be misleading. In fact, many Americans misunderstand the real situation of Social Security, and what it means for them. These misunderstandings can put their own retirement security at risk. When making your retirement plans, it's important to know the facts about the financial condition of Social Security and how you should, and shouldn't, react to it.

Media reports are not the best way to learn about the financial condition of Social Security. They're often incomplete or misleading. The best source is the Annual Report of the Trustees of Social Security. You don't even have to read the full report. The summary gives all the information you need. The report is available on the Social Security website (www.socialsecurity.gov) as is the summary and usually a "Message to the Public." The official title of the report is "The 2020 Annual Report of the Board of Trustees of the Federal Old-Age and Survivors Insurance and Federal Disability Insurance Trust Funds." The report is usually issued in April each year.

But first here's a little background. There are two Social Security trust funds. One trust fund, which is for retirement benefits, is known formally as the Federal Old-Age and Survivors Insurance Trust Fund. The other trust fund, for the disability income program, is known as the Disability Insurance Trust Fund. The trust funds are supposed to have six trustees. Four of them are trustees by virtue of their jobs with the government: the secretaries of Treasury, Labor, and Health and Human Resources, and the commissioner of Social Security. There are also supposed to be two public trustees appointed by the president and confirmed by the Senate. But in recent years one or both public trustee positions have frequently been vacant. The Office of the Chief Actuary of Social Security does most of the work presented in the annual report.

Medicare also has a trust fund with the same trustees. The annual report on the condition of Medicare is included in the Social Security report.

When Will Social Security Go Broke?

The 2020 report from the trustees estimated that the retirement trust fund will run out of funds in 2034, and the disability income fund will be depleted in 2052. What the report refers to as the "combined trust funds" will run out of money in 2035. The 2020 report also said that in 2021 the annual income of the program is expected to be less than the annual costs for the first time since 1982. The income is estimated to be less than the expenses each year after 2021.

The estimated dates when the trust funds will run out of money typically change a little from year to year. As the assumptions that the report is based on are changed, and as the latest year's actual results are better or worse than last year's assumptions, the latest estimates differ from the previous year's. Key assumptions in the report are the rate of economic growth, price inflation, the growth of the labor force, and wage inflation. When the economy goes into a recession, the trust funds are typically estimated to run out of money faster than before the recession. When the economy recovers or has an extended period of growth, the depletion dates are pushed into the future. But for some time the retirement trust fund has been estimated to run out of money during the 2030s.

What Will Really Happen

I have heard people say that when the retirement trust fund runs out of money—in 2034 or whenever it happens—their Social Security benefits will stop. They believe there won't be any more money to pay them. Many younger people believe that they'll never receive retirement benefits from Social Security at all. A 2015 Gallup survey found that six out of ten people between the ages of 18 and 49 did not believe they would receive any benefits from Social Security when they retired. Many people who claim their retirement benefits as soon as they're allowed to, at age 62, give as one of their reasons that they want to receive all the benefits they can before Social Security runs out of money.

Those beliefs are mistaken. They spring from a misunderstanding of the trustees' annual report.

Payroll taxes are paid into the Social Security program every year. For many years, the program collected more in payroll taxes than it was paying in benefits. Those excess tax receipts were put in the trust funds. The trust funds used the money to buy special bonds from the U.S. Treasury. The SSA was lending money to the Treasury to fund the government's annual spending.

As the U.S. population aged, the number of people receiving benefits became a greater percentage of the population and the number of people paying taxes became a lower percentage of the population.

More and more of the annual taxes were used to pay current benefits. In more recent years, the annual taxes plus interest earned by the trust fund bonds were used to pay benefits.

In 2018, the program's total income exceeded the benefits paid by about three billion dollars. The taxes collected were about eighty billion dollars less than the benefits paid. Interest on the trust fund bonds was used to make up the shortfall.

The 2020 report from the trustees estimated that beginning in 2021, the total costs of the program would exceed both the taxes collected and interest received on the bonds. That's the program's first annual deficit since 1982. Annual deficits are estimated to continue indefinitely from that point on, and the trust fund will be reduced as bonds in the trust fund are redeemed and the proceeds are used to pay Social Security benefits and expenses. The bond redemption process will deplete the trust fund fairly rapidly, with the estimated depletion date being in 2034, according to the 2020 trustees' report.

Social Security Still Will Have Money—a Lot of It

A depleted trust doesn't mean there won't be any money to pay benefits, though. Payroll taxes will continue to be received each year and will continue to be used to pay for benefits and expenses.

The problem is the payroll taxes will no longer be sufficient each year to pay all the promised benefits. Absent a surge in the size of the work force (from immigration, for example) or an increase in economic growth that boosts salaries, the payroll tax receipts will always be less than promised benefits. (A decline in the life spans of Social Security recipients also might close the funding gap.)

The trustees' report provides projections for seventy-five years. The projections in the 2020 report are that the annual tax revenues to the program will pay for about 76 percent of the promised benefits each year for the next seventy-five years. In other words, after the trust fund is depleted, the program will be able to pay about 76 percent of promised benefits indefinitely.

Several things could happen with regard to the other 24 percent of benefits. Congress could increase payroll taxes, or other taxes, and use those to fund full benefits. Or Congress could reduce promised benefits. More than likely, Congress will end up doing some combination of raising taxes and reducing benefits.

It also is possible that the assumptions used in the trustees' report are too pessimistic. Tax revenues could be higher than anticipated, and benefits paid could be lower. Then the shortfall would be smaller or even nonexistent. But I wouldn't count on there being a substantial error in the long-term projections.

Social Security's Solvency and the COVID-19 Pandemic

The 2020 report from Social Security's trustees was based on data through the end of 2019. It didn't include any of the effects of the recession associated with the COVID-19 pandemic.

The projections used in the report do assume uneven economic growth over the years, including periodic recessions. Even so, when the next report is issued in April 2021, it could have more negative estimates than the 2020 report. The 2020 report didn't anticipate a recession occurring within months after the report was issued. It's the nature of financial projections that a downturn that occurs soon after projections were made causes worse longer-term results than if a downturn were to occur later.

Another reason the numbers could be worse in the 2021 report is that the 2020 recession is worse than previous recessions in many ways, and it could last longer.

The payment of payroll taxes by both employers and employees is key to Social Security's financial stability. And the rise in unemployment in 2020 was historic. Never before have so many Americans lost their jobs so quickly. When there's a sharp spike in unemployment, payroll tax receipts decline and Social Security has to make up the money elsewhere.

Another pertinent factor is that many people who would have continued working for a few more years before claiming Social Security retirement benefits if the employment market had remained strong lost their jobs in 2020 and decided to claim their retirement benefits instead of looking for new jobs. Thus, the benefits that Social Security is paying will increase at the same time as its payroll tax income is declining.

The real question for Social Security's future is how quickly the employment market will recover, if it can, to the historic strength of late 2019 and early 2020. If the recovery is rapid, the damage to Social Security's finances will be minimal. But if significant job losses linger for years, the exhaustion of the trust fund will be accelerated. Social Security also will suffer if employment returns to high levels but salary levels are reduced from previous highs.

We won't know the damage until the trustees' report is issued in early 2021.

According to a study from the Center for Retirement Research (CRR) at Boston College, the pandemic recession is likely to cause the trust fund to run out of money two years earlier than forecast in the 2020 report from the trustees. But the recession won't fundamentally change the long-term financial status of the program.[1]

Yet those estimates could be too optimistic. If the recession is worse than in CRR's estimates or unemployment remains elevated for longer than they expect, the Social Security trust fund will run out of money sooner.

According to estimates in a report issued by the Penn Wharton Budget Model of the University of Pennsylvania, the trust fund will run out of money only two years earlier than forecast in the 2020 trustees' report if the economy makes a rapid recovery—known generally as a V-shaped recovery—from the 2020 recession. A more gradual recovery, known as a U-shaped recovery, would cause the trust fund to run out of money four years earlier than previously forecast.[2]

What This Means for You

The bottom line is that Social Security won't die anytime soon. As a baseline, regardless of your age, you should plan on receiving at least 75 to 80 percent of currently promised Social Security benefits.

Yet changes will be made at some point. Your retirement plan should anticipate the most likely changes and have some flexibility built into it so that you can respond as changes are made. I'll do my best to explain the likely changes and how those should be anticipated in retirement plans.

The sooner Congress takes action, the less severe the changes to Social Security will have to be. But at present hardly anyone in Washington is willing to even publicly acknowledge problems with the program. President George W. Bush tried to bring attention to the precarious situation of SSA and begin reforming the program. That initiative turned out to be very unpopular and ended quickly. Now it seems unlikely that Congress will even consider taking action until Social Security's inability to fund promised benefits is imminent.

People already receiving Social Security retirement benefits are likely to be sheltered for the most part. Congress is unlikely to reduce benefits for those already receiving them or for those who are close to retirement and have based their plans on the promised level of benefits. A big question is how old a person must be to be considered too close to beginning Social Security to have benefits changed. Five years? Ten years? Longer? I think anyone within five years of retirement at the time changes are made is unlikely to have his or her benefits changed. It's very possible the grandfather period would extend to those ten years away from claiming benefits, or in other words, to those as young as 52.

More Means-Testing for Current Retirees and Near-Retirees Is Likely

Even if Congress grandfathers those who are in and near retirement, there are likely to be exceptions.

The exceptions probably will be beneficiaries Congress considers to be affluent. Beneficiaries above a certain income or wealth level could face an outright benefit reduction, via means testing, or some offsetting tax.

A good example of an offsetting tax is the current Medicare premium surtax on higher income Medicare beneficiaries. Medicare enrollees with incomes above certain levels pay higher Medicare premiums—paid as additions to their income taxes—than other enrollees. The higher the income, the higher the additional premium is.

Some financial advisors say that, to be safe, anyone with a retirement income of $250,000 or higher should assume his or her Social Security benefits will be eliminated or an offsetting tax will be imposed on them at some point. Congress frequently uses a benchmark near that level to define the wealthy. Yet the Medicare premium surtax is imposed at a much lower level.

My best guess is that outright benefit reductions via means testing would be done on a sliding scale based on income. Only those with very high incomes, in the neighborhood of $250,000, are likely to have their benefits fully or substantially eliminated. Those with lower but still above average incomes likely will have some kind of benefit reduction or additional tax. People with expected retirement incomes of $100,000 or above should build enough flexibility into their plans to be able to adapt to a benefit reduction or higher taxes.

The most likely vehicle for effectively reducing the benefits of those already retired or near retirement is changing the formula for paying income taxes on Social Security benefits (see chapter 8). Congress could easily adjust the formula so that higher-income beneficiaries have more of their benefits taxed. Instead of a maximum of 85 percent of benefits being included in gross income, 100 percent of benefits could be included in gross income at some income levels. And the percentage of benefits included as income at different levels could also be increased from current levels.

Larger Changes for Those Not Near Retirement

Another likely change, which would probably affect all beneficiaries, is an adjustment in the annual cost of living allowance (COLA). Any change in the COLA would be likely take effect immediately, affecting current as well as future benefit recipients. The current COLA already is less than general price inflation. The trustees' report assumes that benefits grow one percentage point less than general inflation each year. Several studies have concluded that Social Security beneficiaries lose purchasing power annually because the COLA doesn't keep up with the price inflation they face.[3]

And Congress could easily adjust the COLA formula to reduce the annual increases in benefits, much as it changed many of the inflation adjustments in the tax code in the Tax Cuts and Jobs Act, enacted in 2017. A simple technical redefinition of inflation resulted in smaller inflation increases in various numbers used to figure taxes. Over time, these small changes will compound to meaningful sums.

Another possible change is that people who are years from retirement are likely to pay higher payroll taxes during the rest of their working years once Congress tackles the issue. One simple change would be to increase the wage base on which Social Security taxes are paid.

Higher-income workers and self-employed people pay Social Security taxes on their incomes up to a certain level, known as the maximum wage base, which is adjusted for inflation each year. Congress could increase the income level subject to payroll taxes. The income limit even could be eliminated, as Congress did with the Medicare payroll tax some years ago. Medicare payroll taxes used to be capped at the same income level as Social Security taxes. Now Medicare payroll taxes are paid on each dollar of income, regardless of the level of income. The same thing could be done with Social Security taxes.

It is also likely that benefits formulas will be adjusted so that future retirees receive lower retirement benefits than under the current formulas. One simple change would mean using a different method to index lifetime wages before calculating benefits. (You can review chapter 4 for details of how benefits are calculated now.) The current formula uses general wage inflation. Over time, wage inflation is higher than consumer price inflation, so using wage inflation to index the lifetime earnings record results in higher benefits than if consumer price inflation were used. Many analysts have proposed changing to consumer price inflation.

Another proposal frequently put forward is to increase the age at which retirement benefits can be claimed. Such a change, though, is likely to be especially disadvantageous to lower-income workers. Higher-income workers tend to work at desks in jobs that aren't physically strenuous. So it's easier for them to delay their retirements. Lower-wage workers tend to be on their feet most of the day or engaged in more physically demanding jobs than office workers.

Analysts generally believe that these workers retire earlier than office workers because of the physical demands of their jobs and deterioration of their health. Thus, many analysts have argued that raising the retirement age would harm lower-wage workers and not be feasible for a number of other workers. Changing the retirement age seems less likely than it did a few years ago.

Social Security is heavily means-tested already. As we have seen, higher-income workers receive lower benefits for each dollar in taxes paid than lower-income workers do. Economist William Reichenstein calculated, for example, that a single individual with an annual income of about $34,757 would receive $1.86 of benefits for each dollar of taxes paid, while an individual earning $132,900 would receive only $0.89 of benefits for each dollar of taxes paid.

Even so, many proposals to shore up Social Security's finances suggest increasing means testing—in other words, making the system more progressive. The higher your lifetime income, the more you should expect to be adversely affected by changes in Social Security.

The bottom line is that Social Security retirement benefits aren't going away, but changes will be made at some point. Those already retired or within five years of retirement at the time the changes are made are unlikely to be affected, except perhaps for higher-income retirees. Those further out from claiming benefits need a cushion so they can adjust to any changes without major disruptions in their retirement plans. Most people should assume they'll see a combination of lower benefits and higher taxes equal to about 20 percent, on average, of their estimated or current Social Security benefits. But the higher your income and net worth, the higher that percentage could be.

CHAPTER 15

Social Security and Medicare: How Medicare Premiums Could Wipe Out Your Social Security Income

Though they are separate programs created decades apart, we have already seen that Social Security and Medicare affect each other. You should know about this interaction, because it can have an effect on your income over time.

If you're receiving Social Security benefits as you turn 65, the Social Security Administration (SSA) will automatically enroll you in Medicare Part A at that time. Age 65 is when most people are first eligible to enroll in Medicare, and they pay a penalty if they enroll after age 65.

Each year the SSA tells high-income taxpayers enrolled in both Medicare and Social Security if they will owe the Medicare premium surtax the following year and, if so, how much it will be.

And you can elect to have your premiums for Medicare Parts B and D (or Part C if you're enrolled in a Medicare Advantage program) deducted from your Social Security benefits. That can be a good idea. But before you decide to have your Medicare premiums deducted from your Social Security benefits, you need to understand the consequences.

How Medicare Absorbs Social Security COLAs

One consequence of having Medicare premiums deducted from Social Security is that the Medicare premiums can keep your net Social Security benefits—the cash you receive after deductions—from increasing with inflation.

Unfortunately, the increase in Medicare premiums from one year to the next can absorb the increase in Social Security benefits. Medicare premiums are adjusted each year to match the estimated cost of Medicare the following year. The law requires Medicare premiums to be set at a level that will ensure that the premiums pay for 25 percent of the program's estimated cost for the year. Sometimes there is little or no increase in the premiums from one year to the next. Other years, Medicare premiums increase. The increase can range from a few percentage points to something more substantial.

Social Security benefits receive a cost of living adjustment (COLA) to match any increase in the Consumer Price Index, but Medicare premiums often increase by a higher percentage than Social Security benefits. The result can be that deductions for Medicare premiums absorb all or most of the Social Security COLA.

Suppose you're receiving $2,000 monthly in Social Security benefits and have a Medicare Part B premium of $144 deducted from the benefits before they are paid to you. You receive a net benefit of $1,856 each month. For the next year, the Social Security COLA is 2 percent. That increases your monthly benefits by $40, to $2,040. But the Medicare Part B premium increases by 6 percent, to $152.60. That's a $12.60 increase. Your net Social Security benefit will increase only $27.40.

Beneficiaries who receive a lower monthly Social Security benefit pay the same Medicare Part B premium. The $12.60 increase in that premium takes more of their Social Security COLA, and at some benefit levels will absorb all of it.

Though the headlines may say that Social Security benefits are increasing because of the COLA, if Medicare premiums also increase then many Social Security beneficiaries see little or no increase in the amount of Social Security benefits deposited in their bank accounts.

How Medicare Premium Deductions Save You Money

But there is a positive consequence of having your Medicare premiums deducted from your Social Security benefits.

Under the "hold harmless rule," increases in Medicare premiums cannot cause a reduction in a recipient's net Social Security benefits. If the dollar amount of a beneficiary's Medicare premium increase exceeds the dollar amount of his or her Social Security benefits increase, the beneficiary won't pay the full Medicare premium increase. Only the dollar amount of the premium increase equal to the dollar amount of the Social Security COLA will be deducted from the monthly benefits. The hold harmless rule has been triggered for a majority of Social Security beneficiaries only a few times, but most of those times have been in the last few years.

You may ask, "Who pays the rest of the Medicare premium increase?" The Medicare beneficiaries who don't have their premiums withheld from their Social Security payments bear the burden of the increase. Medicare knows how many of its enrollees have their premiums withheld from Social Security benefits and will be protected by the hold harmless rule, and its actuaries take that number into account in calculating premium increases. The base Medicare premium is increased by more than the increase in the costs of the program in order to ensure that the hold harmless rule doesn't prevent the total premiums from paying for 25 percent of Medicare's costs. The result is that enrollees who don't have the premiums withheld from their Social Security benefits will pay higher premiums than they otherwise would.

That includes new enrollees in Medicare. If they weren't enrolled in Medicare the previous year, they didn't have premiums deducted from their benefits then, so the hold harmless rule doesn't protect them. In a year, the increase in premiums is so high that it triggers the hold harmless rule, new enrollees' first year Medicare premiums will be higher than they would have been without the hold harmless rule, and higher than if they had been enrolled in Medicare the previous year.

Another group that will pay higher premiums are those who enrolled in Medicare because they are age 65 or older but have delayed claiming Social Security to qualify for higher benefit payments later. They also aren't protected by the hold harmless rule and can see more substantial increases in their Medicare premiums than those who are protected.

A third group consists of Social Security beneficiaries who simply chose to pay their Medicare premiums separately instead of having them deducted from their Social Security benefits. They also aren't protected by the hold harmless rule.

Future enrollees also bear part of the cost. The base premium has to increase more than the cost of Medicare in order to cover the premiums that aren't being increased because of the hold harmless rule. This increases the base premium by more than the pro rata cost of the program.

Will Medicare Swallow Social Security?

Medicare premiums increase each year based on expected increases in the cost of the program. This increase isn't just medical price inflation. Inflation is a general increase in prices, for example in medical prices, usually as a consequence of a decline in the value of the currency or in general purchasing power. Medical price inflation is one reason Medicare premiums increase, but it's not the only reason.

Most of the increase in Medicare premiums is due to the fact that the program is spending more dollars per beneficiary because more treatments are available than in the past.

For example, prescription drugs are a major reason people are spending more on medical care. But studies indicate that, for the most part, prescription drug prices aren't rising. There have been a few well-publicized cases of pharmaceutical companies imposing dramatic price increases for certain drugs. But in general, prescription drug prices are stable or falling, especially prices for most generic medicines.

Spending per capita for prescription drugs is increasing, though, because there are drugs available that weren't available in the past, some of them to treat conditions that couldn't be treated in the past. Also, as people age they tend to fill more prescriptions than when they were younger. Longer life expectancies mean people are likely to have more prescriptions than in the past.

The same pattern applies to many other types of medical care. We can take advantage of surgeries and treatments that weren't available in the past. As Medicare enrollees consume those services, the cost of the program increases. These increases are factored into Medicare premiums.

The result is that most years medical spending per person increases at a faster rate than consumer price inflation. Medical care consumes a larger portion of people's annual spending, and Medicare's total spending and its spending per beneficiary increase.

For 2020, the Medicare Part B premium increased 6.7 percent, or $9.10 per month, to $144.60 per month. The COLA for Social Security benefits was 1.6 percent. The average monthly Social Security benefit increased to $1,484 for 2020, so the Part B premium now takes 10 percent of the average Social Security benefit each month. That's the first time Part B premiums have been as high as 10 percent of the average Social Security benefit. Medicare premiums take a greater percentage of the benefits of those receiving Social Security benefits that are less than the average.

From 2000 to 2019, according to the Senior League, Medicare Part B premiums increased 198 percent and Social Security benefits increased only 50 percent.

It's not hard to project that, if this disparity in annual increases continues, at some point many Social Security beneficiaries will see all or most of their monthly benefits go to pay Medicare premiums. Remember, these numbers are only for Medicare Part B premiums. The many beneficiaries who also have Part D Prescription Drug policies and Medicare Supplement policies see even more of their Social Security benefits go to pay for their medical insurance coverage. And when Medicare's deductibles and copayments are included, still more of their monthly Social Security benefits are used to pay for medical expenses.

Some people refer to these Medicare increases as "stealth Social Security cuts." An increase in Social Security benefits due to the COLA is announced, but the increase is effectively taken away by increases in Medicare premiums.

Thus, it is important when making your retirement plans to consider both inflation and how your spending may change over time. Assuming that you begin retirement with a workable balance between income and expenses, you also have to factor in the effects of inflation over future years. Almost everything you will purchase in retirement is going to increase in price. Medical insurance premiums and the cost of healthcare will probably go up faster than inflation in general. In addition, as people age they typically incur more medical expenses. This likely shift in spending has to be considered in your planning.

Either your income has to increase, or your spending in other areas will have to decline.

Medicare premium increases, in particular, have to be factored into your decision of when to claim Social Security retirement benefits. In recent years, the increases in Medicare premiums have been less than the income increase from waiting to claim Social Security benefits. That makes it advantageous to delay Social Security benefits.

But at some point Medicare premium increases may exceed the benefit increases from delayed retirement credits. At that point, the best action might be to claim Social Security retirement benefits, have Medicare premiums deducted from them, and fall under the protection of the hold harmless rule of Social Security. That would ensure that increases in Medicare premiums don't cause a reduction in your net monthly Social Security benefits. We're not there yet, but it could happen.

CHAPTER 16

Thirty-Four Social Security Quirks, Surprises, Misunderstandings, and Key Rules to Know

We have covered a lot of ground in this book. Whether you have read straight through to this point or skipped around for information on the topics that most concern you, you have learned that Social Security can be complicated. In this chapter I'm going to try to put some essential advice in bite-size pieces.

There is not one set of rules applicable to everyone's decisions about Social Security benefits. The best benefit choices depend on a range of factors that vary between individuals and couples, including life expectancy, marital status, the relative earnings of the two spouses, lifetime earnings, expected future earnings, investment assets, other sources of income, children, and other factors. But there are general rules and generally appropriate practices that will help most people maximize their lifetime Social Security benefits.

General Principles

---

1. SSA benefits don't start automatically. You need to claim them.

Not long ago I received an email from a subscriber to my *Retirement Watch* newsletter seeking help on Social Security benefits. He said his mother had complained that she retired some time ago and hadn't received any Social Security benefits. She wanted to know where they were. My answer was that Social Security benefits aren't automatic. Even after you qualify for them, you have to apply for benefits and make clear to SSA the benefits you're seeking.

You have to tell SSA more than your name and Social Security number. To know the benefits for which you're eligible, SSA also needs to know your marital status, information about your current and former spouses, whether you're widowed, and whether you have any dependent children or parents. There are two ways people shortchange themselves when claiming Social Security benefits. One way is not to know all the benefits for which they're eligible. The other way is not to tell SSA all the information it needs to determine the benefits for which they're eligible and the amount that they're due.

2. The SSA says your birth is one day before your birthday.

Under SSA rules, you're treated as attaining a particular age on the day before you reach that age. This matters for the timing of benefits for some people. When you're born on the first of the month, you're treated as attaining the age on the last day of the previous month. People born on the first day of the month will receive their first benefit check one month before people born that same month but after the first day. There's nothing you can do to change this policy, but you can be aware of it so that you won't be surprised at when your payments begin.

3. Social Security benefits are paid one month in arrears.

When you tell SSA the age at which you want benefits to begin, the benefits generally will be paid the following month. If you turn 70 in July and want benefits to begin the month you turn 70, the benefits actually will be paid in August. Again, there's nothing you can do about this, but you should be aware of it when planning cash flow.

4. In estimating benefits, the SSA assumes you'll keep working and earning the same amount until retirement.

The SSA provides estimates of future retirement benefits at different ages through the mail, over the telephone, or online if you open a "my Social Security" account. A number of assumptions are built into these estimates.

One assumption is of concern to people who plan to stop working before age 62, or whatever other age they plan to claim retirement benefits. The SSA estimate assumes that you'll continue working until the date you claim benefits and that you'll continue to earn the same amount you've been earning. If you stop working before the claiming date, in fact you'll be earning zero dollars in the years between retirement and when benefits are claimed. Because of this period without earnings, your actual benefits when you claim them will be less than in the estimates unless you already have thirty-five high-earning years on your record.

The difference in monthly benefits will depend on factors such as the age you stop earning money, the age you claim benefits, and the level of your career earnings. Your benefits could be as much as hundreds of dollars a month lower than the SSA estimates, or it could be only a few dollars less. To get a better estimate of your likely benefits, use the calculators on the SSA website and enter zero dollars for future earnings each year after you plan to stop working. You can use the generic SSA Retirement Estimator or create a "my Social Security" account and use the personalized calculator.

5. Your benefits may increase if you continue working into your seventies.

The maximum retirement benefit is paid beginning at age 70. That means you no longer receive delayed retirement credits by delaying benefits after that age. But your future benefits still might increase if you continue working past age 70.

Each year the SSA recalculates the benefits of any beneficiary who continues working. The thirty-five years of work with the highest earnings are used to calculate your benefits. (See chapter 4 for details on how benefits are calculated.) If your additional earnings after age 70 are higher than your inflation-adjusted earnings for earlier years, the newer earnings will replace earlier earnings among the highest-earning thirty-five years and increase your benefit.

But someone who has been earning at or near the maximum Social Security wage base for thirty-five years won't see benefits increase much from continuing to work. The new earnings, even if they're at the latest maximum wage base, will increase benefits by only a few dollars a month. If the new earnings aren't higher than at least one year already in the highest thirty-five years, the monthly benefits won't go up at all.

6. Social Security retirement benefits are more valuable than most people realize.

Social Security retirement benefits are paid monthly. Estimates of future benefits are expressed as a monthly amount. Because of the emphasis on monthly benefits, many people don't realize how much cumulative Social Security benefits can amount to over their lifetimes.

In addition, Social Security retirement benefits are guaranteed for life and indexed for inflation. There aren't many sources of income that have both of those valuable features.

To determine the value of just the lifetime guarantee, visit a website that tells you how much a commercial insurer would require you to pay to obtain an annuity paying an amount equal to your Social Security benefits (e.g., www.immediateannuities.com or www.stantheannuityman.com). The annuities you'll see on these sites aren't indexed for inflation. With inflation indexing, the annuity would cost even more.

Social Security also provides benefits, based on your earnings, payable to your surviving spouse and dependent children. In addition, Social Security provides disability income if you have to quit working before your full retirement age. These benefits also aren't included in the commercial annuities either, and they add to the real value of your Social Security benefits.

7. Social Security is longevity insurance (so most people should delay claiming their retirement benefits).

The goal of your planning with regard to Social Security benefits shouldn't be to receive as many Social Security checks as possible, or to receive benefits for as many years as possible. The goal should be to maximize lifetime benefits over the various likely scenarios.

There are several ways to compare the different values of the benefits that will be paid beginning at different ages. But the key is how long you live. No matter which method you use, the numbers will show that if you live beyond ages 78 to 80 (depending on when your FRA is), you will receive more lifetime benefits if you wait to claim benefits.

You have fairly high odds of living long enough to make waiting to claim benefits the smart move. The longer you live, the more valuable the higher monthly payments will be to you. Details about realistic life expectancies are in chapter 2. As I explain there, the formulas that the SSA uses to determine the adjustments in benefits for claiming at different ages were set to create a break-even point for Social Security based on the beneficiaries' average life expectancy. Half the beneficiaries would live long enough to receive more in benefits than the average the SSA had budgeted for, and half would pass away before that point, and so receive less in benefits. The system would break even regardless of when individuals claimed benefits. But the life expectancy data that are used to determine the adjustments in benefits for claiming at different ages are from the 1980s. Average life expectancy has increased since then, but the benefits formulas haven't been adjusted. Because people are living longer now than the average in the 1980s, the benefit formulas now favor the beneficiaries who wait and claim higher benefits.

In chapter 13 I show that waiting to claim benefits is a smart move even if you have to draw down your retirement nest egg to pay expenses through age 70. Most of us should wait as long as we can to claim benefits, preferably until age 70.

8. You may be able to make a change if you're already receiving retirement benefits.

In the first twelve months after you initially claim benefits, you can withdraw the benefit application. You'll have to repay all the benefits received to date. After the application to withdraw is accepted, you will be treated as though you never claimed benefits. You can wait to claim benefits, even until age 70, and receive a higher benefit as a result of the delay.

Even after you have received retirement benefits for more than twelve months, you still have an opportunity to change. Once you are at your FRA or older, you can ask SSA to suspend the benefits. You won't be able to start over as though you had never claimed benefits. But once you reach age 70 or ask that benefits be resumed, you'll receive delayed retirement credits for each month that your benefits were suspended. An alternative is to claim a lump sum payment of the suspended benefits. If you do that, you won't receive an increase in the monthly benefits based on delayed retirement after the suspension.

Keep in mind that if you suspend benefits or withdraw your benefit application, benefits will also stop for anyone who was receiving benefits based on your earnings history, such as a spouse (the exception is a divorced spouse).

9. Be wary of collecting retroactive lump sum benefits.

When you apply for retirement benefits after FRA, you're allowed a lump sum payment of up to six months of retroactive benefits. But there's a catch. You'll be treated as having claimed retirement benefits six months earlier than you actually did. Your monthly benefit going forward will be less than it would have been if you had foregone the lump sum retroactive benefits. You'll receive lower monthly benefits each month for the rest of your life. The reduction for taking retroactive benefits doesn't apply to survivor's or disability benefits, but only to retirement benefits.

10. You are deemed to apply for all benefits for which you're eligible (there's an exception for survivor benefits, and this rule does not apply to those born on or before January 1, 1954).

Most people are potentially eligible for more than one Social Security benefit. A person can be eligible for retirement benefits on the basis of his or her own earnings record and also for spousal benefits, ex-spouse benefits, or surviving spouse benefits. A person who has been married more than once could be eligible for benefits based on the earnings records of one or more former spouses.

The SSA doesn't let you pick and choose benefits (though you could before the law was changed in 2015). When you submit an application for benefits, SSA will review all the benefits for which you're eligible, calculate them all, and pay you the one that currently pays the highest monthly amount. You may be able to switch to a different benefit later if it is higher and you become newly eligible for it.

The exception is for surviving spouses. A surviving spouse can make a restricted application for only one type of benefit, either his or her own retirement benefit or the survivor's benefit, and can later switch to the other benefit.

11. Your retirement credits can be delayed.

When you begin retirement benefits after your full retirement age, you receive delayed retirement credits that increase the monthly benefit. The credits apply for each month that you delay benefits, up to age 70. After age 70 there are no additional delayed retirement credits, so there is no advantage to delaying benefits any longer. See more details in chapter 4.

But there's a quirk in SSA's rules that applies to those who begin retirement benefits after FRA but before age 70. In that case, the delayed retirement credits earned in the current calendar year aren't included in the monthly benefit payments until the following January.

Here's an example. Suppose you're age 68 and ask for benefits to begin in July of this year. Your monthly benefits will include all the delayed retirement credits earned through the end of last year. But the credits earned for this year won't be included in your benefit payments until next January. This rule applies only for claims after FRA but before 70. If benefits begin at age 70, all the delayed retirement credits are reflected in the first payment.

Spousal Benefits

12. Spousal benefits are 50 percent of the other spouse's retirement benefit (but only some of the time).

A married person can receive either a retirement benefit based on his or her earnings history or a spousal benefit based on the other spouse's earnings history. As we have seen, you are deemed by SSA to have applied for all benefits available to you, and you'll be paid the higher benefit. Generally, if the other spouse earned significantly more than you over his or her career, the spousal benefit will be higher and you'll be paid that amount.

The base spousal benefit is 50 percent of the other spouse's retirement benefit, but there are exceptions. When the higher-earning spouse delays retirement benefits past full retirement age, he or she will receive a retirement benefit that exceeds the full retirement benefit, or PIA. Details of the increase are explained in chapter 4. But the spousal benefit is no higher than 50 percent of the other spouse's FRB.

Also, if a spouse claims her spousal benefit before her own FRA, that benefit will be reduced. Suppose Lisa is 62 and wants to receive Social Security benefits. Her husband, Dave, earned far more than Lisa during his career, so 50 percent of Dave's benefit is more than Lisa's retirement benefit. But Lisa hasn't reached her FRA. Her spousal benefit will be reduced because she's claiming it early. She'll receive less than 50 percent of Dave's FRB unless she waits until her FRA before claiming the benefit.

13. A spouse may not be able to claim a spousal benefit, at least not yet.

The spousal benefit is not available until the other spouse has claimed his or her retirement benefit. Suppose that in the example above Lisa and Dave are both 62. Dave doesn't plan to claim his retirement benefits until at least his FRA and perhaps later. Thus, Lisa isn't eligible to claim spousal benefits, because her spouse hasn't claimed benefits yet. If Lisa applies for benefits, she'll receive only her retirement benefits, and she will receive a reduced level of those benefits because she's claiming before her FRA.

After Dave claims his retirement benefits, Lisa can switch to the spousal benefit. But it will be less than 50 percent of Dave's FRB. Lisa filed early to claim her retirement benefits, and that early claiming carries over to reduce her spousal benefit when she receives it.

14. Only one spouse in a married couple can receive a spousal benefit.

You can claim a spousal benefit only if the other spouse claims his or her retirement benefit. It's not possible for both spouses in a married couple to receive a spousal benefit at the same time.

15. There are no delayed retirement credits for spousal benefits.

You can maximize your retirement benefits by waiting until age 70 to claim them. Delayed retirement credits after your full retirement age increase your benefit by 8 percent each year. Spousal benefits aren't boosted by delayed retirement credits. Once the spouse reached his or her FRA, there's no benefit to delaying the spousal benefits any longer.

16. Many spouses effectively receive no benefit for the Social Security taxes paid during their lifetimes.

The SSA uses language that makes it appear that people receiving spousal benefits are getting those benefits partly based on their own earnings records. But the truth is that they would receive the same amount of monthly benefits if they had never worked. The same holds for people receiving survivor's benefits.

Suppose you have an earnings history covering thirty-five or more years, and you paid Social Security taxes for all those years. You have a Social Security retirement benefit available to you. But you're married and your spouse earned much more than you did. The spousal benefit of 50 percent of your spouse's FRB is greater than your own retirement benefit.

When you claim spousal benefits, the SSA will say that it is paying you your retirement plus an additional "excess spousal benefit" that brings your total up to the spousal benefit amount. But you would receive exactly the same monthly benefit if you had never worked at a job covered by Social Security. You could have received that same benefit without ever paying a dime in Social Security taxes.

The same applies to a surviving spouse whose survivor's benefits exceed his or her retirement benefits. The SSA will say it is paying retirement benefits plus an "excess survivor's benefit." But the total is the same amount as the survivor's benefit alone and would have been paid if the surviving spouse had never paid Social Security taxes.

17. People between ages 60 and 70 should understand how remarriage will affect their spousal benefits.

Suppose a woman age 61 is engaged to a 72-year-old man. He is already drawing Social Security retirement benefits. Because he had higher career earnings than she did, she expects to draw spousal benefits equal to one-half the 72-year-old's benefits.

The 61-year-old will have to wait a while to collect those benefits. First, spousal benefits can't be claimed until the recipient is at least 62 years old. Second, spousal benefits won't be paid until the couple has been married for at least nine months.

The spousal benefit will be worth 50 percent of the other spouse's FRB, even if the other spouse claimed after his or her FRA and is currently receiving more than the FRB. In addition, if the person claiming the spousal benefit hasn't yet reached his or her FRA, the spousal benefit will be reduced to less than half the other spouse's FRB.

18. Spouses are no longer able to file "restricted applications" for only spousal benefit and later claim their own higher retirement benefits.

Before Congress changed the law in 2015, married couples could dramatically increase lifetime benefits using strategies called the "restricted application" and "claim and suspend."

In the restricted application, the higher-earning spouse would wait until the lower-earning spouse filed for retirement benefits and then file a claim for benefits, but only for spousal benefits. He or she would receive spousal benefits and only later file a claim for retirement benefits. When that higher-earning spouse switched to his or her own retirement benefits, there would be no reduction for having claimed the spousal benefits at an earlier age. The spouse could wait until age 70 to claim retirement benefits and receive the maximum benefit, after having received spousal benefits for years.

In claim and suspend, the higher-earning spouse would file a claim for benefits and then immediately suspend the benefits. This strategy had real advantages. The higher-earning spouse's retirement claim allowed the lower-earning spouse to file and receive spousal benefits right away. But because of the suspension, the higher-earning spouse was effectively treated as having never filed for retirement benefits. When that spouse eventually asked for the suspension to be lifted, he or she would receive the maximum delayed retirement credits payable at that age without any reduction for filing earlier.

Claim and suspend was ended after 2015. You still can file to claim benefits and suspend them, but everyone who receives benefits based on your earnings record also has those benefits suspended. So the spouse who is receiving spousal benefits will have those benefits suspended until you lift the suspension.

Restricted claiming was phased out gradually. In the 2015 legislation it was left in effect for those who reached FRA before January 2, 1954. Everyone who qualified under this grandfathering had reached FRA by the end of 2019.

You might read books and articles published before 2016 that advocate these strategies. Be aware that those publications are out of date and these strategies no longer can be used.

Divorced Spouse Benefits

19. If you're divorced, you may be able to collect benefits on your ex-spouse's earnings record.

Technically, you can claim spousal benefits on the earnings record of your ex-spouse. To do so, you need to have been married for at least ten years to the ex-spouse and currently be unmarried. You can collect once you are age 62 or older and the ex-spouse is at least 62. You also must have been divorced at least two years, unless the other ex-spouse has already claimed retirement or disability benefits. The two-year waiting period can be difficult for those who divorce near age 62.

20. Divorced spouse benefits could be higher than your own retirement benefit.

Since benefits for a divorced spouse really are spousal benefits, a divorced spouse generally is entitled to 50 percent of the other ex-spouse's FRB. When you apply for benefits you'll be deemed to have applied for both your retirement benefits and the divorced spouse benefits. You'll be paid the higher of the two. Reductions for claiming before your FRA apply to either type of benefit.

21. You can receive divorced spouse benefits regardless of what the other ex-spouse is doing.

Once you both turn 62 and the other requirements are met, you're entitled to benefits based on your ex-spouse's work history. In some ways, divorced spouse benefits are more lenient than spousal benefits. You don't have to consult with your ex-spouse before claiming benefits. In fact, there's no reason for the other ex-spouse even to know about your claim. You can claim the benefits even if your ex-spouse isn't yet claiming benefits, something that isn't the case for a current spouse.

22. Consider ex-spouse benefits before deciding to remarry.

Once you remarry, you become ineligible for divorced spouse benefits. If you've already been receiving those benefits, they will stop with your remarriage. Some people will find that the ex-spouse benefits are higher than spousal or other benefits they would be eligible for after a remarriage. They decide they can't afford to remarry and forfeit the ex-spouse benefits.

23. An ex-spouse also qualifies for survivor benefits based on a deceased ex-spouse's earnings history.

Survivor's benefits are higher than spousal benefits, so it might be worth considering survivor's benefits before remarrying. The qualifications for an ex-spouse's survivor's benefits are the same as for divorced spouse benefits, except that you still qualify for survivor's benefits on an ex-spouse's earnings record if you remarried, as long as the remarriage occurred after age 60.

24. Being married more than once can give you more benefit choices.

If you have more than one ex-spouse or deceased former spouse, you could be entitled to benefits based on the earnings records of each of the ex-spouses or deceased spouses. If the ex-spouses still are living, you could qualify for ex-spouse benefits. If an ex-spouse is deceased, you could qualify for survivor's benefits. You'll be paid only one benefit, the highest for which you're eligible. The key is that you must meet the qualifications regarding each spouse. Also, you can't be remarried, unless you're claiming survivor's benefits and you remarried after age 60.

Survivor's Benefits

25. Future survivor's benefits should be the key consideration in married couples' Social Security benefit–claiming decisions.

While both spouses are alive, two Social Security benefits are coming into the household. They might be a retirement benefit plus a spousal benefit or two retirement benefits.

After one spouse passes away, only one Social Security benefit comes into the household. It will be either a survivor's benefit based on the deceased spouse's earnings history or the retirement benefit of the surviving spouse. Whichever it is, the surviving spouse has to continue without one benefit that was coming into the household.

The goal for a married couple should be maximize the benefits that will be paid to the surviving spouse, regardless of which spouse it is. As I show in chapter 2, in almost 75 percent of married couples, one spouse will outlive the other by at least five years. In about 50 percent of couples, the surviving spouse will outlive the other by at least ten years. The probability is very high that one spouse will survive the other by at least five years, and there's a good probability at least one spouse will live well into his or her eighties or beyond.

To protect the surviving spouse, the higher-earning spouse in a married couple should delay claiming retirement benefits for as long as possible. Preferably, the higher-earning spouse should wait until benefits are maximized at age 70. That ensures the surviving spouse has the maximum possible survivor's benefit, and the pain of losing one Social Security benefit is reduced.

26. A surviving spouse has unique claiming opportunities.

Most surviving spouses are eligible for two benefits: their own retirement benefits and the survivor's benefit based on their deceased spouses' earnings histories. Significantly, surviving spouses aren't automatically deemed to apply for all the benefits for which they're eligible and then paid the higher of the benefits. A surviving spouse can choose which benefit to receive first and later switch to the other benefit. A further advantage is that the second benefit won't be reduced if you claimed the other benefit early.

It's important for a surviving spouse to plan the order in which to claim benefits. Retirement benefits and survivor benefits each increase if you delay receiving them. Each is maximized at a particular age. Retirement benefits are maximized at age 70. Survivor's benefits are often maximized at an earlier age.

Here's a general rule for surviving spouses younger than 70. Compare the retirement benefit at age 70 to the survivor's benefit. If the survivor's benefit is less than the age-70 retirement benefit, take the survivor's benefit now and wait to age 70 to claim the retirement benefit. You will probably maximize lifetime benefits by taking the survivor's benefit as early as allowed. But when the survivor's benefit is greater than the age-70 retirement benefit, you should take the retirement benefit early and switch to the survivor's benefit at the age when it is maximized.

27. There may not be an advantage to waiting to take the survivor's benefit.

Unlike retirement benefits, survivor's benefits are maximized before the survivor reaches age 70. There are no delayed retirement credits for survivor's benefits. That means the survivor's benefit is maximized when the surviving spouse reaches full retirement age. Delaying the claim of the benefit past FRA produces no increase in the benefit.

In some cases, there isn't even a benefit to wait until FRA to claim the survivor's benefits. When the deceased spouse claimed retirement benefits before his or her FRA, the survivor's benefits are reduced. The exact age at which the survivor's benefits are maximized depends on how early the deceased spouse claimed retirement benefits. See chapter 6 for details.

28. Before remarrying, a surviving spouse should consider the effect on Social Security benefits.

A surviving spouse can collect survivor's benefits as early as age 60 (50 if disabled). But if the survivor remarries before age 60, he or she can't collect survivor's benefits based on the earnings history of the first spouse. But if the remarriage doesn't occur until after the surviving spouse is age 60, the survivor can still claim benefits on the first spouse's earnings history.

The Earnings Limit

29. Self-employed people have a difficult time avoiding the Social Security earnings test.

The earnings test provides that if you earn "too much" income from employment or self-employment while receiving Social Security benefits, all or part of the benefits may be withheld or suspended. Details about the earnings test are in chapter 5.

You can avoid having the benefits withheld by earning less than the earnings limit for the year. That's hard for self-employed people. The SSA assumes a person with any amount of self-employment earnings isn't retired unless he or she can prove that less than forty-five hours a month are spent on the business. Some advisors recommend that self-employed people form a corporation, pay themselves a salary below the earnings limit, and take out any additional profits as dividends or distributions. The SSA can disrupt this strategy by claiming the salary is set artificially low to avoid the earnings limit. But the SSA also can invoke the forty-five-hour rule and force the beneficiary to prove that he or she spent less than forty-five hours on the business each month.

30. Retirement benefits that are withheld or suspended by the earnings limit essentially are paid back after FRA.

The earnings limit disappears when you reach your FRA. In addition, your benefit amount is recomputed. Say you claimed retirement benefits before your FRA. That's why the earnings test was imposed. Your benefits were reduced to less than your FRB by your early claim, and further reduced by the earnings limit. But when you reach FRA, SSA will recompute benefits, removing the early claiming reduction for months in which you didn't receive your benefits. The recomputation increases the benefits you receive after FRA, so it's the same as if you hadn't applied for benefits early, at least for the number of months your benefits were suspended.

This recomputation applies to retirement benefits. Spousal and parental benefits also can be reduced by the earnings test, and they aren't later recovered through recomputation of the benefits.

31. You can earn as much as you want in the year you first claim benefits without worrying about the earnings limit.

The earnings limit is applied month by month in the year you first claim benefits. So the amount of money you earn during the year in the months before retirement benefits start doesn't count toward the limit. Only earnings during months you are receiving Social Security benefits are applied towards the limit and may cause a withholding of your benefits.

Suppose you want benefits to start in June. From January through May you earn $100,000. You retire and earn nothing after May. The $100,000 of earnings is well above the earnings limit, but it doesn't count against the limit. You earned the money before beginning benefits.

32. The earnings limit applies to more than retirement benefits.

The Social Security earnings limit applies to all benefits received before your FRA. Both spousal benefits and survivor's benefits are subject to the earnings limit. That's why surviving spouses who are still working should consider waiting until their FRAs before applying for survivor's benefits.

Social Security and Medicare

33. Suspending your Social Security benefits could cost you Medicare benefits.

Many people who are receiving Social Security benefits and are also enrolled in Medicare have their Medicare Part B premiums deducted from their Social Security benefits. If you do that, don't forget it if you suspend your Social Security benefits or withdraw the application for them. You have to arrange for Medicare to bill you separately for the Medicare premiums so that you can pay them each month. You also might have other amounts deducted from Social Security benefits, such as federal income taxes or Part D Prescription Drug premiums. Be sure you make other plans to have those items paid as well.

34. Having Medicare Part B premiums deducted from Social Security benefits can save you money over time.

As we saw in the last chapter, the hold harmless provision prevents anyone who has Medicare premiums deducted from his or her Social Security benefits from a net reduction in Social Security benefits if Medicare premiums increase more than Social Security benefits from one year to the next.

Suppose you're receiving $2,000 per month in Social Security benefits and paying $144 per month in Medicare Part B premiums, which are deducted from your Social Security benefits. The cost of living adjustment for your Social Security benefits for the next year increases your monthly benefit by $10. The annual increase in Medicare premiums raises your premium by $15 per month. You'll only pay a $10 increase in Medicare premiums because of the hold harmless provision.

Medicare beneficiaries who don't have their premiums withheld from Social Security benefits don't have this protection. They'll pay the full Medicare premium increase. Over time, the hold harmless provision can save a lot of money for those who have the premiums withheld from their Social Security benefits.

CHAPTER 17

Claiming Your Social Security Benefits: The Nuts and Bolts

Y ou've studied the Social Security benefit options available to you. You have compared the lifetime benefits you would receive under different scenarios. If you're married, you have considered your spouse's needs and potential benefits. You have made a decision about the best claiming strategy for you, or, if you're married, for you and your spouse.

Now it's time to file your application for benefits. The application has to be submitted at the proper time, and its details need careful attention. You don't want to be among the people who selected a claiming strategy but ended up with different benefits from the ones they intended because they misunderstood their options or the rules during the application process. You need to be as diligent and careful when applying for benefits as you were when deciding on your claiming strategy.

When Should You File the Application?
You can claim Social Security retirement benefits to begin as early as age 62 and as late as 70. Other benefits (such as spousal and

survivor's benefits) can be claimed at different ages, as I've discussed in this book. But you need to apply in advance of the date when you want your benefits to start.

You can apply for benefits up to four months before you want them to begin. The SSA will not process an application requesting that benefits start more than four months in the future.

The SSA doesn't give an estimate of how long on average it takes them to process an application and how far in advance you should file to ensure receiving benefits by your target date. The processing time depends on how many other people file applications in the same time period and how complete, clear, and accurate your application is. The SSA may have to contact you to ask questions, clarify issues, get additional information, or request additional documents. In general, it takes three to six weeks to process a typical application. But the SSA usually doesn't make the first payment until thirty to sixty days after the application is approved.

So you should apply for benefits at least six weeks before you want them to start. It's even better to apply as early as you're allowed: four months before you want benefits to begin.

Your age and the date you want benefits to begin determine when you should apply and how much your benefits will be. You probably think you know how old you are. But you haven't read the Social Security rules.

As I explained in the last chapter, the SSA treats the day before your birthday as your birthday. In other words, they count you as having attained an age the day before your actual birthday. So anyone whose birthday is on January 1 is treated as having a birthday on December 31 of the previous year.

Here's a related quirk in SSA's rules you need to know. Benefits are paid one month after the month for which they apply. If you reach full retirement age in June and want to receive that full retirement benefit, technically your benefits will begin as of June but you'll receive the first benefit amount in July. The payments will continue with that one-month lag for the rest of your life. Remember also that SSA usually doesn't make the first payment until thirty to sixty days after the application is approved.

These rules are important when it comes to timing the receipt of your first benefit. If you don't know them, you could receive that first benefit a month later than you intended and have some cash flow problems.

To show how these rules work, let's say you want to begin your benefits as early as possible, at age 62. You will actually be 62 years and one month old before you receive the first benefit payment. You turn 62, and SSA pays the benefit the following month, assuming you submitted the application early enough to have it approved and the benefit processed in time.

Someone whose birthday is on July 1 will be treated as turning 62 on June 30. That person will receive the first benefit payment in July, the month he or she actually turns 62. But if the person's birthday is July 2 or later in the month, the first benefit payment won't be paid until August.

The important point is that you will go without benefits for one month longer than you might expect unless you were born on the first of the month.

There's a further quirk that affects people born on January 2. As we have seen, the SSA treats people who were born on January 1 as if they had been born on December 31 of the previous year. But, in addition, the SSA doesn't recognize January 1 as a birthday. So, because SSA also treats every person as having attained an age the day before his or her birthday, SSA also treats everyone born on January 2 as having been born on December 31 of the year before.

What if you file for your benefits late? You may not have been aware of your benefit options when they were first available, or perhaps you were ill, or you simply procrastinated. Whatever the reason, you can file late for your benefits and have at least some of the benefits paid retroactively. The SSA will pay up to six months of retroactive benefits in a lump sum if you are at least full retirement age. So, if you recently turned 68 and only recently realized that the best strategy would have been for you to claim benefits at age 66, go ahead and file the application for benefits listing age 66 as your desired entitlement date. After the application is approved, you'll receive a lump sum equal to six months of benefits, and thereafter will receive monthly benefits. But you won't receive benefits for the first six months after age 66. You'll be treated as having begun benefits at age 66 and six months.

How Should You File for Benefits?

You can choose from four different methods of filing a claim for Social Security benefits:

- Obtain and complete a paper application. Then mail the application or take it to the nearest SSA office.
- Visit the nearest SSA office and complete an application with the assistance of an SSA representative.
- Telephone the SSA at 800-772-1213 and complete the application over the phone with the assistance of an SSA rep.
- Open a *"my* Social Security" account on the SSA's website and complete an online application.

Each of these methods has its own advantages and disadvantages. The paper application process involves more time. You have to obtain the application. You can get it through the SSA's website, by visiting the nearest SSA office, or by telephoning SSA and requesting the application. The SSA can't process the application until it is delivered to them. There's always the concern that the application won't be delivered by the USPS or won't be delivered in a timely manner, delaying the processing of your application and the start date of your benefits. And of course, it's always possible that some of your writing on the forms may be misread when the application is processed.

Visiting the SSA office eliminates a number of the disadvantages of mailing a paper application. But if you choose to visit the SSA, be sure you have an appointment. A lot of people arrive at SSA offices without appointments and have to wait until the SSA reps have handled both those who walked in earlier and those who have appointments. Those with appointments are given priority.

Applying at an SSA office does come with the risk that you won't bring some information or documents that are needed to complete the application. You may need to schedule another appointment and return with the information and documents.

Before deciding to apply through an SSA office, read chapter 3 of this book. Anecdotes from a number of sources indicate that the SSA rep you are assigned may not be aware of all the rules governing the strategy you're considering and might even try to talk you into making a different choice that isn't optimal for you. You need to go into the office armed with a thorough understanding of the strategy you want to pursue. When possible, bring documentation that shows you're allowed to claim the benefits you have decided on. And above all, be sure to read the completed application thoroughly to be sure it reflects your choices before signing. If you apply through an SSA office, you should be careful that you receive both a copy of your completed application and documentation stating when it was filed.

Calling the SSA is convenient. You don't have to leave your home, and you will have access to the documents and information needed for the application. Phone calls to the SSA are handled in the order they are received, and it's not unusual for a caller to be on hold for an extended period before an SSA rep is available. The waiting time varies based on the time of day as well as the day, week, and month you call.

Unfortunately, the telephone option probably increases the potential for miscommunication and errors. It's easy for people to misunderstand each other when dealing with complicated issues over the telephone.

As with the office visit option, read chapter 3 before using the telephone option. There's a real potential that the SSA rep won't be well-informed on your strategy or will try to convince you to take a different claiming option, which may not be optimal for you.

The online option is the final method. For many people, it is the best option. You have to open a "*my* Social Security" account on the SSA website at www.socialsecurity.com to complete an online application. Assuming you are comfortable doing things online or have a trusted friend or relative who can help, the online option avoids many potential problems. There's no risk someone will misread the handwriting on a paper application or the words said in person or over the telephone. You don't have to wait. There's also no delay between the time you complete the application and when it is available to the SSA to process.

When you're applying online, everything you need is likely to be readily available. You can consult other pages on the SSA website if you have questions about the rules and your choices. You can fill out the online application from home, where you probably have all the personal information and documents you will need for the application.

An online application doesn't have to be completed in one sitting. You can save the partially completed application and return to it hours or days later. When you're done, you'll receive a receipt indicating that you filed the application on that date. The online process allows you to check the status of your application beginning one month before you are scheduled to receive benefits.

Another advantage of online filing is that an SSA rep isn't able to try to talk you into a different claiming strategy. When you've done your homework and decided on a strategy, you can go online and complete the application to reflect the strategy you want. If you have questions or need help with an issue, you always can seek the answer on the SSA website or by calling the SSA.

You can find details of how to file online at this link: https://www.ssa.gov/benefits/retirement.

The Most Important Part of the Application

As you prepare the application to claim your benefits, it's important to remember a few key points touched on throughout this book.

First, don't forget that you can't always rely on an SSA rep to know what's best for you, or even to know all the rules. (See chapter 3 for examples of some problems that erroneous, bad, or incomplete advice from SSA has caused.)

Also, remember that details are important. Your benefit amount can change based on a small factor, and the difference will compound the longer you live.

And don't forget that when your choices are unclear, the SSA uses default options that may not be the best for you. For example, anyone who claims benefits after full retirement age is assumed to want a lump sum of six months of benefits in return for a lower monthly benefit for life. This might not be the best choice for you, and you can opt out of it. See chapter 11 for details. To give another example, a widowed person may want to apply only for retirement benefits now and defer an application for survivor's benefits until later. (Or in some cases, the other way around. See chapter 6 for details.) Yet the SSA will assume you're applying for all benefits for which you're eligible unless you clearly state you aren't.

Another point to consider is that after you apply for benefits, the application will be reviewed manually at the SSA. The review will include a final calculation of your monthly benefit amount and verification that you are eligible for the benefits. The reviewer also will examine your benefit selections. At this point the reviewer may make unwarranted assumptions about your benefit choices or apply SSA's defaults and change things from what the applicant intended to the SSA default options. He or she may assume, as in the examples above, that someone applying for retirement benefits after FRA wants the lump sum option or that a widowed individual wants the higher of available benefits instead of opting for a lower benefit now while allowing the other benefit to increase over time.

You can avoid having the application changed during the manual review process.

The way to maximize the probability of receiving the benefits you want and to have them start on the date you want is to make use of the Remarks section on the application. You should reiterate the benefits you want in the Remarks section, even if you believe the intention should already be clear from the application. The remarks don't have to be long. Usually one sentence or two will suffice to make your point clear so that your choices aren't changed.

Let's take the example of the widowed individual who wants to file only for retirement benefits now and wait to receive survivor's benefits later when a higher amount will be paid than would be available today. In the Remarks section, the applicant should write a statement such as, "I am filing only for retirement benefits and want to exclude survivor's benefits from this application." That should be sufficient to ensure the intended benefits will be received.

Or suppose you are applying for benefits at age 70. You want the maximum benefit available from delayed retirement benefits. But if you aren't clear, SSA may pay a lump sum of six months of retroactive benefits and change your monthly benefit to the benefit due at age 69 and 6 months. You should include in the Remarks section a statement such as, "I want my entitlement date to be age 70. I do not want retroactive benefits to which I might be entitled."

In the Remarks section you should always state clearly the age you want to be on the beginning date (which SSA calls the "entitlement date") of your retirement benefits. You want the Remarks section of your application to state your intentions clearly, whether you fill out your application online, on paper via snail mail, over the telephone, or in person at an SSA office. That's one reason that when you file an application in person at an SSA office, you should be sure to review it carefully before signing and submitting it.

The importance of the Remarks section is highlighted in SSA's rule book, the Program Operations Manual System, or POMS, which says that an applicant may restrict the application using the Remarks section. But the statements in the Remarks section of the application must be clear and unequivocal. Any hedging or qualifying phrases will cause the statement to be ignored. A qualifying phrase is one such as "at this time" or one that explains future plans.

POMS gives, "I filed on (DATE) for all benefits for which I may be eligible except_____" as an example of a clear statement that the SSA can act on. Another example is, "I wish to exclude _____ benefits from the scope of this application."

When There's a Mistake

Despite all these efforts, there could be a mistake in the process, and you could begin receiving a benefit different from the one you wanted. Don't give up at that point. You might not be stuck with the benefits SSA says it is awarding you and has begun paying. You can appeal an SSA decision or action.

An appeal has to be made within sixty days of the date you receive a letter from the SSA informing you of its decision on your benefits application. You can appeal if your application is denied, but also if you believe that the amount you're being paid is wrong or not what you applied for.

The easiest way to appeal is to ask for a reconsideration of the decision. This doesn't involve going to court. Instead, you notify SSA in writing that you are appealing the decision. You can use the official SSA form or send SSA any writing that includes your Social Security number stating that you are appealing.

At this first level of appeal, someone at SSA who was not involved in the initial decision on your application reviews all the evidence that was used to make the first decision and any additional evidence that you provide. If the reconsideration doesn't change the decision, you can ask for a hearing before an administrative law judge, who also had no part in the original decision.

Any letter that you receive from the Social Security Administration should have information about how to appeal the SSA's decision, and the SSA website also has details on the appeal option.

I also recommend that you consider involving your U.S. representative. Most members of Congress have staff devoted to helping constituents who are having problems with federal agencies, and each agency has employees who work directly with congressional staff on constituent complaints. Don't resort to these resources for a small or routine matter. But if you believe that the facts are on your side and SSA is not handling your application properly, contacting your congressional representative's office can be an effective option. At a minimum, it often will expedite decisions.

An alternative action is to simply withdraw your application for benefits and reapply. As we have seen, you can withdraw your application within the first twelve months of receiving benefits as long as you repay all benefits received to date. Then you'll be treated as though you never applied for benefits. You can start over and file a new application for benefits any time you want. Details are in chapter 12. The disadvantage is that there will be a delay in when benefits begin being paid to you.

The Surprising Estate-Planning Step to Protect Your Social Security Benefits

You probably know that as part of your estate plan, you should have a financial power of attorney that designates one or more people to manage your finances when you aren't able to. You also may need someone to manage your Social Security benefits, but the Social Security Administration (SSA) doesn't recognize powers of attorney.

Instead, you contact the SSA and make an advance designation of a representative payee.

This feature, created under a 2018 law, allows you to choose one or more individuals to manage your Social Security benefits. You can name up to three people as advance designees and rank them in order of priority. The SSA is then required to work with the named individual or individuals in most cases. If the first one isn't available or is unable to perform the role, the SSA will move to the next person on the list.

Anyone already receiving Social Security benefits may name an advance designee at any time. Someone first claiming benefits can name the designee during the claiming process.

You can name your designee using your *"my* Social Security" account on the Social Security website, by contacting the SSA by phone (800-772-1213), or at the local field office. Designees also can be named through the mail by using Form SSA-4547 – Advance Designation of Representative Payee.

You can change your designees at any time.

First, the SSA will evaluate a designee to determine the person's suitability to act on your behalf. Once accepted, a designee becomes the representative payee for your benefits. The payee receives the benefits on your behalf and is required to use the money to pay for your current needs.

A representative payee generally must be an individual, but it can also be a social service agency, nursing home, or one of several other organizations recognized by the SSA to serve as payees.

If you don't name a designated appointee and the SSA decides you need help managing your money, the SSA will name a representative payee on your behalf. Relatives or friends can apply to be representative payees, or the SSA can choose someone else.

Being named a designated representative doesn't confer any legal authority or power over any other aspect of your finances or personal life.

Representative payees generally can't charge fees for their services unless they receive authorization from SSA or are court-appointed legal guardians authorized to charge fees.

Once the SSA approves a designated payee, that individual or organization has to file an annual report with SSA detailing how the benefits were spent. Receipts and records must be retained in case a state agency asks to review how the funds were spent. The SSA has a booklet explaining the duties and responsibilities of a representative payee, "Guide for Representative Payee," which is available for free through its website, toll-free telephone number, and local offices.

Most people don't realize that the SSA doesn't recognize a power of attorney. Only a designated payee is recognized by SSA as the person who can receive and manage a person's Social Security benefits.

If you don't name one or more authorized designees as part of your estate planning process, someone will have to apply for that position later, or the SSA will designate someone on its initiative.

CHAPTER 18

How to Avoid Social Security Scams

" **H**ello, this is the Social Security Department. Because of suspicious or fraudulent activity, your Social Security number has been suspended. Please contact us to have it reinstated."

Millions, perhaps tens of millions, of Americans have received telephone messages similar to this one in recent years and continue to receive them. The calls are from fairly sophisticated international con artists. Though the callers are often based outside the U.S., technology allows them to use local telephone numbers to fool caller ID into reporting that the calls are from the Social Security Administration (SSA).

Sometimes the calls are prerecorded, but other times the callers are live people. In the latter case, when the target of the scam answers the phone, the caller will say the call needs to be transferred to a Social Security representative to have the Social Security number reinstated. The person to whom the call is transferred will claim that there's an urgent need for immediate action and ask for key personal information such as Social Security number, birth date, and perhaps even bank account information. In addition to taking all the personal information, the scammer will often ask the victim to pay a fee to have his or her Social Security number reinstated. The victim is usually asked to pay by means of a gift card.

Sometimes the fraud call is less threatening. The caller says that Social Security's computers are down and the government needs to confirm the person's Social Security number to keep it from being suspended or to have it reinstated.

Other variations of the scams make the same claims through emails purported to be from the SSA. The recipient will be advised to click on a link in the email and follow the instructions on the webpage it brings up. The webpage will ask the person to enter in personal information and perhaps pay a fee via credit card or gift card.

Scams of this sort typically used to involve crooks posing as Internal Revenue Service (IRS) employees. Through telephone calls and emails, the thieves attempted to convince people that they were in serious trouble with the IRS and that the trouble could be resolved only by immediate payment using gift cards.

The IRS impersonation scams still are around, but have dwindled. The IRS issued alerts warning about the scams, and the alerts received a lot of publicity. That warned people about the scams and made them ineffective. In addition, the main scammers were traced to call centers in India, where law enforcement arrested many of the perpetrators.

Why Social Security Scams Are Growing

But scams and cybercrimes are constantly evolving. As law enforcement and the public become aware of one scam and it is shut down or becomes less effective, the criminal world develops a new approach. The scammers appear to have shifted their schemes from the IRS to the SSA. And, as we have seen, the perpetrators of today's scams are much more sophisticated than the thieves who used to go

from mailbox to mailbox looking for Social Security checks to steal. These days, theft of Social Security benefits takes place primarily through email and automated telephone calls. Technology allows crooks to craft emails so they appear to be official communications from a government agency. Thieves also can make low-cost and untraceable calls that appear to be coming from the local number of a government agency. Caller ID is no defense against these scams because, as we have seen, it can be deceived about the origin of a call.

Many of the thieves aren't content with stealing your Social Security number and personal identity; they want to steal your Social Security benefits. And yes, as I'll explain shortly, your retirement benefits can be stolen.

Though the scams are constantly modified, you should be aware of some consistent factors, and of what you can do to protect yourself.

The thieves are most likely to contact you over the telephone or through email. Their specific message isn't important because it changes over time. What's important is that the Internal Revenue Service, Federal Trade Commission, and Social Security Administration have all advised that they won't initiate contact by email or telephone for any such issues. If there's some problem with your account or Social Security number, or if there's any other issue, you'll be contacted by old-fashioned mail, now often called snail mail, through the U.S. Postal Service.

The SSA does send emails reminding people to review their benefit statements to ensure their earnings history is correct. But you'll get those emails only if you have established a *"my* Social Security*"* account on the Social Security website and provided an email address.

To be on the safe side, though, don't click on any links in an email purporting to be from SSA or any other government agency. You can't be sure if the email is legitimate or a scam. If you want to

check your earnings history or other information, open your internet browser and manually enter the address of the Social Security website: www.socialsecurity.gov. Or call the SSA using a published telephone number such as 800-772-1213.

Sometimes the communications from thieves are easy to identify. They contain obvious mistakes, such as misspellings or poor grammar, which betray the fact that the scammers aren't fluent in English and didn't take the trouble to have someone who is fluent in English review their material. Another typical mistake is the one in the sample scam script at the beginning of this chapter. In fact, there's no "Social Security Department." The proper name is the "Social Security Administration." Details such as that can help an informed citizen tell when a communication is fraudulent.

At other times, however, the cyber thieves go the extra mile to make an email or phone call appear authentic. They'll use the logo of the government agency, which can easily be obtained online or from an official publication. There also might be authentic telephone numbers and addresses for the government agency listed in the email.

Key Rules to Follow to Foil the Crooks

Because these fraudulent communications can appear to be authentic, it's important to remember these key rules.

Rule #1: Remember that government agencies won't initiate contact through email or telephone. If there is an issue the SSA needs to discuss with you, you'll first be notified through regular first-class mail.

When you have initiated contact with an agency or have had a continuing back-and-forth, the agency may telephone you or send an email regarding that issue. For example, if you have applied for Social Security benefits, you are likely to receive a follow-up phone call from someone at SSA. Calls are typically made to confirm information in

the application and to ask for supporting documents, such as a birth certificate. If you aren't sure the telephone call is legitimate, don't worry. The SSA representatives are aware of cybercrimes, and they expect people to be skeptical. If you're wary, the rep will offer to give you a telephone number and extension so that you can call them directly. Or you can call the main Social Security number, 800-772-1213, and ask to be put through to the representative who called you. This could take some time, but it provides valuable protection.

Rule #2: Government employees won't ask for payment through gift cards, cash, or wire transfers. They'll request a check made out to the government agency. An IRS employee also might recommend online payment using the online Electronic Funds Transfer Payment System or the Direct Pay feature on the IRS website.

Rule #3: A genuine representative of the government won't ask for your Social Security number or other personal information over the telephone. The exception is when you yourself make a call to the government agency. In that case, the agency needs to verify that you are who you say you are before discussing your account with you. So don't provide key personal information over the telephone to someone who initiated the call.

Rule #4: Never click on a link in an email unless you are certain of the source and confident the link is legitimate. If you need to do business on a government agency's website, open a web browser and type in the agency's web address. It may take some time to get to the webpage you need, but the extra steps provide valuable protection.

Rule #5: Don't worry about brushing off or hanging up on someone who calls you unexpectedly and claims to be from a government agency. If it's a real government agency and there's a real problem, they'll understand, and you'll receive a letter. You always can look up the agency's legitimate telephone number and call back directly to see if the person who called had a legitimate reason for getting in touch with you.

How Thieves Can Steal Your Social Security Benefits, and How to Stop Them

Stealing Social Security benefits is a relatively new but fast-growing cybercrime. You may have heard of the old-fashioned crime in which thieves would go down a residential street pulling mail out of the mailboxes, and after stealing Social Security checks would try to cash them.

That crime is rare now. Most Social Security benefits are deposited electronically into the financial accounts of the beneficiaries. Other beneficiaries receive benefits through a debit card. The odds of a thief finding a Social Security check (or almost any other kind of check) in a mailbox are low. In addition, the crime is very labor intensive, and it's easy for the thief to be caught.

Today, stealing Social Security benefits is the domain of cybercriminals.

There are two ways people now steal Social Security benefits. Both involve using a *"my* Social Security" online account in your name on the Social Security website. (See chapter 17 for details about the accounts.)

They use one method when you're already receiving benefits. First, the thieves have to obtain your personal information, something they can do through a number of methods. They can use one of the scams that I've already described. Or they can purchase the information online, on what's known as the "dark web." By now, most Americans have had their personal information stolen and put up for sale on a website. (Unfortunately, today you have to assume that most of your personal information is available for sale.)

However they obtain your personal information, the thieves use it to hack into your *"my* Social Security" account. Once they're into your account, the thieves revise the settings to redirect your benefits to their bank account. To learn more details of how this can work, you can read an article at the AARP website: "YouTube Stars Once Stole Social Security Benefits: 20-Somethings Ripped Off People Old Enough to Be Their Grandparents."[1]

The cyberthieves use another method if you aren't yet receiving benefits but are eligible. For example, you might be 64 years old, but you're not planning to claim retirement benefits until at least full retirement age, though you were eligible to begin benefits as early as age 62. The cyberthieves will go online and initiate benefits in your name but have the benefits deposited into their bank account.

If you haven't created a *"my* Social Security" account, the thieves will create one in your name. That's probably the best scenario for the thieves. They can purchase your personal information from the dark web to set up the new account. If you have already created an online account, the thieves will try to hack into it and use it to apply for benefits in your name. Of course, they'll request that the benefits be deposited in their bank account, not yours.

You can see that theft of Social Security benefits is a problem even for those who aren't receiving benefits. Someday the victims of this scam will actually apply for their retirement benefits, and after submitting the application, they'll be told they've been receiving benefits for some time.

Fortunately, the SSA is aware of the benefit-stealing scams and won't penalize the real beneficiaries. It will take some time, but the mess will be straightened out. You'll receive the benefits you want based on the beginning date you intended. The future benefits will be deposited in the right account. But there will be a waiting period.

The SSA doesn't release information on identity theft and related incidents involving benefits. But a 2015 Inspector General's (IG) report, which sampled some data from 2013, found that about $20 million in benefits intended for 12,200 recipients had been misdirected to the wrong bank accounts. That comes to less than 2 percent of online bank account deposits of benefits. The IG also found the agency was able to prevent the misdirection of another $6 million owed to 5,300 beneficiaries.

Key Steps to Avoid the Theft of Your Benefits

The problem is only going to get worse as more of the large Baby Boom generation reach Social Security eligibility age.

You should take steps to protect your Social Security benefits, whether you are receiving them yet or not. As you approach age 62, the benefits will be attractive to thieves. You should take preventive actions even if you don't plan to apply for benefits for years.

The best way to protect your benefits is to set up a "*my* Social Security" account on the Social Security website at www.socialsecurity.gov. As we have seen, the account lets you estimate the benefits you'd receive under different claiming scenarios, check the accuracy of your earnings history, and apply for benefits online when you're ready. But another advantage of the "*my* Social Security" account is that you can check any activity related to your Social Security number.

So if someone applies for benefits in your name or tries to change your address or the bank account to which your benefits are deposited, you'll see it in your "*my* Social Security" account. That's why the best protection against Social Security scams is to set up the account and check it periodically to see if there has been any activity. Then contact Social Security if you see any suspicious activity, such as benefits applied for in your name.

An alternate preventive action is to call Social Security's toll-free number periodically to ask if there has been any activity in your account. You also can ask what your latest estimated benefits are or check your earnings history.

When you're receiving benefits, be sure the benefits are being deposited in your bank account on a timely basis. When a deposit isn't made on time, contact Social Security. A delay could be the first sign that thieves have obtained your information and used it to divert the benefits to their bank account.

Social Security is good about restoring benefits once you alert them to the theft and convince them you didn't authorize the change. But the faster you act and the more steps you take to prevent the theft or catch it early, the easier it will be to resolve the problem and restore your benefits.

Cybercrime is something we have to deal with today. Even people who don't use much technology and consider themselves to be "off the grid" have to be aware that they are targets. Know the indicators or red flags of an attempted identity theft or other cybercrime. Keep your guard up. Don't be worried that you'll be penalized for hanging up on a suspicious telephone call or failing to respond to an email. Government agencies are aware of the scams and risks people face. If the SSA or some other government agency needs to be in touch with you, it will contact you through first-class mail.

CHAPTER 19

How the Disabled Can Boost Their Benefits

Retirement benefits are the main part of the Social Security program and the focus of this book. But they are far from the only benefits available under Social Security. We have already covered spousal and survivor's benefits, and a few others as well.

Social Security also provides disability benefits, and they are valuable to those who qualify for them. Total disability benefits paid by Social Security have increased significantly over the years but declined in the last few years, as I explain below.

There are two disability programs in Social Security.

One is known as Supplemental Security Income (SSI). It pays benefits primarily to disabled adults and children who have limited income and resources. Its main beneficiaries are those who haven't been able to work most of their lives and haven't established a work record that qualifies for other benefits. I won't go into the details of SSI.

The other disability program is Social Security Disability Insurance (SSDI). SSDI pays disability benefits to a qualified disabled worker and certain family members. A beneficiary qualifies for SSDI by working long enough in covered employment and then becoming disabled. The program pays about $160 billion annually in benefits to those who meet its definition of disabled and to their family members. About 90 percent of those payments go to the disabled workers and 10 percent to their families.

The disability programs have a separate trust fund under Social Security. In the 2020 Annual Social Security Trust Fund Report from the Trustees of Social Security, it was estimated that the reserves of the disability trust fund will be depleted in 2052. That's later than the 2034 date estimated for the retirement trust fund. Only a year earlier, though, the two trust funds were estimated to be deleted at about the same time. Before that, the disability trust fund was estimated to be depleted earlier than the retirement trust fund.

The turnabout was the result of the economy and workforce recovering from the financial crisis. Following the financial crisis of 2008–2009, applications for disability benefits increased and were approved at a higher rate than in the past. As the economy improved, disability applications declined. There also are indications that approval standards were tightened. The result is that both applications for and approvals of disability benefits have declined. In fact, since 2014 the number of disabled worker beneficiaries has decreased. It's too soon to know if the effects of the coronavirus pandemic will change the trend.

Who Qualifies?

Qualifying for SSDI is not easy. In most years, fewer than half of the applicants for SSDI benefits are approved. Even after appeals, which often are pursued with the help of attorneys, most applications aren't approved. The approval rates vary greatly around the country. Some analysts attribute the differences to variations in the nature of work and the workforce around the country. For example, some areas have more jobs that are dangerous, leading to higher rates of disability. Other analysts believe the differences in approval rates occur because approval standards differ around the country, especially among the Social Security judges who hear appeals of benefit denials.

SSDI is for all qualified disabled persons and their dependents. The payments can go to the disabled workers, their spouses, and their children. Benefits are paid monthly to a qualified worker who is unable to work for a year or longer because of a disability. The benefits will continue until the person is able to work again on a regular basis or reaches retirement age.

You must have worked long enough to qualify for disability benefits under Social Security, and the work must have been relatively recent. You may recall that to qualify for retirement benefits, you need a minimum of forty credits of work. The number of work credits required to qualify for SSDI are on a sliding scale that varies with your age and when you became disabled.

The general rule is that to qualify for SSDI you need forty credits, twenty of which were earned in the last ten years, ending with the year you became disabled. As we have seen, you can earn up to four work credits each year. A credit is an amount of income earned by working, and the amount of income needed to earn a work credit varies. In 2020, for example, you earned one credit for each $1,410 in wages or self-employment income. When you earned $5,640, you had earned your four credits for the year. Notice that you don't have to work all year. You only need to earn a minimum amount of money during the year to earn the maximum credits for that year.

But, as I said, the basic credit requirement is adjusted by age for SSDI. If you're younger than 24, you may qualify for SSDI with as few as six credits earned in the three-year period ending when your disability starts. From ages 24 to 31, you can qualify if you have credit for working half the time between age 21 and the time you become disabled. For example, if you become disabled at age 27, you would need credit for three years of work (twelve credits) from the past six years (between ages 21 and 27).

From ages 31 through 42, you need twenty credits to qualify. After that, the number of credits required increases by one for each year you become older. For example, at age 43 you need twenty-one credits, at age 44 you need twenty-two credits, and so on, until at age 62 or older the full forty credits are required.

Who Is Disabled?

Besides having enough work credits, you have to show Social Security that you're disabled.

SSDI has its own definition of disability, which is considered to be among the strictest definitions—stricter than the definitions of disability in most disability insurance policies, or to qualify for the disability benefits available through pension plans.

To qualify for SSDI you must be totally disabled. That means you're unable to do the work you were doing before or to adjust to other work because of your medical or physical condition. In other words, you have to be physically unable to do any kind of work. By contrast, some disability insurance policies pay benefits when the insured person is unable to perform work similar to the job that he or she was doing before the disability.

For example, a surgeon can qualify as disabled under most insurance policies if an injury or medical condition affects his (or her) manual dexterity so that he can no longer perform surgery. The surgeon's mind and the rest of his body might be fine, so that he was able to perform a wide range of other jobs. But under the definition of disability in the insurance contract, the surgeon would be disabled and qualify for benefits.

SSDI goes beyond that. To qualify, the applicant can't be able to perform any type of work. In this example, the surgeon wouldn't qualify for SSDI because he would be able to do a wide range of jobs that don't require a high level of manual dexterity.

In addition, the disability must have lasted or be expected to last for at least one year or to result in death. Benefits aren't awarded for short-term and temporary disabilities. There are also no benefits under SSDI when it's possible that you might recover enough within a year to be able to do some kind of work.

Even after a person qualifies for SSDI, the SSA will periodically review the beneficiary's physical condition to determine whether the person has improved enough to be able to return to work. If he or she is deemed to have recovered enough to return to work, SSDI benefits will be discontinued.

The Qualification Process

Social Security uses a multi-step process to determine whether someone is totally and permanently disabled.

The first test is to determine whether the disability significantly limits the person's ability to do basic work, which is defined as lifting, standing, walking, sitting, and remembering. Any inability to do basic work must be expected to last at least twelve months.

The second test is to review the list of medical conditions maintained by Social Security. These conditions are considered to be so severe that being diagnosed with any of them prevents a person from engaging in gainful activity. When someone has been diagnosed with a condition on the list, it is likely the application will be approved. There are some diagnoses (Lou Gehrig's disease, pancreatic cancer) that usually qualify a person for disability insurance as soon as they are diagnosed. In other cases, the SSA uses a computer program to identify those that have a high probability of being approved.

Finally, the SSA determines whether you can do the work you did previously and, if not, whether there are any other types of work you can do. When the applicant can't do any type of work, the application is approved. But if it is found that the applicant can do some type of work, he or she won't qualify for SSDI. Notice that you don't have to be able to actually obtain other work. To be denied SSDI, it only has to be shown that you can do some type of work.

The SSA does take education into account in determining whether an applicant is able to perform other work. For many years, the inability to communicate in English was also a factor in determining whether an applicant was able to work. But in 2015 the Inspector General (IG) of the SSA recommended that this policy be reconsidered, and in 2020 SSA announced a change in the policy. Research indicated that an inability to communicate in English is not a good indication of a person's education level or ability to engage in work. So the SSA adopted a new rule that de-emphasizes the ability to communicate in English as a factor in determining whether an applicant is disabled and unable to do any work.

As I said, the SSDI definition of disability is a strict one. A low percentage of applicants qualify for the benefits.

How Much Are the Benefits?

For people who do qualify, there are several unique features to SSDI benefits. Each month the SSDI beneficiary receives the equivalent of the full retirement benefits for which he or she would qualify at full retirement age, without a reduction for taking them early. The payments are called disability benefits, but essentially you are receiving your full retirement benefit early.

The benefits continue as long as the person remains disabled. Once the beneficiary reaches full retirement age, the benefits are automatically converted from SSDI to retirement benefits. There's no change in the amount of the benefits (except for annual COLAs). There's only a change in SSA's records of the type of benefits being paid.

The potential downside is that the SSDI beneficiary has no opportunity to increase his or her benefits through delayed retirement credits. Because the benefit is automatically converted from SSDI to retirement benefits at full retirement age, the beneficiary doesn't have the opportunity to maximize the monthly benefit the way a non-disabled person can by waiting until age 70 to receive retirement benefits. And the disabled person also doesn't have the opportunity to increase the retirement benefits through additional lifetime earnings.

When a person begins to receive SSDI, family members may also qualify for benefits on his or her earnings record. Family benefits can be paid to a spouse, divorced spouse, children, disabled children, and adult children who were disabled before age 22. Spousal benefits under SSDI can be claimed when the non-disabled spouse is age 62, regardless of the age of the disabled spouse.

Each eligible family member can receive monthly benefits of up to 50 percent of the disabled worker's monthly SSDI payment. The catch is that there's a monthly maximum family amount limiting total benefits. The maximum family amount ranges between 150 percent and 180 percent of the disabled worker's monthly benefit. When the total benefits to family members exceed that maximum, the benefit of each eligible family member will be reduced proportionately.

Spousal and Survivor's Benefits for the Disabled

An SSDI beneficiary who also is eligible for spousal benefits on the non-disabled spouse's earnings record isn't deemed to be applying for both benefits when applying for SSDI. That rule can be helpful if the spousal benefit on the non-disabled spouse's earnings record will be higher than the SSDI beneficiary's full retirement benefit.

Here's how the rule can play out. An SSDI beneficiary who is younger than FRA can receive the SSDI benefits based on his or her own earnings record. And then, upon reaching FRA, the beneficiary can apply for spousal benefits based on the non-disabled spouse's earnings history. This delay allows the non-disabled spouse's earnings history to increase the amount of benefits payable. And the spousal benefit to the disabled spouse won't be reduced because he or she was receiving the SSDI benefits before full retirement age. The same rule applies when the SSDI beneficiary is a divorced spouse who can claim higher benefits under the other ex-spouse's work record.

When a disabled individual is eligible for survivor's benefits because of the death of a spouse or divorced spouse, the disabled individual can apply for the survivor's benefits as early as age 50. A non-disabled survivor must wait until at least age 60 to apply for survivor's benefits.

The disabled survivor faces no additional reduction in benefits for claiming at age 50 instead of 60. The benefits are reduced the same amount as they are for a non-disabled survivor who claims at age 60.

Another unique rule for the disabled comes into play when the surviving disabled spouse reaches full retirement age. Suppose the disabled individual began receiving survivor's benefits between age 50 and full retirement age and therefore received a reduced survivor's benefit. When the disabled survivor reaches full retirement age, the survivor's benefit might be increased to its full level. That will occur only if the beneficiary began receiving SSDI before or at the same time as the survivor's benefits. If the individual began taking the survivor's benefit before full retirement age and later began receiving SSDI, there won't be an increase in the survivor's benefit at full retirement age.

To begin survivor's benefits as early as age 50, however, the surviving spouse must have become disabled within seven years of the other spouse's death. And that seven-year period can't include any period during which the surviving spouse was collecting a surviving parent's benefit because he or she had care of a child under 16, or a disabled child, or the deceased spouse.

A final important point is that a disabled person is often eligible for other benefits such as workmen's compensation, SSI, and perhaps some state benefits. It's likely that the monthly SSDI benefits will be reduced by any other benefits received or will cause other benefits to be reduced. So before applying for SSDI, you should check to see if an approval would cause other benefits to be reduced or eliminated.

The Language of Social Security

S ocial Security has its own vocabulary. It's important to understand the different terms if you want to maximize your Social Security benefits. In this appendix the essential terms of Social Security are defined. I also include some all-important acronyms.

Average Monthly Indexed Earnings (AIME)

Your Social Security benefits will be based on your record of lifetime earnings. First, though, the SSA goes through a series of calculations with the data. Each year of earnings is adjusted, or indexed, in line with changes in the average worker's wages through the years. This indexing updates wages from earlier years to reflect the comparable purchasing power in current wages. After the indexing, the workers' highest-earning 35 years are added. Then divide the total by 420, which is the number of months in 35 years. The result is your Average Monthly Indexed Earnings, or AIME. When a worker doesn't have 35 years of earnings, $0 is used in those years without earnings.

Bend Points

The bend points are particular income levels that the SSA uses to compute your monthly primary insurance amount (PIA), also known as your full retirement benefit (FRB), in order to ensure that retired workers with lower lifetime incomes receive a higher percentage of their career earnings in benefits than higher-income workers do. In other words, the benefit formula is legally mandated to be progressive. The bend points in the formula change each year with inflation. You can find a table of the bend point amounts that have been used each year in the past on the SSA website at: https://www.ssa.gov/OACT/COLA/bendpoints.html.

Cost of Living Adjustment (COLA)

Social Security benefits are indexed, or adjusted for inflation, each year. When overall prices, as measured by the Consumer Price Index (CPI), increase, the monthly benefit amount for the following year is increased by the same percentage. Each December the SSA announces the COLA that will take effect for the following year, based on the twelve-month increase in the CPI as of September of that year. The COLA applies only after your first year of benefits. If there is no increase in the CPI, there is no COLA for the following year. But if the CPI declines, there is no reduction in Social Security benefits for the following year. The COLA is meant to ensure that benefits retain their purchasing power over time. But some studies have concluded that the COLA doesn't preserve full purchasing power for retirees, as we saw in chapter 14.

Covered Earnings

Most employers in the United States are required to withhold Social Security taxes (also known as FICA or OASDI taxes) from each employee's wages. The withheld wages are deposited with the IRS. The employer also has to pay a matching amount to the IRS. Self-employed individuals are required to pay similar taxes through the self-employment tax. The earnings from a job or self-employment on which these taxes are paid are known as covered earnings. Covered earnings are included in the worker's Social Security earnings work history, and those earnings are used to compute the worker's eventual Social Security benefits.

Not all earnings paid to citizens and residents of the U.S. are covered earnings. Wages from some state and local governments and non-profit organizations are exempt from Social Security taxes. Their employees don't receive Social Security benefits based on the non-covered earnings. Employment outside the U.S. or with U.S. subsidiaries of some foreign-based companies also might not be covered work.

Not even all wages in covered employment are subject to Social Security taxes. When total annual earnings (including those from self-employment) exceed a level known as maximum taxable earnings or the Social Security wage base, the earnings above that level aren't subject to Social Security taxes and aren't included in the worker's earnings history used to compute benefits. The maximum taxable earnings amount changes with inflation each year. The Social Security wage base for 2020 was $137,700.

The Death Benefit

Upon the death of a worker or retiree covered by Social Security, the SSA pays a flat, one-time payment of $255. The payment is made only to a surviving spouse or minor child of the deceased. This payment used to be referred to as "funeral expenses." But the amount wasn't indexed for inflation, and now it is too low to cover funeral expenses. So now it's generally known as the death benefit.

Deeming

One general rule of Social Security is that when a person applies for one benefit, he or she is deemed to apply for all benefits for which he or she is eligible. A person may be eligible for more than one benefit, but he or she will be paid only one benefit at a time. The deeming rule was put in place to prevent people from applying for one type of benefit while letting another type of benefit grow from delayed retirement credits, or by the application of other rules.

Survivor's benefits are an exception to the deeming rule. A surviving spouse who is eligible for both retirement benefits and survivor's benefits can submit an application restricted to only one type of benefit, receive that benefit for years, and then apply for the other benefit later, after it has reached the maximum level.

The deeming rule also doesn't apply when a person is eligible for one benefit and only later becomes eligible for another benefit. For example, a married person might be eligible for a retirement benefit but not be eligible for a spousal benefit because the other spouse hasn't applied for retirement benefits yet. After the other spouse claims his or her retirement benefits, the first spouse can switch from retirement benefits to spousal benefits if the spousal benefits are higher.

Delayed Retirement Credits (DRCs)

When retirement benefits are not claimed by full retirement age, the benefit that will eventually be paid is increased for each month that benefits are delayed. The benefit increases above the full retirement benefit by 8 percent for each full year the claim is delayed after full retirement age, or two thirds of 1 percent per month. The increases are known as delayed retirement credits or DRCs. Maximum DRCs are earned the last month you are age 69. No additional DRCs are earned for delaying your claim for retirement benefits past the month when month you turn 70.

Divorced Spouse's Benefits

Under some conditions, a divorced spouse can claim spousal benefits based on the earnings history of the other divorced spouse. Each spouse must be at least age 62, and the marriage must have lasted at least ten years. In addition, the couple must have been divorced for at least two years before divorced spouse benefits can be claimed. The former spouse claiming the benefits must be unmarried at the time of the claim.

The deeming rule applies to divorced spouse's benefits. You won't be paid divorced spouse benefits if you are eligible for other benefits and they are higher. Divorced spouse benefits are the same as the basic spousal benefit: 50 percent of the other spouse's PIA, with reductions for early claiming.

Divorced Spouse Survivor's Benefits

A divorced spouse may be able to claim surviving spouse benefits after the other former spouse passes away. The two spouses must have been married at least ten years, and the former spouse claiming the benefits must be at least age 60 (age 50 is disabled). The spouse claiming the benefits must be single or not have remarried until after age 60. The deeming rule applies. So, the divorced surviving spouse benefits won't be paid if the spouse seeking the benefits is eligible for other benefits that are higher.

Early Retirement Reduction

You can claim retirement benefits as early as age 62. But when you claim benefits before full retirement age, your benefits are reduced below your full retirement benefit. The reduction in benefits is made for each month before full retirement age benefits are claimed, and so the total reduction varies with the number of months that benefits are claimed before FRA. The extent of the reduction is detailed in chapter 4 and shown in Table 4.2.

The early retirement reduction can apply to benefits other than retirement benefits, such as spousal benefits and survivor's benefits.

The early retirement reduction has nothing to do with whether the beneficiary is actually working. It is imposed whether the beneficiary is fully retired or still working. What matters is the age at which benefits are claimed.

The Earnings Test or Earnings Limit

If you are receiving Social Security benefits before your full retirement age and are also still working for pay, some or all of your benefits will be suspended if you earn more than a ceiling amount known as the "earnings limit." Both the earnings limit and the amount of benefits suspended depend on the beneficiary's age. There is one earnings test for the years before the year in which the beneficiary reaches full retirement age and another for the months in the calendar year in which the beneficiary reaches FRA. The earnings limit is adjusted annually for inflation. See the details in chapter 5.

Full Retirement Age (FRA)

The full retirement age is the age at which full retirement benefits (FRB), also known as the primary insurance amount (PIA), are payable. Despite the name, the FRA is not defined by whether the beneficiary is retired or still working. All that matters is the beneficiary's age. A beneficiary's full retirement age depends on the year of birth. Table 4.1 in chapter 4 shows the FRAs for different birth years.

When benefits are claimed before FRA, the early retirement reduction is imposed. When benefits are claimed after FRA, the delayed retirement credits are applied to increase the benefit over the amount of the FRB.

Full Retirement Benefit (FRB)

The full retirement benefit is the monthly amount that will be paid if the beneficiary claims benefits at his or her full retirement age. This also is known as the primary insurance amount (PIA).

Government Pension Offset (GPO)

The government pension offset is imposed when a worker receives a pension from work not covered by Social Security and is also eligible for Social Security benefits, such as spousal or survivor's benefits, on the basis of someone else's earnings record. The GPO reduces the amount of Social Security benefits by two-thirds for any beneficiary who began receiving a pension from non-covered work after December 1984. See the details in chapter 9.

Maximum Taxable Earnings

See "Covered Earnings" for details on maximum taxable earnings, also known as the Social Security wage base.

Primary Insurance Amount (PIA)

The PIA, also known as the full retirement benefit (FRB), is the amount of monthly benefits that will be paid when the beneficiary claims benefits at full retirement age. When benefits are claimed at an age other than FRA, the amount paid is adjusted. The amount paid is reduced below the FRB by the early retirement reduction when benefits are claimed before FRA. The amount paid is increased above the FRB by delayed retirement credits when benefits are claimed after FRA. Details are in chapter 4.

Retirement Insurance Benefit Limit (RIB-LIM)

The RIB-LIM is a limit imposed on the survivor's benefits of a surviving spouse whose deceased spouse claimed retirement benefits before his or her full retirement age. While computing the limit is complicated, the RIB-LIM means that a survivor's benefit is limited to the higher of 82.5 percent of the deceased spouse's FRB or 100 percent of the benefit the deceased spouse was actually receiving at the time of death. Because of this limit, the survivor's benefit is often maximized before the surviving spouse's own FRA.

Social Security Administration (SSA)

The Social Security Administration is the government agency that administers all the benefits under Social Security, including retirement, spousal, survivor's, disability, and more. The SSA is an independent agency. In other words, it isn't part of any other federal government agency and doesn't report to a cabinet secretary. (From 1953 to 1994, the SSA was part of the Department of Health, Education, and Welfare, now known as the Department of Health and Human Services.)

Social Security Disability Insurance (SSDI)

This program provides benefits to workers who meet Social Security's definition of being disabled. It also provides benefits to family members of disabled workers. See chapter 19 for details of the program.

The Social Security Wage Base

The Social Security wage base also is known as the maximum taxable earnings. See the entry for "Covered Earnings" above for details.

Spousal Benefits, or the Spousal Insurance Amount

In general, a married person can claim the higher of the retirement benefit based on his or her own earnings history or half the full retirement benefit of the other spouse. Under the deeming rule, you apply for all the benefits for which you are eligible, and SSA will pay you the higher of the benefits. When you're eligible for both spousal benefits and your own retirement benefits, you'll be paid the retirement benefits unless they are less than half of your spouse's full retirement benefit.

But spousal benefits won't be paid until the other spouse files to claim his or her retirement benefits. A spouse who wants to receive benefits before the other spouse claims retirement benefits can first claim his or her own retirement benefits and later switch to spousal benefits after the other spouse claims retirement benefits.

Spousal benefits will be reduced by the early retirement reduction if they're claimed before full retirement age. But spousal benefits won't be increased by waiting past full retirement age to claim them.

Survivor's Benefits

A surviving spouse can claim either his or her own retirement benefits or survivor's benefits. Unlike other beneficiaries, a surviving spouse can file a restricted claim for one type of benefit and later switch to the other benefit after it is maximized.

A surviving spouse is eligible for the survivor's benefit at age 60 (50, if disabled) if the couple was married at least nine months. A divorced spouse also can qualify for survivor's benefits if he or she hasn't remarried.

The amount of the survivor's benefit depends on the survivor's age when benefits are claimed and when the deceased spouse claimed retirement benefits. If the deceased spouse claimed benefits early, survivor's benefits may be reduced by the Retirement Insurance Benefit Limit (see above).

See chapter 6 for details.

Windfall Elimination Provision (WEP)

The Windfall Elimination Provision is imposed on people who have earned a pension in a job that isn't covered by Social Security but also qualify for a Social Security retirement benefit. Ordinarily, the computation of your full retirement amount (FRA), also known as the primary insurance amount (PIA), especially the bend points in that calculation, is progressive. In other words, workers with lower career earnings get relatively higher benefits. That computation doesn't take into account the fact that a worker might have significant earnings in non-covered work and receive a pension based on those earnings. The WEP was designed to adjust such a worker's Social Security retirement benefits to take account of the other pension. See details in chapter 9.

Supplemental Security Income (SSI)

SSI is a program administered by the SSA to pay monthly amounts to aged, blind, and disabled people who have limited income and wealth. The program is not funded by Social Security taxes.

NOTES

Chapter 1: You're Richer Than You Think—and Can Become Even Richer

1. The Harris Poll, "Social Security Consumer Survey," Nationwide Retirement Institute, July 2020, https://mutualfunds.nationwide.com/media/pdf/NFM-19602AO.pdf.
2. Matt Fellowes et al., "The Retirement Solution Hiding in Plain Sight," United Income, June 28, 2019, https://unitedincome.capitalone.com/library/the-retirement-solution-hiding-in-plain-sight.
3. Ibid.
4. Ibid.
5. Ibid.

Chapter 2: The Key to Making the Right Social Security Decisions for You

1. Matt Fellowes et al., "The Retirement Solution Hiding in Plain Sight: How Much Retirees Would Gain by Improving Social Security Decisions," United Income, June 28, 2019, https://unitedincome.capitalone.com/library/the-retirement-solution-hiding-in-plain-sight.
2. Tom Foster, "A Regrettable Decision," Mass Mutual, August 2, 2019, https://blog.massmutual.com/post/wp-social-security-timing.
3. Fellowes, "The Retirement Solution"; "Social Security Planning: Things to Consider When Deciding When to Claim Social Security," T. Rowe Price, n/d, https://www.troweprice.com/personal-investing/advice-and-planning/retirement-planning/social-security.html; William Reichenstein and William Meyer, "Social Security Strategies for Couples," *AAII Journal*, December 2013, https://www.aaii.com/journal/article/social-security-strategies-for-couples; William Reichenstein and William Meyer, "Social Security Strategies for Singles," *AAII Journal*, November 2013, https://www.aaii.com/journal/article/social-security-strategies-for-singles.

4. Jafor Iqbal, "The Retirement Income Reference Book: Fourth Edition," LIMRA Secure Retirement Institute, October 29, 2018, https://www.limra.com/en/research/research-abstracts-public/2018/the-retirement-income-reference-book-fourth-edition.

Chapter 3: You Can't Depend on the Social Security Administration for the Right Answer

1. Social Security Administration, "Higher Benefits for Dually Entitled Widow(er)s Had They Delayed Applying for Retirement Benefits (A-09-18-50559)," Office of the Inspector General, February 2018, https://oig.ssa.gov/sites/default/files/audit/full/pdf/A-09-18-50559.pdf.
2. Social Security Administration, "Retirement Beneficiaries Potentially Eligible for Widow(er)'s Benefits (A-13-13-23109)," Office of the Inspector General, June 2020, https://oig.ssa.gov/sites/default/files/audit/full/pdf/A-13-13-23109.pdf.

Chapter 4: What You Need to Know about Your Social Security Benefits

1. On a side note, one proposal to bolster the solvency of Social Security—an issue you can read more about in chapter 15—is for the SSA to make this adjustment to your earnings in past years using a lower level of inflation than wage inflation. This change would have the effect of lowering future Social Security benefits indirectly.
2. Emily Brandon, "The Most Popular Ages to Collect Social Security," *U.S. News & World Report*, January 22, 2020, https://money.usnews.com/money/retirement/social-security/articles/the-most-popular-ages-to-collect-social-security.
3. James Poterba, Steven Venti, and David Wise, "The Composition and Drawdown of Wealth in Retirement," *Journal of Economic Perspectives* 25, no. 4 (Fall 2011): 95–118, https://www.aeaweb.org/articles?id=10.1257/jep.25.4.95.

Chapter 5: What If I Keep Working?

1. Gila Bronshtein et al., "The Power of Working Longer," *NBER Working Paper Series*, no. 24226 (January 2018): 1–46, https://www. nber.org/papers/w24226.

Chapter 6: The Solo Years: Social Security When You're Widowed

1. Social Security Administration, "Old-Age, Survivors, and Disability Insurance," Annual Statistical Supplement, 2020, Table 5.F13, https:// www.ssa.gov/policy/docs/statcomps/supplement/2020/5f.html#table5. f13.

Chapter 8: When Your Social Security Benefits Will Be Taxed

1. William Meyer and William Reichenstein, "Social Security: When to Start Benefits and How to Minimize Longevity Risk," *Journal of Financial Planning* 23, no. 3 (March 2010): 49, http://connection. ebscohost.com/c/articles/4853 8138/social-security-when-start-benefits-how-minimize-longevity-risk.

Chapter 12: How the Right Social Security Decision Will Make Your Nest Egg Last Years Longer

1. David M. Blanchett, "The Impact of Guaranteed Income and Dynamic Withdrawals on Safe Initial Withdrawal Rates" *Journal of Financial Planning* 30, no. 4 (April 2017): 42–52, https://search. proquest.com/openview/1a266a1642f962f6eb759b5c12e2dd26/1 ?pq-origsite=gscholar&cbl=4849.
2. William Meyer and William Reichenstein, "How the Social Security Claiming Decision Affects Portfolio Longevity," *Journal of Financial Planning* 25, no. 4 (April 2012): 53–60.

Chapter 13: How to Fund a Social Security Delay and When Not to Delay

1. Wenliang Hou et al., "Why Are U.S. Households Claiming Social Security Later?" Center for Retirement Research at Boston College, CRR WP 2017-3 (April 2017): 1–25, https://crr.bc.edu/wp-content/uploads/2017/04/wp_2017-3-2.pdf.
2. Gila Bronshtein et al., "The Power of Working Longer," *NBER Working Paper Series*, no. 24226 (January 2018): 1–45, https://www.nber.org/papers/w24226.pdf.
3. Steven A. Sass, "Should You Buy an Annuity from Social Security," Center for Retirement Research at Boston College, no. 12-10 (May 2012): 1–7, https://crr.bc.edu/wp-content/uploads/2012/05/IB_12-10-508.pdf.
4. Wade Pfau, *Reverse Mortgages: How to Use Reverse Mortgages to Secure Your Retirement* (McLean: Retirement Researcher Media, 2018).

Chapter 14: The Future of Social Security and What It Means to You

1. Alicia H. Munnell, "Social Security's Financial Outlook: The 2020 Update in Perspective," Center for Retirement Research at Boston College, no. 20-7 (April 2020): 1–9, https://crr.bc.edu/wp-content/uploads/2020/04/IB_20-7_.pdf.
2. Sophie Shin and Yan He, "The Impact of the Coronavirus Pandemic on Social Security's Finances," Penn Wharton Budget Model, May 28, 2020, https://budgetmodel.wharton.upenn.edu/issues/2020/5/28/social-security-finances-coronavirus.
3. See, for example, Mary Johnson, "2018 Loss of Buying Power Study," The Senior Citizens League, June 2018, https://seniorsleague.org/assets/2018-Loss-of-Buying-Power-Report.pdf.

Chapter 18: How to Avoid Social Security Scams

1. Katherine Skiba, "YouTube Stars Once Stole Social Security Benefits: 20-Somethings Ripped Off People Old Enough to Be Their Grandparents," AARP, December 26, 2019, https://www.aarp.org/money/scams-fraud/info-2019/florida-social-security-fraud.html.

INDEX

401(k), 53, 136, 141, 157, 186, 188, 190

A

Actuaries Longevity Illustrator (ALI), 27
adjusted gross income (AGI), 132
after-tax return, 29, 74, 186, 192
American Samoa, 131–32, 141
Average Indexed Monthly Earnings (AIME), xii, 53–56, 149–50

B

Baby Boomers, 6, 14, 22, 113, 256
bend points, xiv, 55, 269–70, 278
break-even analysis, 30, 32–33

C

capital gains, 74, 142–43
Center for Retirement Research (CRR), 187, 190, 200
child benefits, 45, 52
Congress, 37, 61, 86, 129, 148–49, 153, 172, 199, 201–4, 226, 244
Consumer Price Index (CPI), xii, 8, 47, 54, 178, 208, 270
coordinating decisions, 24, 91
cost of living adjustments (COLA), xii–xiii, 48, 57, 208, 234, 270
covered earnings, 53–54, 56–57, 149, 155, 270–71
cyber thieves, 252

D

deferred annuities, 143
delaying benefits, 10, 14, 34, 37, 48, 59–60, 66, 69–70, 83, 99, 182–83, 218, 222
Department of Labor, 77
disability benefits, 45, 52, 162, 221, 227, 259–62, 264

E

earned income limit, 85–88, 109, 170
ex-spouse benefits, 52, 221, 228–29
excess survivor's benefit, 101–2, 225

F

federal income taxes, 109, 129–30, 132–34, 136, 145, 234
Federal Insurance Contributions Act (FICA), xiii, 17, 34, 52, 55–56, 147, 270
Federal Old-Age and Survivors Insurance Trust Fund, 195–94
Federal Trade Commission, 251

G

Government Pension Offset (GPO), 148, 153–56, 275
Great Depression era, 85

H

higher-earning spouse, 30, 63, 68, 71–72, 96, 99–100, 108, 175, 223, 226, 230

highest-earnings years, 48, 79, 100, 218, 269
hold harmless rule, 209–10, 213, 234

I

income-producing assets, 143–44
Internal Revenue Service (IRS), 39, 87, 131–32, 134, 139, 250–51, 253
investment portfolio, 12, 36, 140, 177–78, 180–81, 190

L

late-in-life divorces, 113
lifetime earnings, 14, 35, 49, 53–54, 70–72, 79–80, 88, 94, 116, 161, 204, 215, 265, 269
LIMRA Secure Retirement Institute, 23
longevity insurance, 33–35, 37, 65, 108, 219
longevity risk, 15, 24–25, 33, 69–71, 177–79
loss regret, 32
lump sum benefits, 4, 158, 162–63, 171, 221

M

marginal tax rate, 134–35, 137
married couples, xiii, 2, 23, 29, 70–72, 91, 100, 138, 226
maximizing benefits, 72
maximum retirement benefit, 218
maximum taxable earnings, xiii, 271, 275–76
medical insurance premiums, 132, 212

Medicare Part B premium, 208, 211–12, 233–34
Medicare payroll taxes, 204
modified adjusted gross income (MAGI), 132–33, 137–44

N

National Average Wage Index, 54
Nationwide Retirement Institute, 6

O

Office of Inspector General (OIG), 41–42, 111

P

Puerto Rico, 131–32, 141

R

retirement income, 5, 7, 11, 39, 51, 202–03,
Retirement Insurance Benefit Limit (RIB-LIM), 96–98, 275, 277
Retirement Watch, 13, 39, 158, 216
Roth IRA, 141

S

scams, 249–51, 253–57
self-employment, 17, 45, 52–54, 87, 109, 157, 231–32, 261, 270–71
Social Security Disability Insurance (SSDI), 259–67, 276
Social Security earnings test, 231
Social Security Solutions, 50, 73, 83
Social Security–claiming decisions, 19, 37, 69–70, 91, 181
SSA calculator, 49
Stealth Taxes, 135

T
Tax Cuts and Jobs Act, 203
total disability benefits, 259

U
U.S. citizens, 133, 147
United Income, 7, 9, 14, 19
University of Michigan Health and
  Retirement Study, 9

W
windfall elimination provision
  (WEP), 148–56, 277–78

Z
zero-earnings years, 54